Workers Leaving the Studio.
Looking Away from Socialist Realism.

Punëtorët dalin nga studioja.
Duke mos parë më realizëm socialist.

First published in 2015 by Punctum Books, Brooklyn, NY, USA & The Department of Eagles, Tirana, Albania.

Botuar për herë të parë në 2015 pranë Punctum Books, Brooklyn, NY, SHBA & Departamenti i Shqiponjave, Tiranë, Shqipëri.

ISBN-13: 978-0-692-48041-0
ISBN-10: 0-692-48041-2

Cover image
Në kopertinë
National Gallery of Arts, Tirana ·
Galeria Kombëtare e Arteve, Tiranë

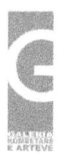
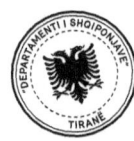

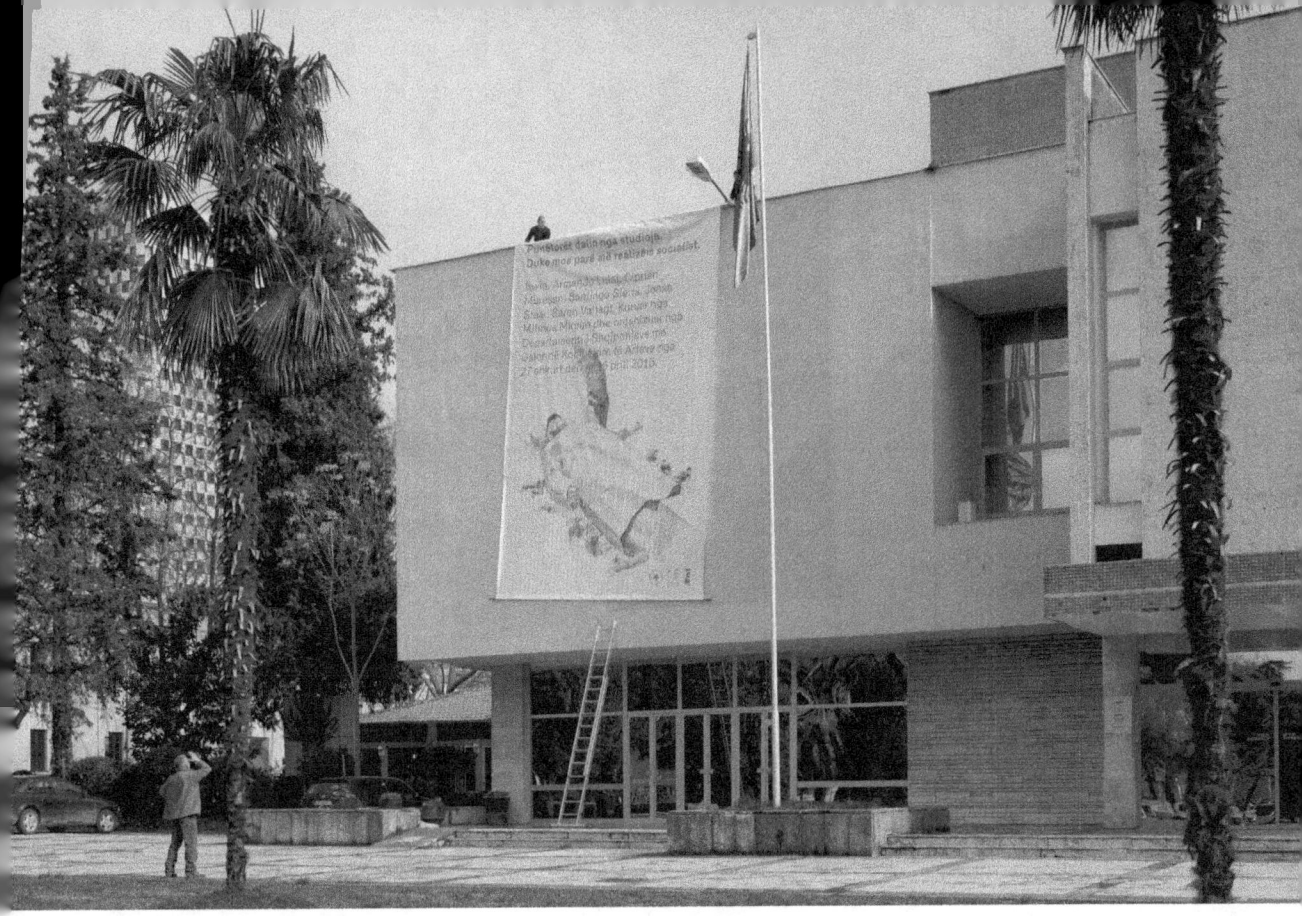

Workers leaving the studio.
Looking away from socialist realism.

Punëtorët dalin nga studioja.
Duke mos parë më realizëm socialist.

Irwin, Armando Lulaj, Ciprian Mureşan,
Santiago Sierra, Jonas Staal, Sarah Vanagt.

Contents · Përmbajtje

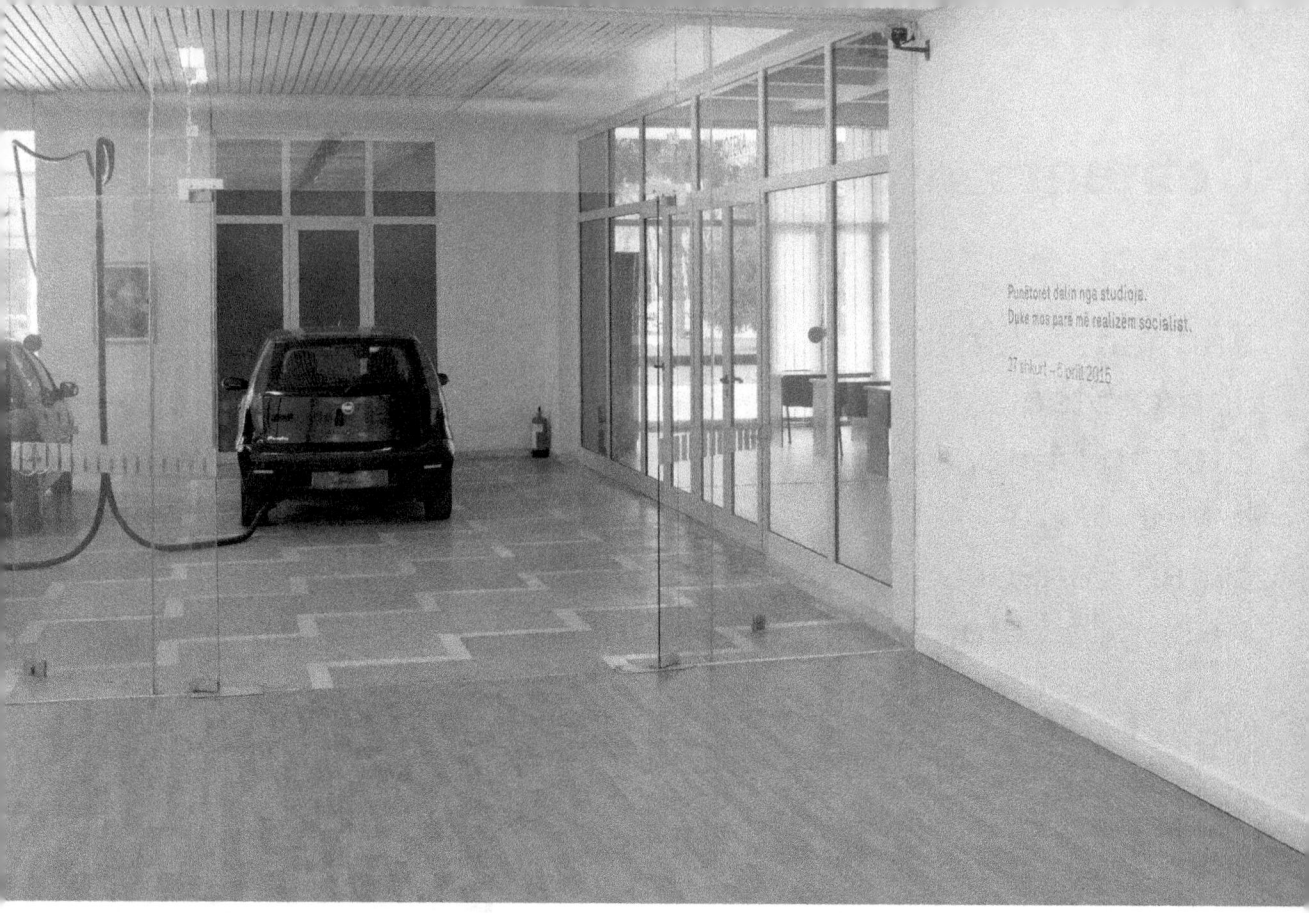

Exhibition view.

Pamje ekspozite.

Parathënie

Ekspozita *Punëtorët dalin nga studioja. Duke mos parë me realizëm socialist* përcjell një këndvështrim të veçantë mbi marrdhënien mes artit bashkëkohor sot, dhe artit të krijuar gjatë periudhës së realizmit socialist në Shqipëri, një nga vendet më misterioze dhe represive të bllokut lindor gjatë Luftës së Ftohtë, një zemër e vërtetë e errësirës komuniste.

Fragmente nga arti i realizmit socialist që përmban koleksioni i Galerisë Kombëtare, krijuar në Shqipëri dekada më parë, kuratori Mihnea Mircan i risjell me një forcë të ripërtërirë në dialog me dishepujt më të rinj të së njëjtës optikë: një kombinim i pazakontë mes impulseve politike dhe estetike për të prodhuar rezultate të papritura.

Suksesi i ekspozitës qëndron në artikulimin qartë të një pyetje të rëndësishme: nëse vërtetë "mandati i artit për të protestuar kundër gjendjes së jolirisë nuk ka skaduar ende", si shkruan Martin Jay në parathënien e një libri të rëndësishëm mbi këtë subjekt.

Ekspozita të tilla me një theks të fortë mbi politiken në art, në një vend e kontekst të tejmbushur me politikë, Galeria Kombëtare e Arteve ka kënaqësinë ti propozojë për një publik – lokal, kombëtar e ndërkombëtar – gjithmonë e më shumë indiferent karshi propozimeve të saj të lodhshme, dhe konfuze, pas kolapsit të modernizmit, dhe të narrativave triumfaliste historike, sociale, politike dhe shoqërore të komunizmit. Eshtë me vend të nënvizojmë se qëndrimet politike të artistëve të përfshirë në këtë ekspozitë janë qëndrimet e tyre individuale.

Gjej rastin të falënderoj me shumë dashamirësi dhe respekt të gjithë artistët shqiptarë, edhe ata që nuk jetojnë, të cilët me një gatishmëri për tu admiruar i bënë veprat e tyre pjesë të këtij projekti. Dua të falenderoj veçanërisht familjarët dhe trashëgimtarët e artistëve që nuk jetojnë më, të cilët me shumë përgjegjësi e nuhatje intelektuale treguan se gjëja më e mirë që ndodh me një vepër arti është kur ajo ekspozohet dhe hyn në sferën e përbashkët të debatit artistik dhe memories kolektive pamore.

Realizimi i kësaj ekspozite nuk do të kishte qenë i mundur pa dedi-
kimin e stafit kuratorial (Mihnea Mircan dhe Vincent W.J. van Gerven
Oei), pa përkushtimin e gjithë stafit të Galerisë Kombëtare të Arteve,
dhe pa ndihmën financiare të Fondacionit "Prins Claus" në Hollandë.
I falenderoj të gjithë përzemërsisht për realizimin e kësaj ekspozite, që
uroj, dhe jam i sigurtë, do të mbahet mend gjatë, jo vetëm për pyetjet
që shtron por edhe për përgjigjet që rreket të japë.

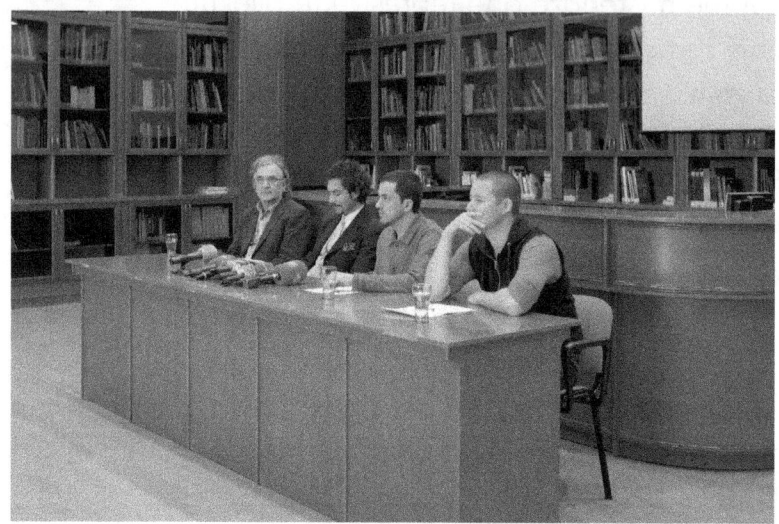

Press conference.

Konferencë për shtyp.

Curatorial Note

Film begins in 1895, when female workers exit the factory and walk in front of their employers' camera, pacing the space of the frame quickly to keep up with the reel's running time. "It's the invention of a new physics, operating by the pressure of time spans on the body, by the condensation of space within the frames": the act of producing new rhythms for new bodies. Cinema is to do with representation, but also with a "morphological inflection, resulting from the meeting between the rotating metal teeth of a machine, the reaction time of silver salt and the body of a worker."[1]

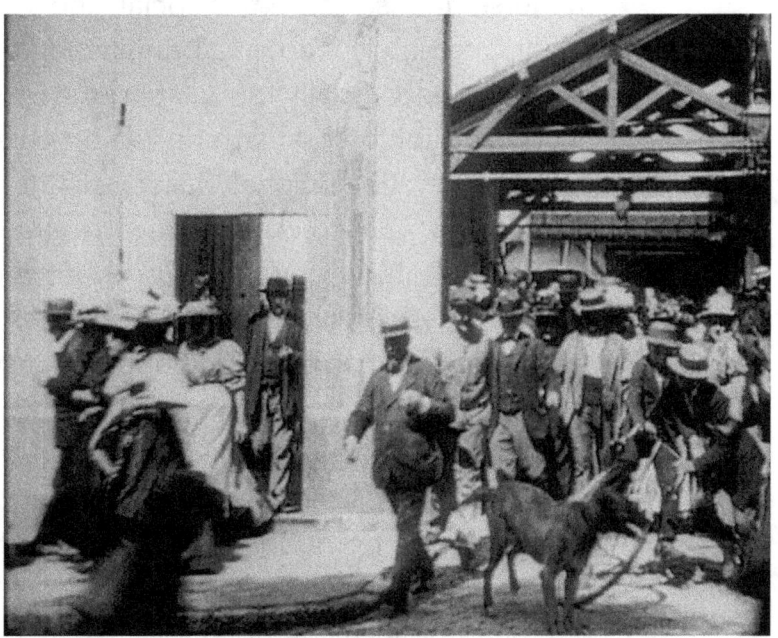

The present exhibition reflects on another projection machine, whose history and consequences, unlike cinema, are circumscribed by national boundaries, specific histories, and ideological configurations. The regime of production and representation of socialist realism radicalizes the violence that the creation of a new image does to its subject: it intensifies the fraught relation between refashioned repre-

Still image from Louis Lumière, *Workers Leaving the Factory in Lyon*, b/w film, 0'46", 1895.

Pamje nga Louis Lumière, *Punëtorët dalin nga fabrika në Lyon*, film bardhezi, 0'46", 1895.

sentation and that which is represented. Its insistence on a particular, projective notion of reality is commensurate with the coercion of daily – cultural, social, emotional – life into a grid whose perspective lines and vanishing points carry heavy ideological charges. It enforces what it represents onto that which it represents, so that representation would replace reality.

Regardless of differences between national variants, the main ones being propagandistic intensity and iconographic proliferation, socialist realism glorifies labor, and – directly or obliquely – the power in whose service labor toils. To return to the project's title, workers are symbolically locked up in the factory, fabricating, hammering away, chiseling and polishing new realities: an exit from history through communism's triumph. Artists, on the other hand, leave the studio and immerse themselves in this social landscape of permanent productivity (or, alternately read, in a brutal world of faceless collectivism), both capturing and visually formulating the process.

This exhibition is an attempt to articulate specific fragments of the collection at the National Gallery of Arts in Tirana and contemporary art projects whose concerns revolve around the notion of realism. It works through two hypotheses about the realism of socialist times, the two ways in which that discourse did not end. The heroic drive in those images, banishing metaphor but having it return as Freudian slip, undermines and corrodes their realist aspirations, and deflates the mimesis of a world "to come." On the other hand, the relations between artistic freedom and political subservience that underpin socialist realist art production radicalize an equation that contemporary engaged practices must also respond to, even if within a different regime of political interlocution.

Socialist realism did not prevail over art-historical conventions, while the political complicities that propelled it might have something to say about – and to – contemporary art at large, bring a corrective to its claims of emancipation and engagement. Though often disavowed as naive within artistic discourse, the relation between visual language and economic and political hegemonies as constantly emphasized in socialist realism remains a fact to this day, in spite of the many continually renewed claims to art's autonomy; an autonomy that can only be maintained precisely because of the economic and political structures that profit from art's image as autonomous. Socialist realist art was never able to internalize the revolutionary changes in political and social life it was expected to depict, nor was it able to withstand that shock wave of liberalization that obliterated them. A social realist art "to come" is a renewed articulation of the links between art and politics, between the impossibility of art's autonomy and the impossibility of its impotence. Here are some examples.

1.   Fabien Giraud & Raphaël Siboni, notes on their multi-part video project "The Unmanned," 2009– ongoing.

Shënim kuratorial. Kinematografia fillon në 1895, kur punëtoret dalin nga fabrika dhe ecin me hap të shpejtë para hapësirës që po xhirohet me kamera prej punëdhënësve të tyre, për të qenë në sinkron me tempin e xhirimit të filmit. "Kjo është shpikje e një fizike të re, që vepron nga presioni i fragmenteve kohore mbi trupin, nga ngjeshja e hapësirës brenda kornizave": akti i prodhimit të ritmeve të reja për trupa të rinj. Kinemaja ka të bëjë me paraqitjen, por gjithashtu edhe me një "modulim morfologjik, që rezulton nga takimi mes dhëmbëve metalikë të një makine, me kohën e reagimit të kripës së argjendit dhe trupin e një punëtori."[1] Ekspozita aktuale reflekton mbi një makinë tjetër projeksioni historia dhe pasojat e së cilës, ndryshe nga kinemaja, janë të diktuara nga kufijtë kombëtarë, historitë e veçanta dhe konfigurimet ideologjike. Regjimi i prodhimit dhe paraqitjes në realizëm socialist radikalizon dhunën që krijimi i një imazhi të ri ushtron mbi subjektin e vet: ai intensifikon marrëdhëniet e tensionuara midis paraqitjes së rimodeluar dhe subjektit të paraqitur. Insistimi i tij në një nocion të

posaçëm, projektues të realitetit është proporcional me shtrëngimin që i bëhet jetës së përditshme – kulturore, sociale, emocionale – për ta futur atë brenda një suaze, linjat dhe drejtëzat e së cilës shkojnë drejt pikës fundore të perspektivës së mbarsura me ngarkesa të rënda ideologjike. Realizmi socialist përforcon atë çka paraqet në kurriz të asaj që paraqitet, në mënyrë që ri-paraqitja të zëvendësojë realitetin.

Pavarësisht dallimeve mes varianteve kombëtare të tij – ku kryesore janë intensiteti propagandistik dhe riprodhimi i shumëfishtë ikonografik – realizmi socialist ngre në piedestal punën dhe – drejtpërsëdrejti apo tërthorazi – atë pushtet që vë punën dhunshëm në shërbim të vetes. Për t'iu kthyer titullit të ekspozitës, punëtorët, në mënyrë simbolike, janë të mbyllur në fabrikë duke prodhuar, rrahur me çekan, gdhendur e lustruar realitete të reja: një dalje nga historia përmes triumfit të komunizmit. Artistët, nga ana tjetër, dalin nga studio dhe kridhen në këtë peizazh social të produktivitetit të përhershëm (ose, lexuar ndryshe, në një botë brutale të kolektivizmit anonim), duke bërë njëkohësisht të dyja: edhe kapjen, edhe formulimin nga ana pamore të procesit.

Kjo ekspozitë është një përpjekje për të hedhur dritë mbi fragmente të veçanta të fondit të Galerisë Kombëtare të Arteve në Tiranë, dhe atyre projekteve të artit bashkëkohor që fokusin e kanë rreth nocionit të realizmit. Ajo ngrihet mbi dy hipoteza për realizmin e kohëve socialiste, mbi dy mënyrat sesi diskursi i asaj periudhe nuk mori fund. Shtysa heroike në ato vepra, që dëbonte metaforën e cila më pas rikthehej si një lapsus frojdian, minon dhe gërryen aspiratat e tyre realiste, dhe mpak *mimesis*-in e një bote "të ardhshme". Nga ana tjetër, marrëdhëniet mes lirisë artistike dhe shërbimit politik, shtylla ku mbështetet prodhimi i artit realist socialist, shtrojnë një ekuacion për të cilin praktikat e angazhuara të artit bashkëkohor patjetër duhet të japin një përgjigje, edhe atëherë kur gjenden brenda një regjimi të ndryshëm të bashkëbisedimit politik.

Realizmi socialist nuk triumfoi mbi konvencionet artistiko-historike, ndërsa makinacionet dhe bashkëfajsitë politike që e ngritën dhe e mbajtën në jetë mund të thonë diçka në lidhje me (dhe për) artin bashkëkohor në përgjithësi, duke i hequr një vijë korrigjuese deklamacioneve të tij për emancipim dhe angazhim. Edhe pse shpesh i braktisur si naiv brenda diskursit artistik, lidhja mes gjuhës pamore dhe hegjemonive ekonomike–politike, të theksuara vazhdimisht në realizëm socialist, mbetet fakt edhe sot, pavarësisht pretendimeve të shumta e të vazhdueshme për autonominë e artit; një autonomi që mund të mbahet në këmbë vetëm për shkak të strukturave ekonomike dhe politike që përfitojnë nga imazhi i artit si autonom. Arti i realizmit socialist nuk qe kurrë në gjendje të asimilonte ndryshimet revolucionare të jetës politike dhe sociale që pritej të paraqiste, e nuk qe në gjendje as të përballonte dallgën e shokut të liberalizimit që i rrafshoi ato. Një art realist social "i ardhshëm" është një artikulim i ripërtërirë për lidhjet mes artit dhe politikës, mes pamundësisë për autonominë e artit dhe pamundësisë për pafuqinë e tij. Këtu kemi disa shembuj.

1.   Fabien Giraud & Raphaël Siboni, shënime mbi projektin e tyre video me shumë seri "The Unmanned", 2009–në vazhdim

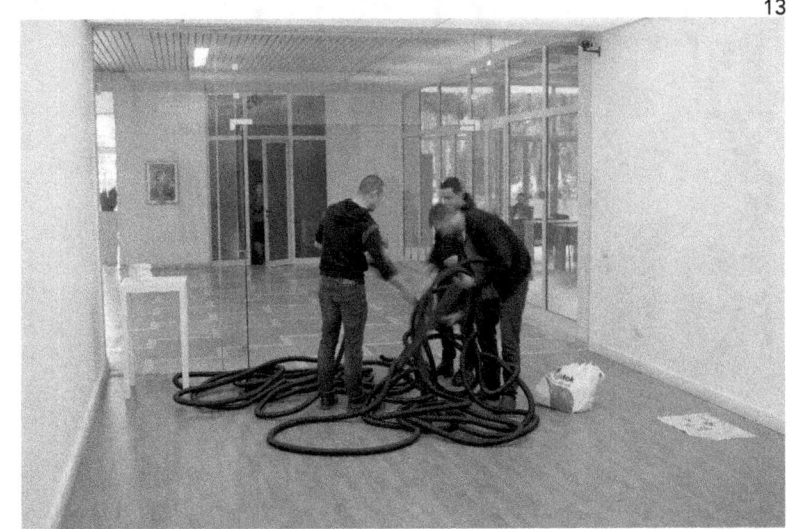

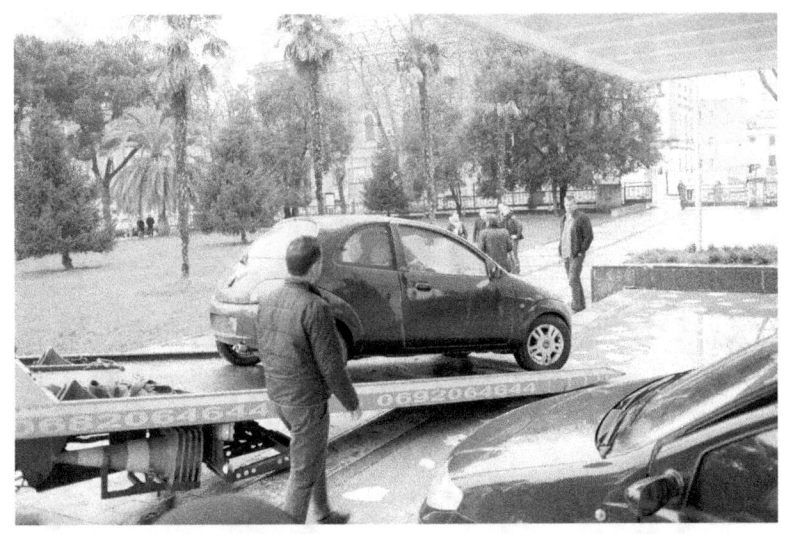

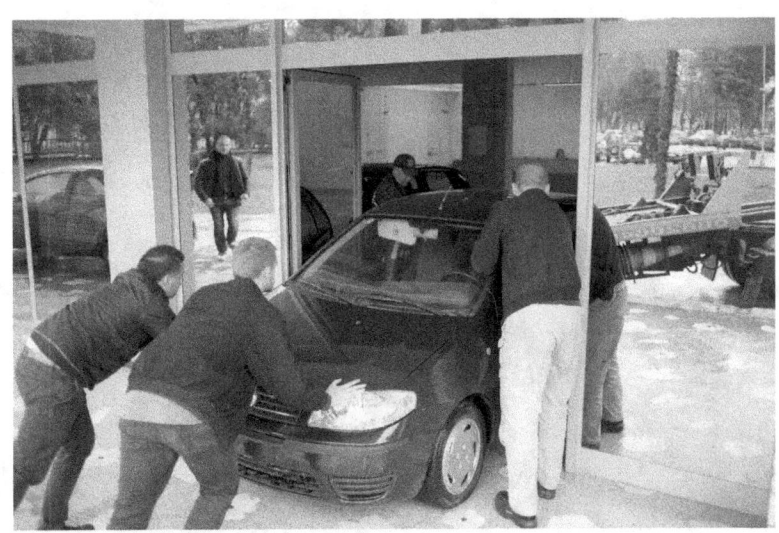

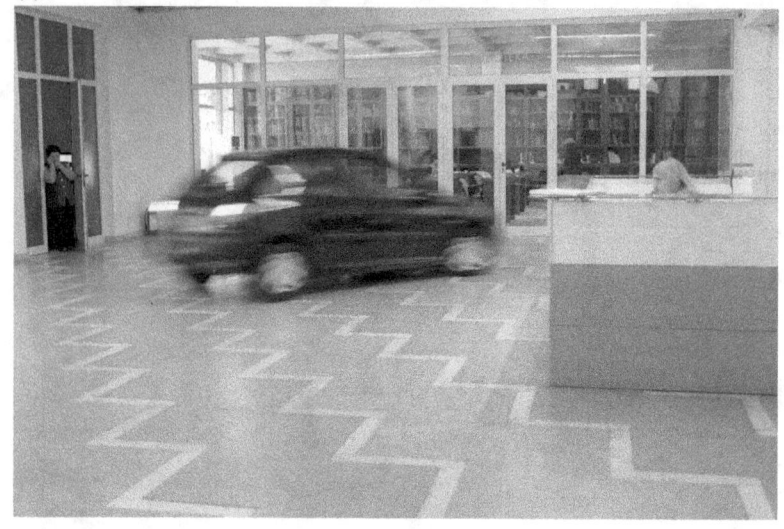

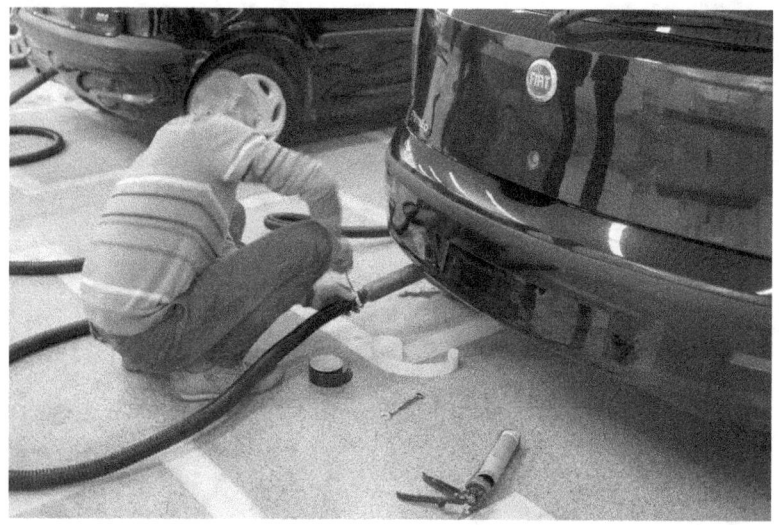

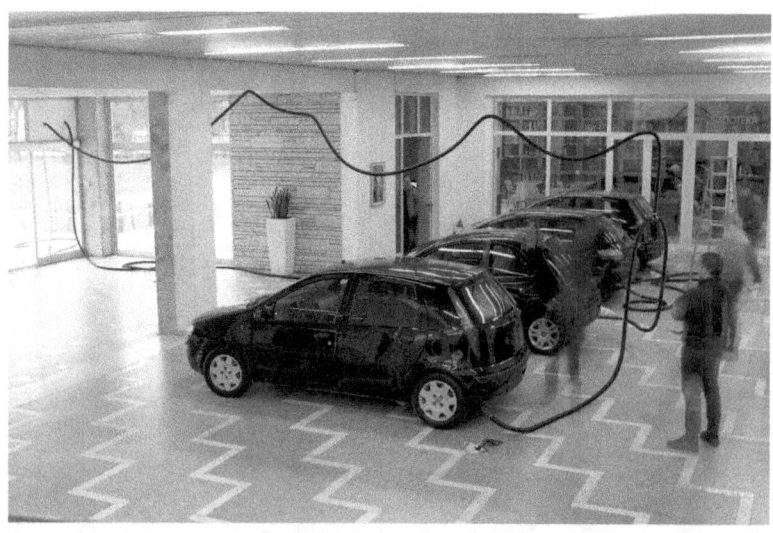

Santiago Sierra: Four Black Vehicles with the Engine Running inside an Art Gallery

Santiago Sierra's work insistently deals with the contradictions of capitalist modes of production and the logic of the art space. In this installation, four black vehicles with the engine running throughout the duration of the exhibition are located in the interior of the museum, while the smoke produced by the engine is deviated with tubes from the vehicle's exhaust to the outside of the gallery. A symbolic threshold separates a situation that would be perfectly tolerable on the street in front of the art gallery, the space of "life," but a different set of reaction once the cars contaminate the space of "art." The four black cars' mechanical hum is also a powerful response to a plethora of ecologically-minded projects in recent art, whose utopian promises fail to (cor)respond to the day-to-day reality of environmental gridlock.

Santiago Sierra: Katër automjete të zeza me motor ndezur brenda një galerie arti. Puna e Santiago Sierra-s shqyrton me këmbëngulje kontradiktat e mënyrës kapitaliste të prodhimit dhe logjikën e hapësirës së artit. Në këtë instalim, katër automjete të zeza me motor ndezur gjatë kohëzgjatjes së ekspozitës vendosen në hollin e galerisë, ndërsa tymi i prodhuar nga motori devijohet me tuba nga pjesa e pasme e automjetit në pjesën e jashtme të galerisë. Një prag simbolik ndan një situatë që do të ishte e krejtësisht e tolerueshme në rrugën para galerisë, hapësirën e "jetës", por që shkakton një reagim ndryshe kur makina infekton hapësirën e "artit". Zhurma mekanike e katër makinave të zeza është gjithashtu një reagim i fuqishëm kundër një shumice projektesh me prirje ekologjike në artin e kohëve të fundit, premtimet utopike të të cilave nuk arrijnë dot t'i japin përgjigje realitetit të përditshëm të paralizuar mjedisor.

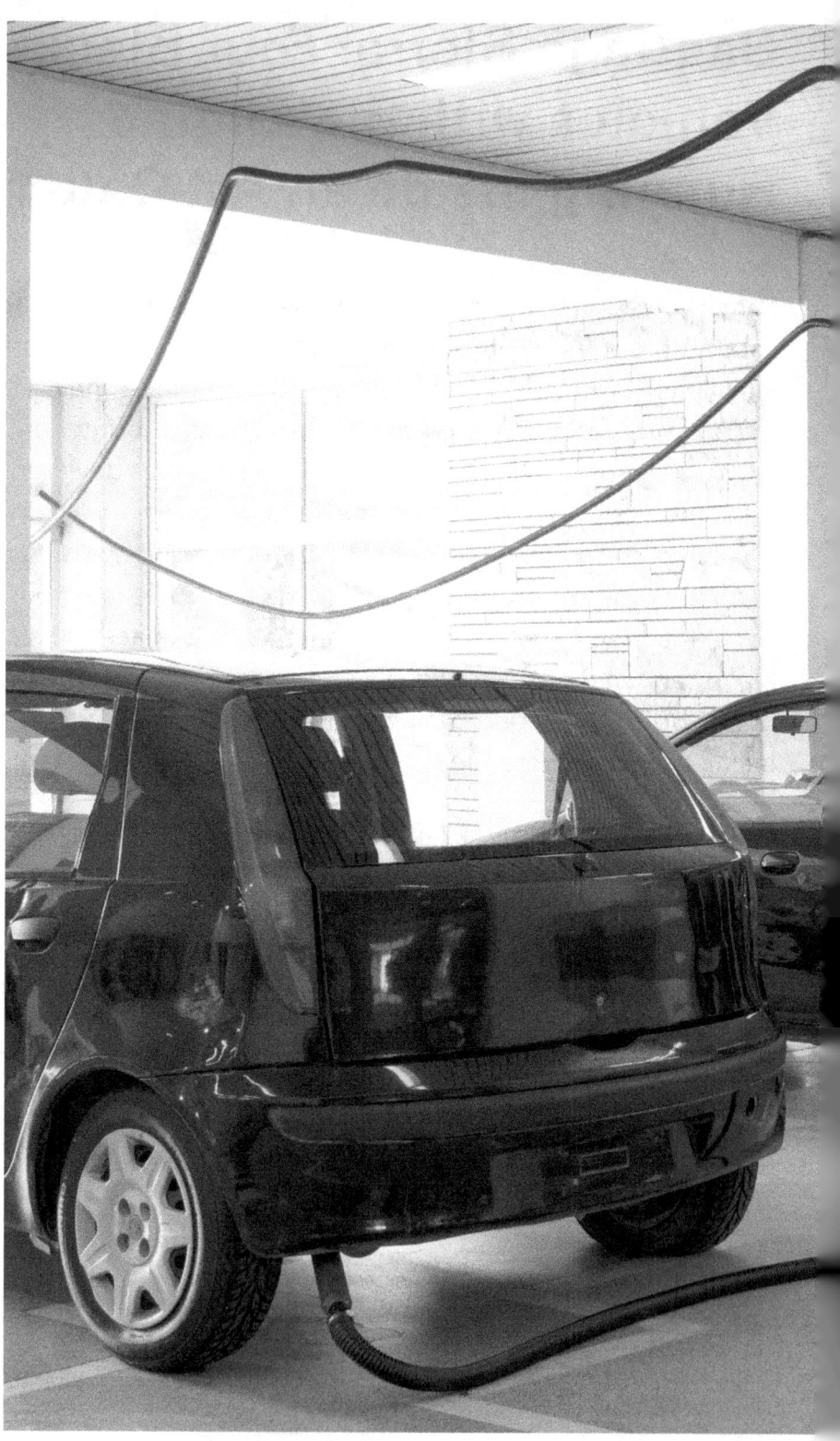

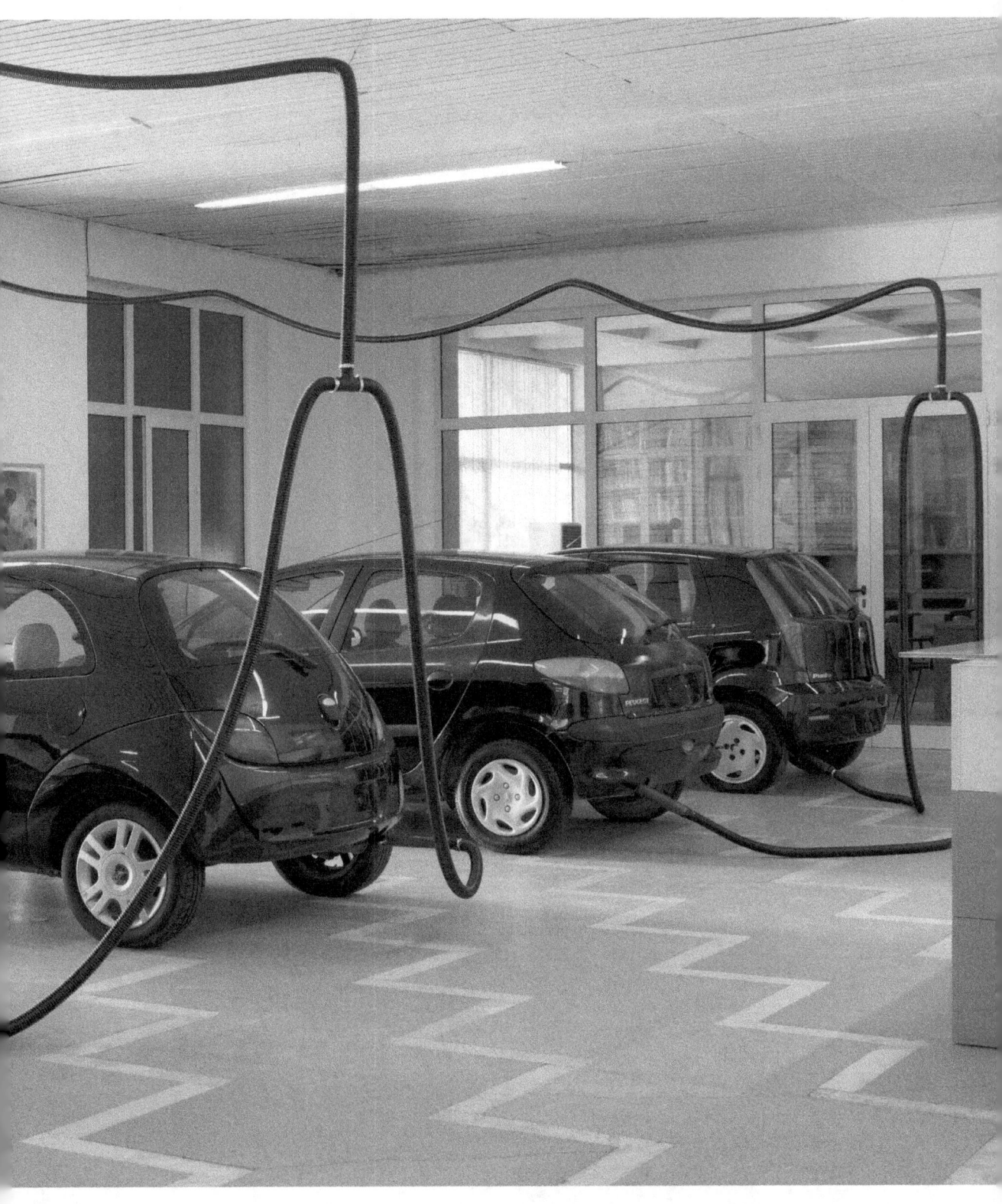

Santiago Sierra, *Four Black Vehicles with the Engine Running inside an Art Gallery*, mixed media, National Gallery of Arts, Tirana, Albania 2015.

Santiago Sierra, *Katër automjete të zeza me motor ndezur brenda një galerie arti*, media e përzier, Galeria Kombëtare e Artit, Tiranë, Shqipëri, 2015.

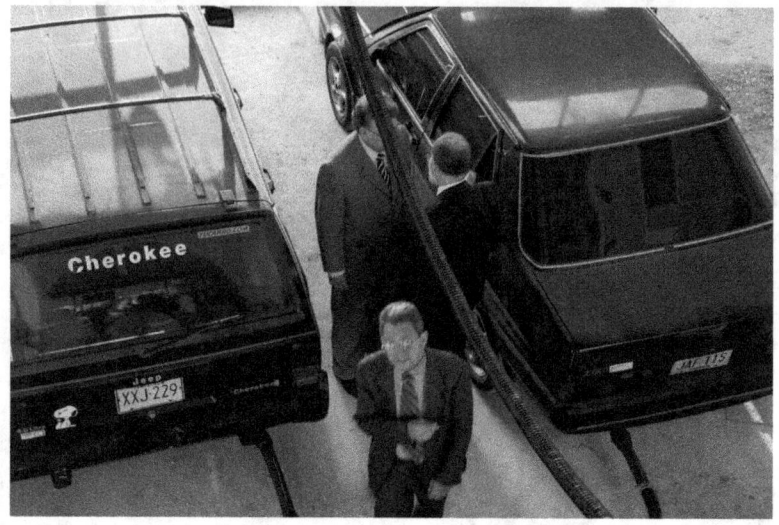

Santiago Sierra, *Four Black Vehicles with the Engine Running inside an Art Gallery,* mixed media, Sala Mendoza, Caracas, Venezuela, 2008.

Santiago Sierra, *Katër automjete të zeza me motor ndezur brenda një galerie arti,* media e përzier, Sala Mendoza, Karakas, Venezuelë, 2008.

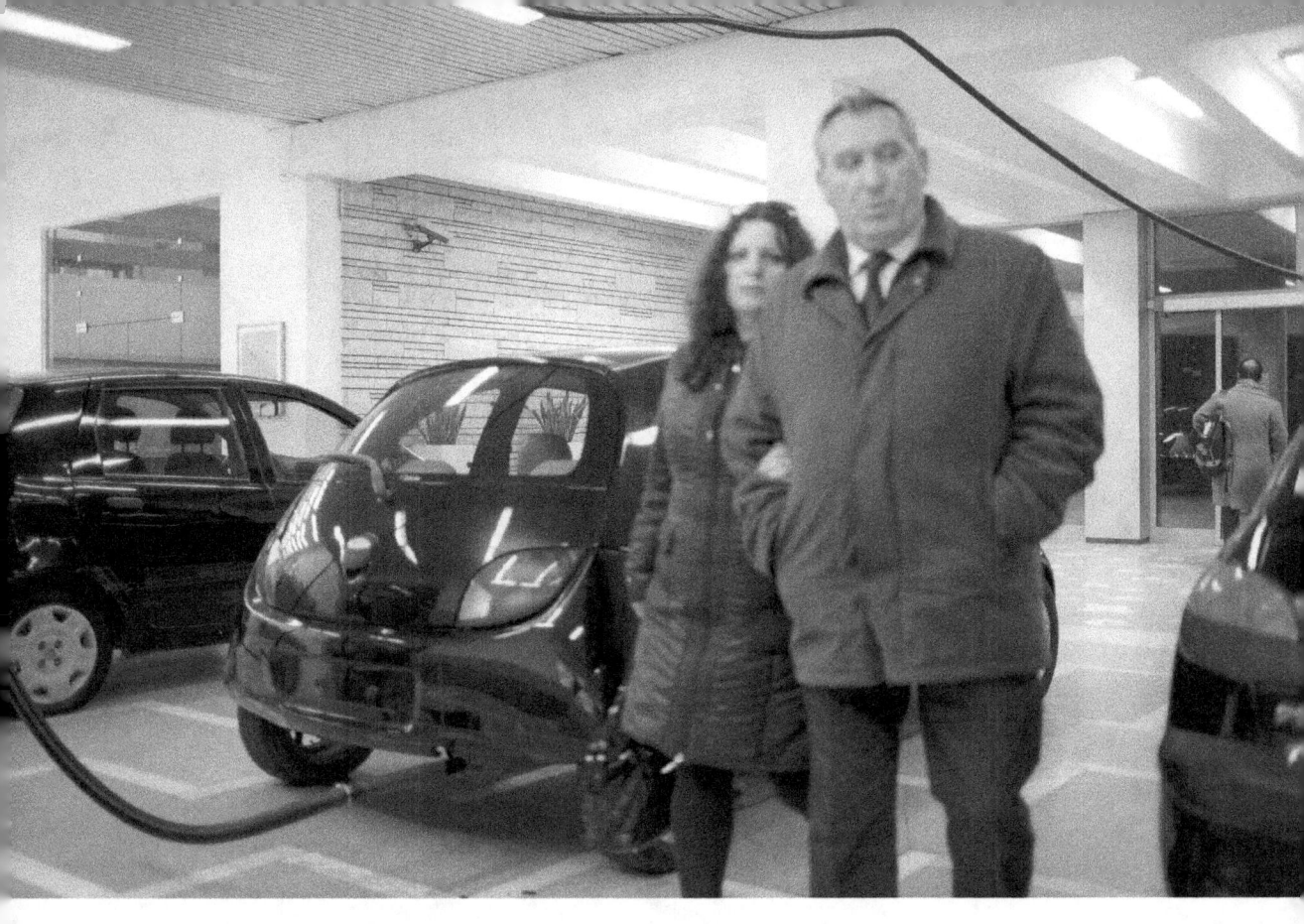

Santiago Sierra, *Four Black Vehicles with the Engine Running inside an Art Gallery*, mixed media, National Gallery of Arts, Tirana, Albania 2015.

Santiago Sierra, *Katër automjete të zeza me motor ndezur brenda një galerie arti*, media e përzier, Galeria Kombëtare e Artit, Tiranë, Shqipëri, 2015.

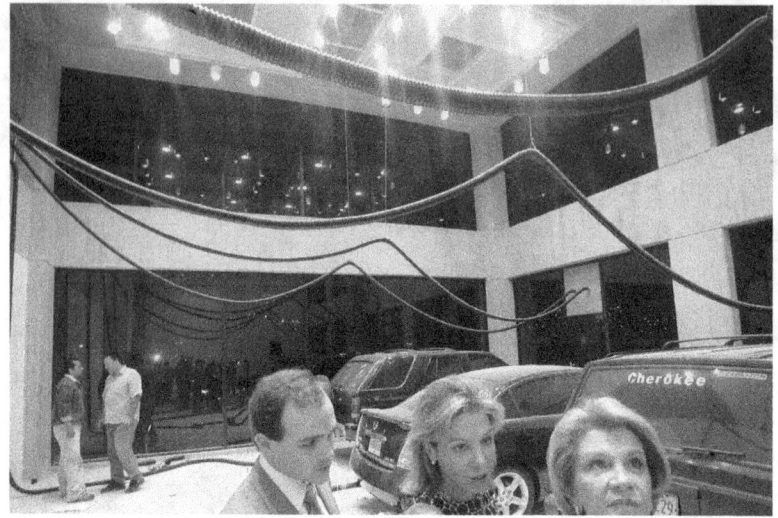

Santiago Sierra, *Four Black Vehicles with the Engine Running inside an Art Gallery*, mixed media, Sala Mendoza, Caracas, Venezuela, 2008.

Santiago Sierra, *Katër automjete të zeza me motor ndezur brenda një galerie arti*, media e përzier, Sala Mendoza, Karakas, Venezuelë, 2008.

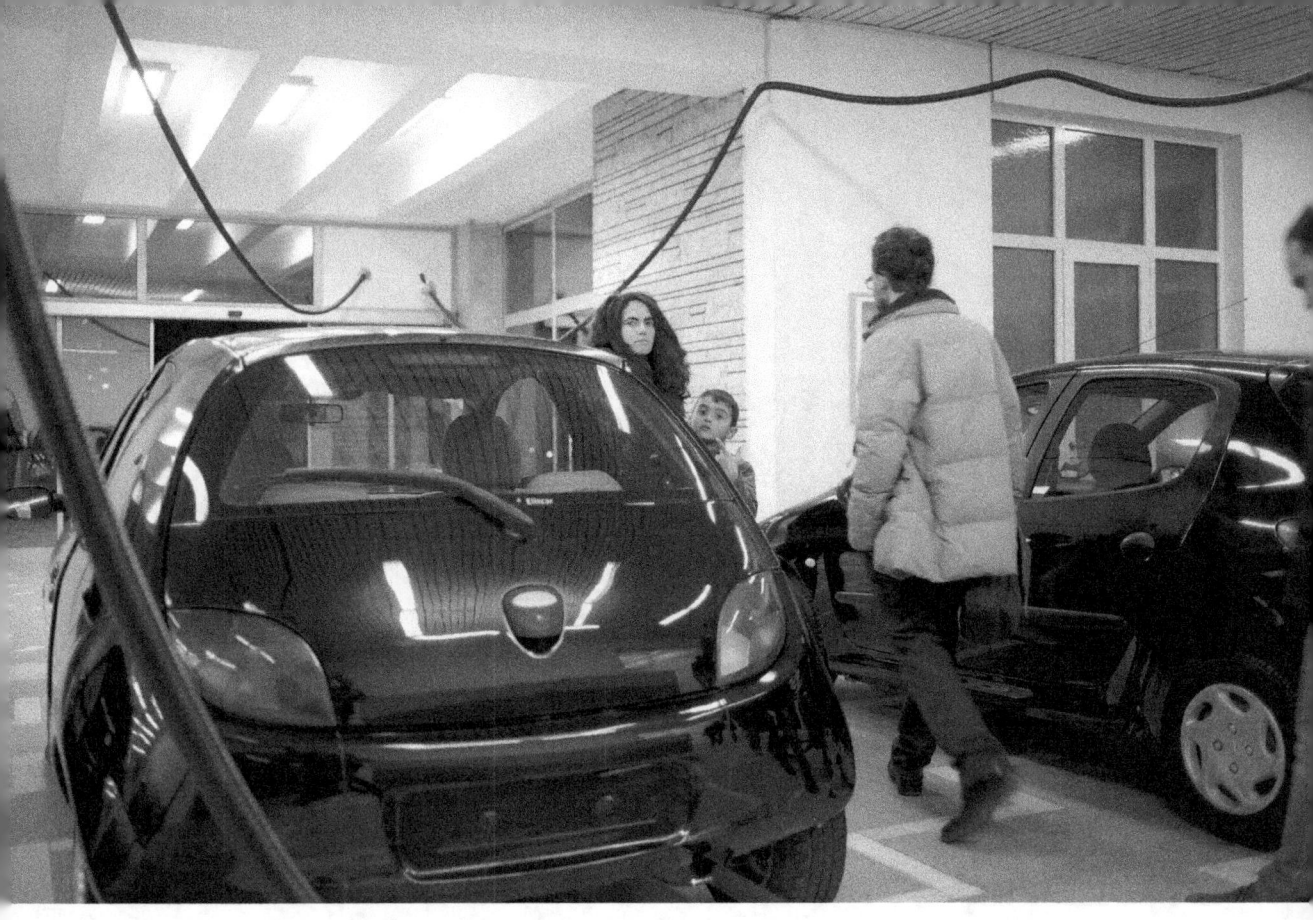

Santiago Sierra, *Four Black Vehicles with the Engine Running inside an Art Gallery,* mixed media, National Gallery of Arts, Tirana, Albania 2015.

Santiago Sierra, *Katër automjete të zeza me motor ndezur brenda një galerie arti,* media e përzier, Galeria Kombëtare e Artit, Tiranë, Shqipëri, 2015.

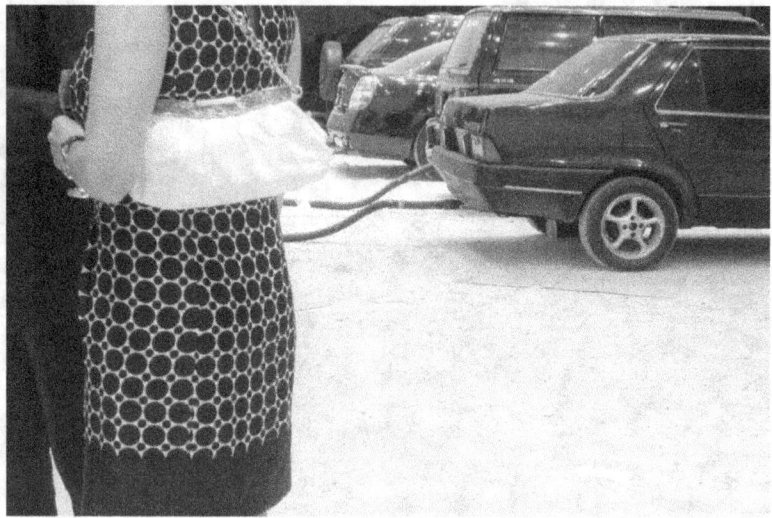

Santiago Sierra, *Four Black Vehicles with the Engine Running inside an Art Gallery,* mixed media, Sala Mendoza, Caracas, Venezuela, 2008.

Santiago Sierra, *Katër automjete të zeza me motor ndezur brenda një galerie arti,* media e përzier, Sala Mendoza, Karakas, Venezuelë, 2008.

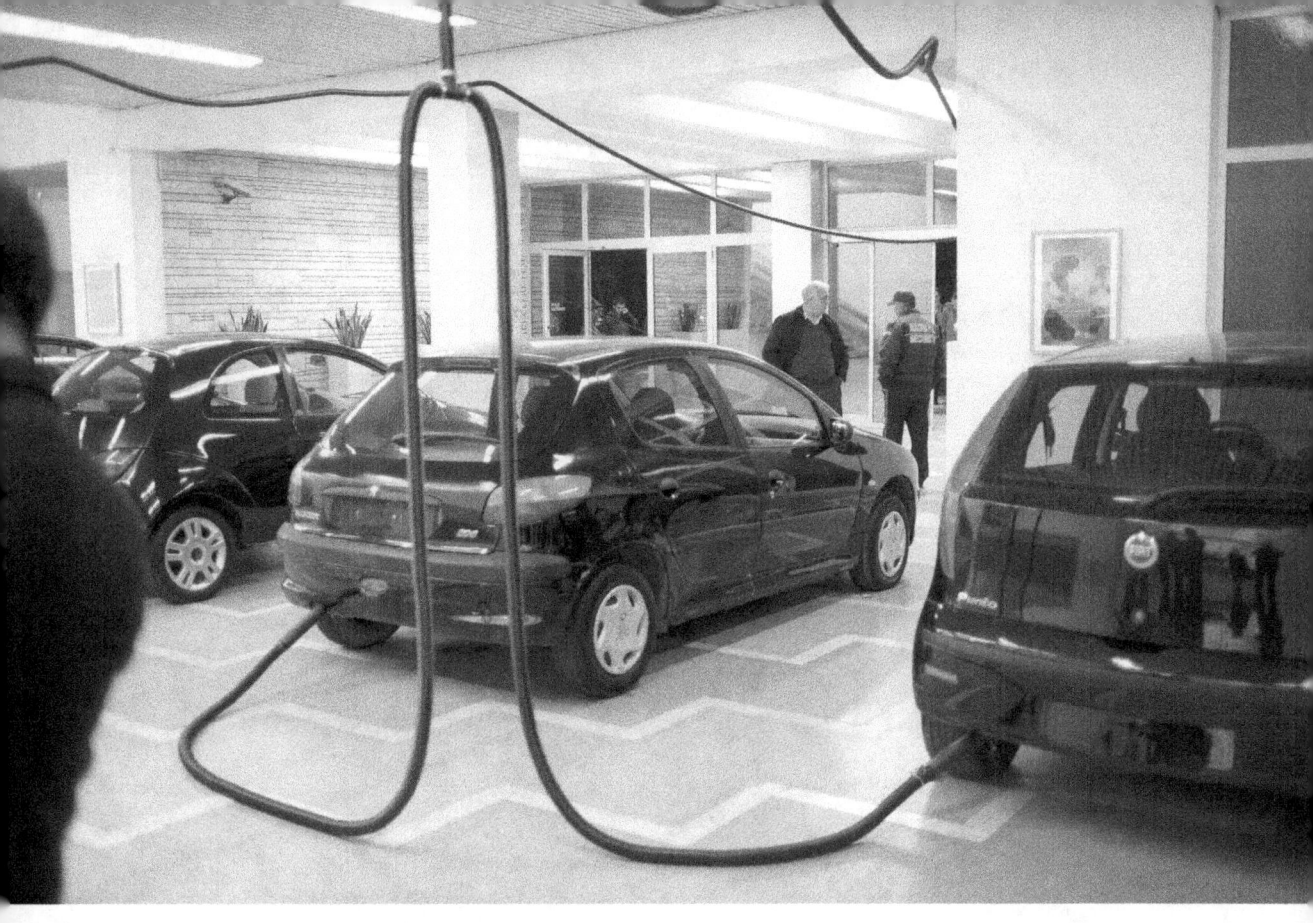

Santiago Sierra, *Four Black Vehicles with the Engine Running inside an Art Gallery*, mixed media, National Gallery of Arts, Tirana, Albania 2015.

Santiago Sierra, *Katër automjete të zeza me motor ndezur brenda një galerie arti*, media e përzier, Galeria Kombëtare e Artit, Tiranë, Shqipëri, 2015.

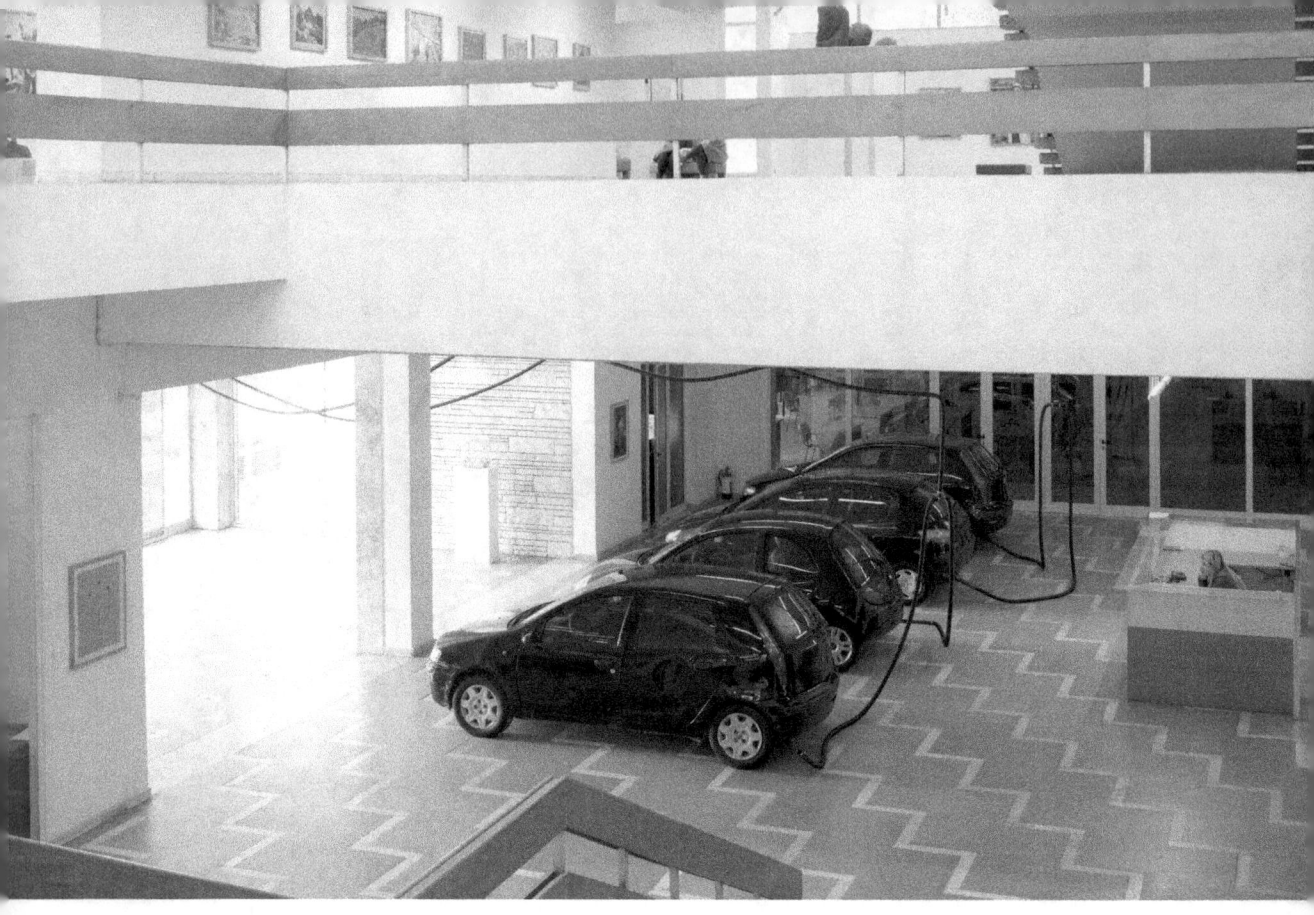

Exhibition view.

Pamje ekspozite.

Sali Shijaku's Zëri i Masës and the Metaphysics of Representation in Albanian Socialist Realist Painting

1. Introduction

The innovative aspect of this painting is not that the painter invited several other people into the studio, and depicted them alongside himself. Its innovative, and national, character comes from the fact that it incorporates [class-]conscious workers, that their thoughts and their ideology are included within it. [...] The image's novel quality stems not from any new technical innovation or display of virtuosity, but from the artist's attitude towards the working class and towards our new reality.[1]

Thus did sculptor Kristaq Rama describe Sali Shijaku's *Zëri i Masës* [*Voice of the Masses*] in a 1977 lecture devoted to images of socialist life and the positive hero in the figurative arts. Let us, for the moment, take Rama at his word, and accept that insofar as Shijaku's painting represents an innovation, a new comportment towards artistic creation that accords itself to the ideological framework of the socialist "New Life," it does so because at its conceptual and compositional center stands the worker. This, of course, leaves open the question that Rama's lecture – which takes *Zëri i Masës* as its point of inception – never fully answers. Namely: what is the relationship between art, the working class, and "our new reality" as it *actually appears* in the painting?

On the one hand, we must keep in mind that this ambiguity was not only endemic to the aesthetic criticism of the socialist period in Albania, but was in fact an integral part of its function. It was just such an ambiguity that allowed the idea of 'reality' to remain so nebulous

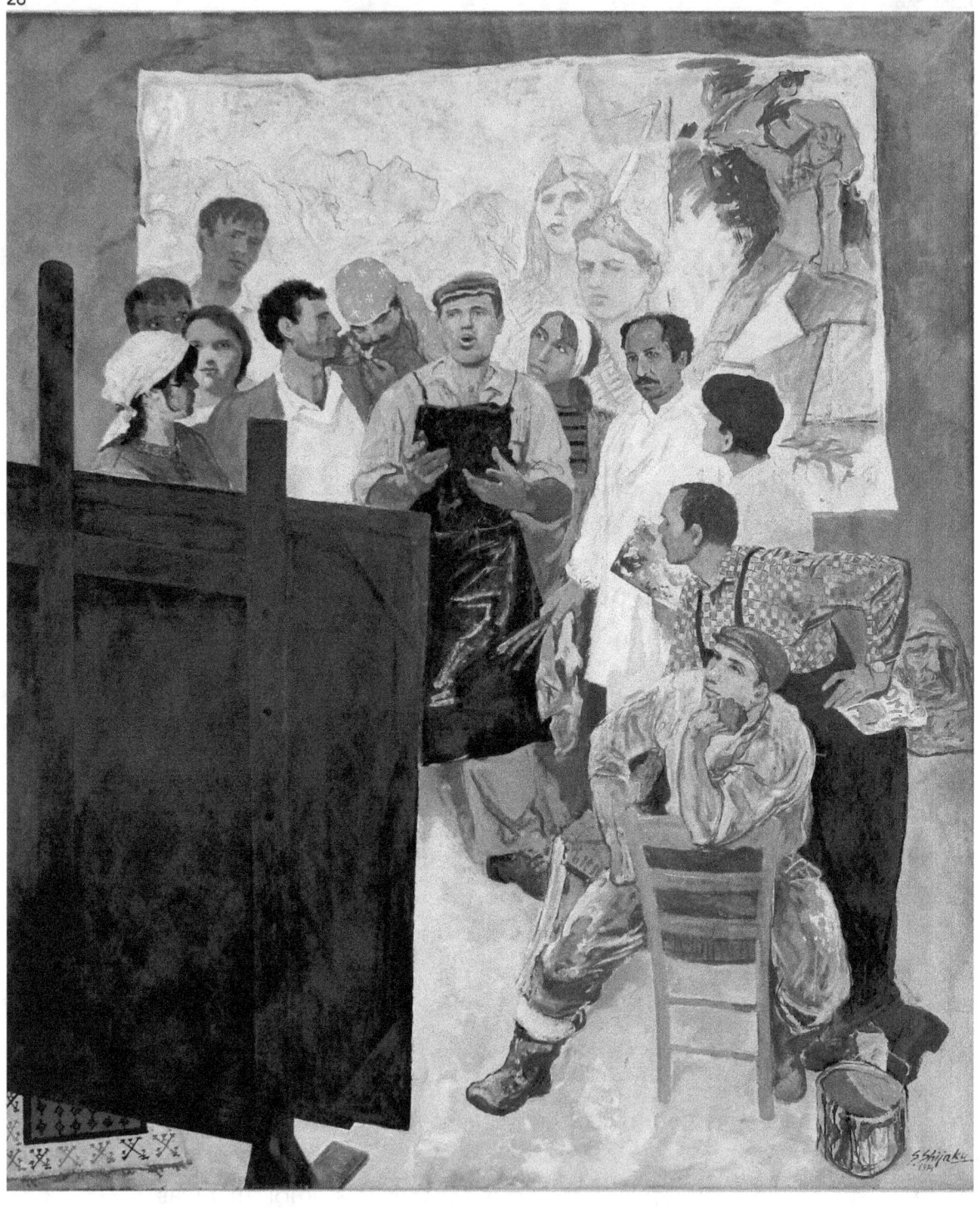

Sali Shijaku, *The Voice of the Masses,*
oil on canvas, 250 x 206 cm, 1974.

Sali Shijaku, *Zëri i Masës,* vaj në
kanavacë, 250 x 206 cm, 1974.

and elusive, simultaneously promised by the future and embodied in the present. At the same time we must acknowledge that the socialist realist system possessed a great sense for metaphor, for the discovery of hidden associative meanings. That is, it understood the possibility that the signs of subversive, revisionist ideology could appear anywhere, at any time, and thus that a heightened hermeneutical sensitivity was always necessary, especially when encountering works of art. Thus, no matter how superficial Rama's critical treatment of a work like *Zëri i Masës* must seem at first glance, this should not prevent us from approaching the work as a complex system of meanings, and from realizing that this complexity would have characterized the work in the context in which it was created and viewed.

Of course, there is a *right way* to view and understand the painting – that is precisely what Rama's description gives us – but that *right way* is not as reductive as it might seem, for it involves understanding how the totality of the painting's diverse threads of meaning are to be united in the correct aesthetic comportment towards the new Albanian socialist existence.

2. Producing the Image of the Production of Socialist Reality

Sali Shijaku (b. 1933) emerged as one of the most important painters of socialist realism during a crucial period of transition in the visual arts in socialist Albania (and indeed his works often occupied an aggressive formal periphery within official art of the period). Like many other Albanian artists of his time, he first attended the Jordan Misja Lyceum in Tirana, where his professors included Abdurrahim Buza and Nexhmedin Zajmi, and later the Ilya Repin Academy of Fine Arts in St. Petersburg.[2] After completing his studies in 1962, Shijaku became one of the artists whose works epitomized the dynamic possibilities of socialist realist representation in Albania.[3]

In the late 1960s and early 1970s, Albanian socialist realist art developed and diversified in a number of ways, and the first years of the 70s are typically regarded as representing a period of relative openness towards more overtly Modernist models of representation in the fine arts.[4] The stylistic and thematic diversity of these years (which, when it drifted too far became "eclecticism" and eventually forth-rightly "bourgeois-revisionism"[5]) can, in another sense, be seen as endemic to what Katerina Clark has called socialist realism's "modal schizophrenia, its proclivity for making sudden transitions from realis-tic discourse to the mythic or utopian."[6] Shijaku's own paintings, which ranged from monumental depictions of partisan heroes (such as his well-known *Vojo Kushi*, 1969) to vibrant images of landscapes and ag-ricultural workers, certainly embody the paradoxes of socialist realist modality. Within the artist's oeuvre, however, and indeed among other works from this period in Albanian history, *Zëri i Masës* represents a particularly sophisticated aesthetic topology of the character of "our new reality."

In 1970, dictator Enver Hoxha asserted that "in the greater part of our country's literary and artistic production … our New Man finds himself. In it, he sees the vitality of our socialist people and fatherland, he hears the fiery and beloved words of the Party, and he is filled with courage to continue onward on his ascent up the steps of life."[7] Shijaku's painting attempts to represent precisely this situation of re-flection wherein the New Man finds himself in art, to depict the meta-physical movement whereby art "takes its inspiration from the people and returns it to them."[8] To arrive at this representation, Shijaku cre-ates an image that both explicitly establishes itself in the tradition of *realist* painting tout court, *and* treats the uniqueness of the socialist context for the production of works of art.

Put plainly: *Zëri i Masës* depicts a system that encompasses the creation and reception of works of Albanian socialist realism. It de-scribes a visual (and conceptual) hierarchy of the materialization of ideas as well as of modes of perception and contemplation. In the de-piction of this system, it engages with certain well-known tropes from the history of painting (the representation of the interior of the artist's studio, of the creative process, of the absorbed reception of art, and of the blank back of the canvas, for example). Despite this clear refer-ence to traditions of picture-making, however, Shijaku has not merely changed certain thematic elements to make the painting at home in its contemporary political-historical context, but has in fact attempted to introduce a new *structure*. This structure is not wholly innovative or without precedent, but it is true that endemic to this structure is *the production and sustenance of the new reality*. The work makes this structure apparent by playing upon the same kinds of ambiguity that characterize Rama's critical appraisal of the painting, by revealing the origin and reception of its reality *without ever actually attempting to reflect or depict the reality itself*. In this way, the work is perhaps one of the most honest works of Albanian socialist realism (a description that I will qualify below, for it certainly demands qualification). It is also one of the most successful, in that it understands the reality of socialist realism to be, as Evgeny Dobrenko puts it, the image of production of socialist reality itself.[9] In other words, the painting is a machine that produces socialist reality by showing the inner workings of the production of socialist reality.

3. The Shape of Zëri i Masës

At the center of the painting stands the worker – but at first we need merely note that the painting *has a center*, that all the elements and implied movements that make up the work as a whole take up their places around this center (which is, however, not necessarily the only 'center' of the work in a phenomenological sense). Let us also note, following Kujtim Buza, that the worker is the only figure really *moving*, and it is his motion that puts into play all the surrounding figures.[10] But for the moment we set aside the worker, caught mid-sentence, hands raised in the midst of explication, not because his role in the painting is merely formal (necessitated, for example, by the aesthetic demand for *centrality* in socialist realism) but because we will not fully understand his role until we examine the other elements of the painting.

If the worker is the source of motion in the image, we can identify two major movements that stem from his vitality. The first is a kind of ebb and flow that centers on his gesticulation, both reflecting his own oratory back at him and spinning it out into the small groups of onlookers – and even into the depicted canvas itself, seen only from the back. The second movement is the more quintessentially metaphysical one, the one that moves from the top of the canvas to the bottom and that, at first glance, seems to represent the movement from abstract ideas to concrete materializations of socialist reality. This movement is tripartite: from the wall behind the group, to the central gathering of figures, to the worker at lower right and the back of the canvas, which seem most convincingly to join *our* space. (Although the movement is spatial, there is also an element of the flow from the past to the present.) Both movements pass through the worker, and as such he functions as the medium through which they become tangible and comprehensible to the viewer. However, both also ultimately draw the viewer's attention down to the lower left of the painting, to the back of the canvas that the onlookers are gathered to contemplate and discuss. Since the front of the canvas remains a mystery, it is left to the viewer to (re)construct the content of the work from the reactions and attitudes of the *depicted* viewers.

The unseen painting within the painting thus functions as a second center, absorbing the viewer into its ambiguous space (since it occupies roughly a quarter of the work) and then redirecting her attention back to the various modes of attention modeled by the onlookers in the studio. These onlookers – a group that contains several recognizable types, including both villagers and workers – display various levels of engagement with both the painting and the worker-orator at center. Two on the right (one of whom – possibly a reporter – has a copy of *Drita*, the weekly publication of the Albanian Union of Writers and Artists, shoved in his back pocket, revealing a literary and ideological preparation to engage with works of art) gaze raptly back towards the worker who is speaking. Some of those to the left seem absorbed in their own activity, such as the man lighting a cigarette, while others either look to the worker, to the canvas at lower left, or – in case of one of the women – stare directly out of the painting.

The artist himself stands unmoving just to the right of the speaking worker, his gaze fixed on the work that he has either just completed or is still in the process of creating. His lowered hands, one holding his palette and the other his brushes, offer a counterpoint to the expressive gesture of the worker's hands, and together the two suggest a definite parallelism: there is *expression* to be found in the work of

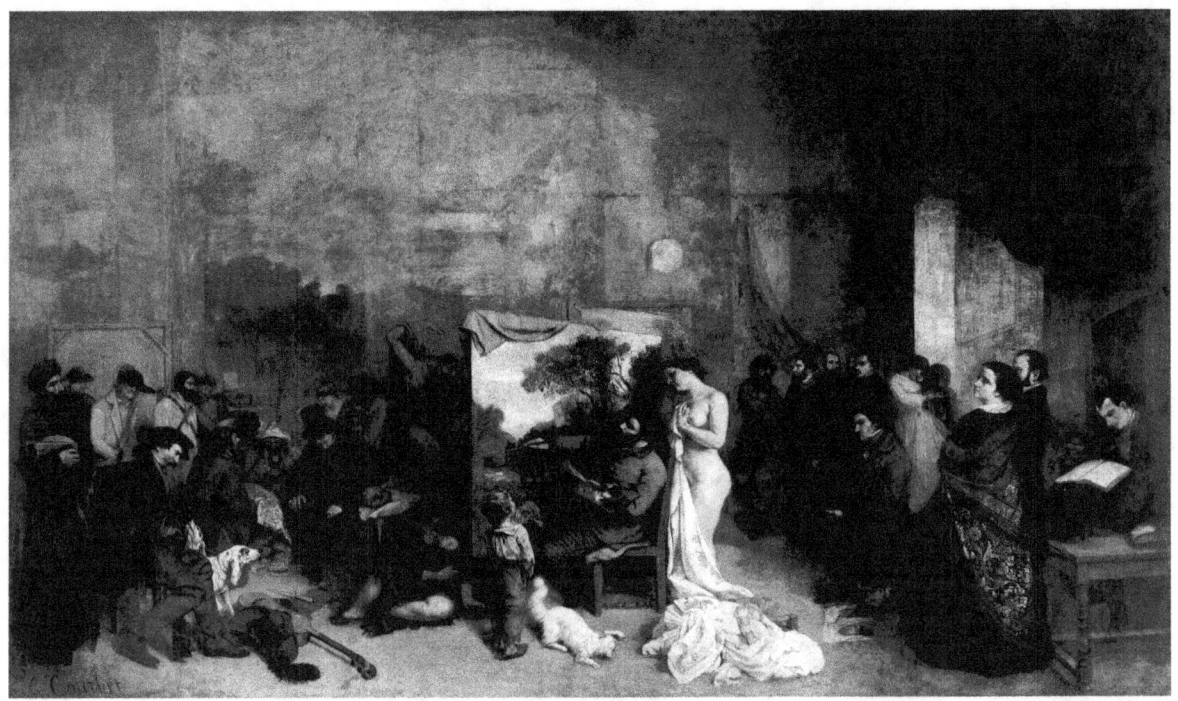

the hands of both the artist and the laborer, both produce the kind of meaning that ecstatically pours forth (through the mysterious concealed image and through the worker's narration) by means of *gesture*. This emphasis on the emphatic and expressive gesture of the hand is predicted in the sketch for *Vojo Kushi* hanging behind the gathering, where the figure's aggressive heroism is concentrated in the one hand prying open the tank and the other preparing to hurl the grenade. On another level, the very materiality of the work – of Shijaku's signature painterliness and effective use of impasto passages – reinforces the connections between the *work* of the artist's hands and the production of socialist reality that the worker undertakes.

Finally, the worker at the lower right – presumably a painter by his dress and the bucket next to him[11] – sits, seemingly wholly absorbed in the contemplation of the canvas, his face cradled by a hand in turn braced upon his knee in an undeniably classical pose. There is a sort of triangle formed by the central worker (the orator), the second worker (the contemplator) and the looming back of the canvas. In a certain sense, the canvas works as a second center to the painting. It not only

Gustave Courbet, *The Painter's Studio, Real Allegory Determining a Phase of Seven Years in My Artistic and Moral Life*, oil on canvas, 361 x 598 cm, 1855.

Gustave Courbet, *Studioja e piktorit, alegori e vërtetë që përcakton një fazë shtatë-vjeçare në jetën time artistike dhe morale*, vaj në kanavacë, 361 x 598 cm, 1855.

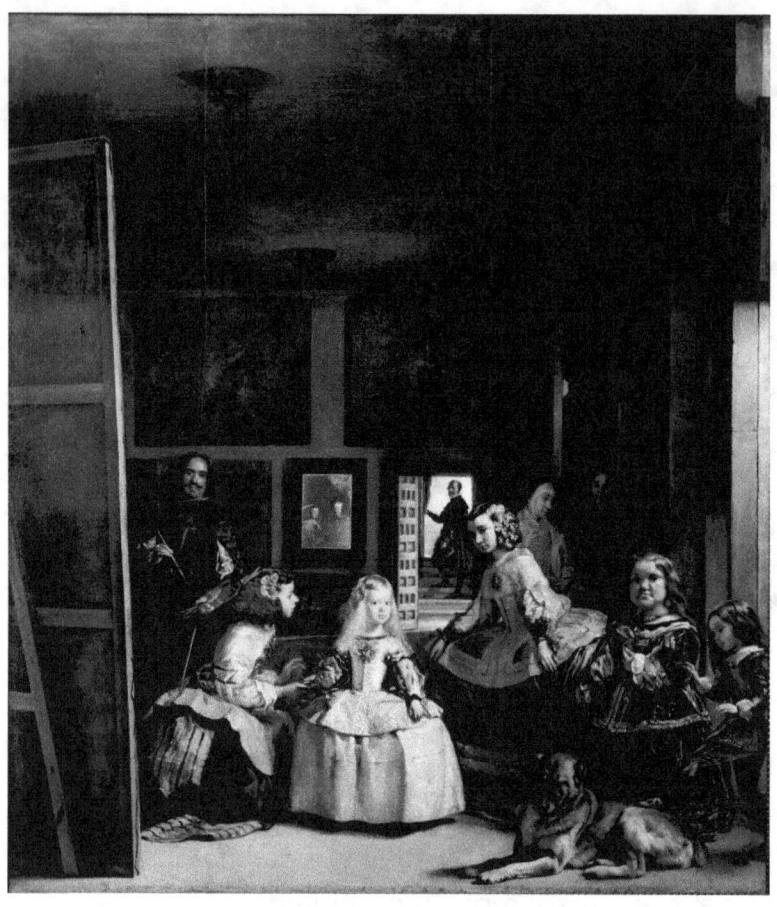

conceptually anchors the gathering of figures in *Zëri i Masës*; it also visually holds sway over all other elements present, drawing the eye to its broad brown swath, even occluding part of the central worker's body with its corner. Above all, the blank back of the canvas creates an air of mystery that pervades the experience of the painting: one wonders what is depicted on its surface. The final version of one of the sketches found on the wall behind the figures? Some other scene entirely? Perhaps even a depiction of the very people present in the room? – for one possibility is that the hidden canvas is a double of the work we are in the process of viewing, creating an infinite loop of viewing that includes both the viewer and all those present in the scene…in fact, all of *reality*.

In both theme and the ambition of its meta-pictorial commentary,

Diego Velázquez, *Las Meninas*, oil on canvas, 320 x 276 cm, 1656.

Diego Velázquez, *Las Meninas*, vaj në kanavacë, 320 x 276 cm, 1656.

the clearest realist predecessor to *Zëri i Masës* is Gustave Courbet's massive *The Painter's Studio, Real Allegory Determining a Phase of Seven Years in My Artistic and Moral Life* of 1854-55. In Courbet's image, the artist sits at the center of the composition, engaged in painting a landscape, surrounded by a collection of viewers (a naked muse, a cat, a young peasant, several of the artist's friends and intellectual champions, and a collection of general types). Courbet's iconic painting depicts the central role of the artist in synthesizing and representing the whole of reality, even as – in the title's assertion that the work is a *real allegory* – it broaches the complex and contradictory character of the relationship between the act of painting and the real. Shijaku does not, however, borrow Courbet's compositional schema.[12] The more direct reference goes back two centuries more, to Diego Velázquez's *Las Meninas* of 1656.[13] It is deeply significant that Shijaku would turn to the Baroque – and in particular, to an image like *Las Meninas* – as a paradigm for the painting of socialist reality.

Michel Foucault most famously analyzed Velázquez's painting as a the representation of a whole system of (Classical) representation, a representation in which the subject-viewer "has been elided" – leaving behind an "essential void."[14] Shijaku's painting is certainly the representation of representation itself – specifically, of the production of the representation of socialist representation. But it is perhaps easier to read the image along the lines of Svetlana Alpers's interpretation of *Las Meninas*, as an image that straddles two systems of representation: one in which the artist looks out at the world and one in which the world projects itself onto a surface.[15] For Alpers, the tension between these two systems – seeing and being seen – is fundamentally unresolvable in Velázquez's painting, and the lack of resolution is the key to the work's poignancy. A similar point could be made regarding *Zëri i Masës*, though the movement of *reflection* has perhaps been heightened even though Shijaku replaces the mirror of *Las Meninas* with the sketches covering the back wall of the studio. Here, the tension is one endemic to socialist realist art, as outlined in Enver Hoxha's statement above: that between the artist observing the New Life and depicting it, and the New Life projecting itself in its dynamism. In either case, *Zëri i Masës* raises the question of our access to the New Life in art, and part of the key to its elaboration of this tension is the back of the canvas shown in the image. It would benefit us, however, to return to a careful spatial analysis of the painting.

At the uppermost level, the level of the artist's sketches mounted on the wall, is the realm of ideas. The world of ideas is largely indistinct – devoid of color except in the case of the brilliant red and black of Vojo Kushi – and amorphous. Several different scenes form the white register, as if this ideal realm was coterminous with the artist's mind. However, since the artist is not the central figure, it seems unlikely that the upper register of the painting merely offers a psychological snapshot, an inventory of creative ideas present for the artist, waiting to be (more) fully realized. Instead, I think that the upper level of the painting is meant to represent the metaphysical primacy of the images portrayed, and it is significant for this primacy that they are linked to the past. Images of war heroes, of the mountainous terrain of Albania itself: these images form part of a realm of primordial myth that both acts as the foundation for and is transformed by "our new reality." This transformation occurs through the artist, but his action alone is not sufficient to establish the full significance of the new reality – his bringing it to vision does not suffice to make it a part of the New Life. This, I think, is one reason why we do not, and need not, see whether or not the images the artist has sketched find themselves realized on the canvas. The New Life projects itself, but at the same time this projection *exceeds the need for re-presentation*. If we are somehow blocked from the space of *Zëri i Masës* by the canvas, if the dialogue between the spaces it depicts seems self-contained, then the painting functions by producing an unrepresentable excess, the impossibility of showing reality even as it shows the production of reality.

Below the realm of myths and ideas is the space of the painter's studio, where the motley group described above are gathered. In some cases (such as the man at far left) the transition between the sheet with the artist's sketches and the figures present in the studio seems sufficiently ambiguous to warrant the assumption that there is an intentional and significant spatial bridge between the two; certain figures seem to occupy both spaces, or to be emerging from the upper space into the middle space (whose ambiguous flatness also suggests its continuity with the paper hung on the wall behind). It is in this middle space that the worker first enters the painting (and with him, Rama argues, his ideology and worldview, giving the work its revolutionary quality). Even the centrality of the worker who is explicating the canvas before him, however, cannot compete with the movement that draws the viewer's attention down to the back of the canvas and, at the same time, over and down to the worker who silently contemplates this canvas.

The vast expanse of the back of the canvas, placed so far forward in the scene, serves in some way to block off the space depicted within the work from the space of the viewer, but in doing so also employs the well-worn strategy of drawing the viewer into the work by just such an impediment. At the same time, the placement of the canvas (nearly, but not quite, reaching to the bottom of the painting) contributes to the hierarchical arrangement of space mentioned above, which maps the flow from ideas to their concrete materialization along the axis from the top of the painting to its bottom edge, which in turn suggests the transition to our space. What is closest to us is most "real" – although there is also the suggestion that it is meant to be more "real" than us. Since we cannot see what is depicted on the canvas, we must default not only to the worker-orator at center, but also to the worker (the painter) seated at lower right. In fact, if anything, we are more directly tied to this worker, since he models, in his rapt contemplation, the comportment towards the canvas that – presumably – we are meant to hold toward *Zëri i Masës*.

4. Voice of the Masses, Words of the Party

If the worker at lower right (who is also the final point of a sweeping diagonal beginning from the floating bust of the man at upper left), is meant to model our own engagement with the work (with a work of socialist realism in general), it is also important to note that his absorption in the work is not merely visual. After all, the very title of the painting – *Voice of the Masses* – reminds us that Shijaku's painting is also about *listening*. Here again, through the figure of the worker gazing at the canvas we cannot see, Shijaku references a rich tradition in painting and sculpture of people *absorbed* in listening (to music, to speech). At the same time, he creates an inner world for the worker who gazes at the canvas. This inner world is not one already populated with ideas and emotions; instead it is a world that exists only in relation to the prior two levels (the realm of ideas and the realm of the studio). (Here, we might observe, is the production of the space of the socialist subject, who can then be filled in with the ideological substance of the more metaphysically primary levels. At the same time, this filling-in is a paradoxically reflective process, in which the worker's reality is created for him, but shown to him as if it had existed before, in him.)

In fact, nearly all of the figures in *Zëri i Masës* appear absorbed in listening – including the artist, whose gaze appears to be one not of visual concentration but of immersion in listening to the ideas expressed by the worker speaking. The worker-orator and the work whose image we cannot see *function together* to synthesize, clarify, and expound the truth of socialist Albanian life. To encounter a work of socialist realism – and thus to encounter socialist reality – the worker at lower right shows us, is both to look *and to listen*, to be shown *and to be told*. As Enver Hoxha asserted, in the work of socialist realism, one not only sees the vision of the New Life but also "*hears* the fiery and beloved words of the Party." One need only consider the role played by radio and television, by *speeches*, in the life of citizens of socialist Albania to understand the phenomenological situation that Shijaku has translated into a strictly visual medium. The oration of socialist Albania – the one transmitted through radio and television, written in newspapers and books – has been theorized as, fundamentally, a form of totalitarian monologue.[16] While it is true that some aspect of this monologic quality is to be found in *Zëri i Masës* (for no one but the worker speaks, and his speech is decisive), I think that reading the image too strongly along these lines is reductive. For Shijaku's painting is importantly about the *dialogue* between voice and image: their mutual reinforcement and, I now wish to argue, their irreconcilable schism in the space of representation.

As Mladen Dolar writes, the voice has long been associated with the metaphysics of presence, conceptualized as "the privileged point of auto-affection, self-transparency, [and] the hold in presence."[17] The voice of the worker in *Zëri i Masës* would *seem* to perform precisely this function: it indicates the absolute self-presence of the workers' ideology and thought, the coincidence of the new reality with itself. And yet, in pairing the representation of speech with the impossibility of representing socialist reality (the canvas with its back to us), Shijaku has in fact drawn attention to the difficulty of representing "our new reality" as a condition of self-presence. Just as the worker's voice both is and is not the words of the Party[18] (which exist through him, but also before him), so the painting of Albanian socialist realism both is and is not the production of reality. The way to show this paradox, as Shijaku has done, is to draw attention to the constitutive discontinuities in the metaphysics of representation. The artist alone does not shape the image of reality, the worker also shapes it. The image alone does not define reality, it is also expressed and understood through absorption in the voice. The image of socialist reality is not simply its own picture, it is also the meta-picture of its production. This is Shijaku's *realism*.

5. Conclusion

Allow me to restate some of the principal points outlined above, and hopefully to clarify my thesis about how Shijaku's painting *works* as a paradigm of socialist realism. Put simply, and perhaps too bluntly, the painting shows that to understand reality is both to contemplate it and to listen to the explanation of what reality is. It is to understand reality as something that can never be represented as the product of a completed synthesis, for our contemplation, our narration, is always already part of the production of reality. The image depicted upon the canvas is not just a mystery to us – insofar as we viewers imagine it is some recognizable scene of socialist life or national history – but it is also superfluous in an important sense to the process Shijaku is depicting. This is what is most radical about *Zëri i Masës*: in this in-novative example of socialist realism the artist has shown the futility of *comparing* art to reality, as if we could hold reality and art as objects alongside each other, examining the canvas with an eye towards its correspondence to some element of lived experience. Such an encounter with the image would be futile not because no such correspondence exists, but because we would learn little about "our new reality" from such an encounter. The artist has chosen instead to show the new reality as a reality of mechanisms, the mechanisms of the metaphysics of aesthetic creation, interpretation, and representation. The reality of the painting is that it depicts the artistic process – both practical, in the sense of the physical production of the artwork in the space of the studio, and metaphysical, in the sense of the relationship between nascent ideas and myths and their materialization in the artwork – that gives rise to works of socialist realism. This artistic process is both visual and auditory, and it is both conceptual and ideological in addition to its aesthetic aspects. It is not individual, but fundamentally collective. The outcome of this process is not simply the work of art depicted in the image but, by metaphorical extension, the whole "new reality" occupied by we the viewers.

I said at the outset that Shijaku's painting was one of the most *honest* examples of socialist realism. I hope it has become clearer what I mean by this: that the work frankly depicts the production of a reality, its imposition and ideological strengthening, its genesis through different levels of metaphysical and ideological clarity to arrive in the world, together with its discontinuities and fundamental irreconcilabilities. The truth of *Zëri i Masës* is that the image of Albanian socialist reality is the image of image production. To reflect this reality is not to reflect a finished object, but to reflect the mechanisms by which a viewer (and an artist) is created who knows the right way to encounter the world, to understand the ideological production of the world *as* reality.

1.   "Aspekti novator i kësaj tabloje nuk qëndron në faktin që autori futi disa njerëz nëstudio dhe i piktoroi ata bashkë me piktorin. Tingullimi novator dhe kombëtar i kësaj tabloje qëndron në faktin që këtu u futën punëtorët e ndërgjegjshëm, u fut medimi i tyre, ideologjia e tyre. [...] Aspekti i ri i kësaj tabloje nuk qëndron në ndonjë shpikje të re teknike, apo në ndonjë farë virtuozizmi të të pikturuarit, por në qëndrimin që mban artisti ndaj klasës punëtore, ndaj realitetit tonë të ri."

Kristaq Rama, "Tablotë e Gjera të Jetës dhe Heroi Pozitiv në Artet Figurative," *Nëntori* 24.5 (May 1977): 227–8. (The issue is devoted to the proceedings of the 1977 Plenum of the Albanian Union of Writers and Artists, held on March 11–14.)

2. See Ylli Drishti, Suzana Varvarica Kuka, and Rudina Memaga, *Monografi: Me artistë shqiptarë të shekullit XX* (Tirana: Galeria Kombëtare e Arteve, 1999), 110–11, and Llambi Blido, *Shënime për pikturën dhe skulpturën* (Tirana: Naim Frashëri, 1987), 66–9.

3. Kujtim Buza, *Sali Shijaku: Piktor i Popullit* (Tirana: Galeria Kombëtare e Arteve, 1986), 3–5.

4. Edi Muka, "Albanian Socialist Realism, or, the Theology of Power," *East Art Map: Contemporary Art and Eastern Europe*, ed. Irwin (London: Afterall, 2006), 133.

5. It is interesting, for example, to consider the reception of Edison Gjergjo's 1971 painting *Epika e Yjeve të Mëngjesit* [*Epic of the Morning Stars*], another important image of oration and listening from the same period. In 1971, critic and art historian Andon Kuqali called it "expressive, but also eclectic." (See Kuqali, "Shprehëse, por edhe Eklektike," *Drita*, December 19, 1971.) A few years later, Gjergjo was imprisoned on the basis of his artistic production.

6. Katerina Clark, *The Soviet Novel: History as Ritual*, 3rd ed. (Bloomington: Indiana University Press, 2000), 37.

7. "Në pjesën më të madhe të krijimtarisë sonë letraro-artistik [...] njeriu ynë i ri gjen vetëveten, sheh vitalitetin e popullit dhe tëatdheut tonë socialist, dëgjon fjalën e dashur e të zjarrtë të Partisë dhe mbushet me kurajë dhe guxim për t'i ngritur kurdoherë e më lartë shkallët e jetës." Enver Hoxha, "Përshëndetje e Komitetit Qendror të PPSh dejtuar Shkrimtarëve dhe Artistëve me Rastin e 25-vjetorit të Themelimit të Lidhjes së Shkrimtarëve dhe të Artistëve të Shqipërisë," in *Mbi Letërsinë dhe Artin* (Tirana: 8 Nëntori, 1977), 314.

8. "[...] frymëzimet i merr nga populli dhe ia kthen ato prapë atij [...]." Ibid., 315.

9. Evgeny Dobrenko, *Political Economy of Socialist Realism*, trans. Jesse M. Savage (New Haven: Yale University Press, 2007), xviii.

10. Buza, *Sali Shijaku*, 5.

11. The identity of this worker as a painter suggests a further parallel between laborer and artist: it is in fact the painter who is the most enthralled viewer of the canvas, as if her were both its most enlightened critic of the mage and the most receptive to the reflection of his reality *in* the image.

12. Although if – as I argue – Shijaku's composition is fundamentally tripartite, then it bears comparison to Courbet's tripartite painting.

13. I am certainly not the first to note the influence of Velázquez and Courbet on Shijaku's painting. This has been done by Ermir Hoxha, in his article "Studio e Artistit, Krahasim mes Velaskesit, Kurbesë dhe Sali Shijakut," *Shekulli*, 17 March, 2008, 14-15 (available from: http://www.arkivalajmeve.com/Studio-e-artistit.27308/, accessed 5 March, 2015). Hoxha's analysis is perceptive, especially in his discussion of the relationship established between the face of the partisan on the wall behind the group, who gazes directly at a canvas we cannot see. However, he does not explore the full significance of the fact that we cannot see the painting being discussed, and thus does not arrive at as nuanced an analysis of the relation between artistic representation and socialist reality as I aim to provide here.

14. Michel Foucault, *The Order of Things: An Archaeology of the Human Sciences* (New York: Vintage, 1970), 16.

15. Svetlana Alpers, "Interpretation without Representation, or, the Viewing of *Las Meninas*," *Representations* (Feb., 1983): 36–7.

16. See Artan Fuga, *Monolog: Mediat dhe Propaganda Totalitare* (Tirana: Dudaj, 2010).

17. Mladen Dolar, *A Voice and Nothing More* (Cambridge, MA: MIT Pess, 2006), 37.

18. In an important way, but one beyond the scope of the current discussion, Shijaku's painting can be read in terms of Dolar's distinction between the word and the voice – and thus between the writing of the Party and the speech of workers (pictured in *Zëri i Masës* in the interesting juxtaposition of the newspaper *Drita* and the speech of the central orator).

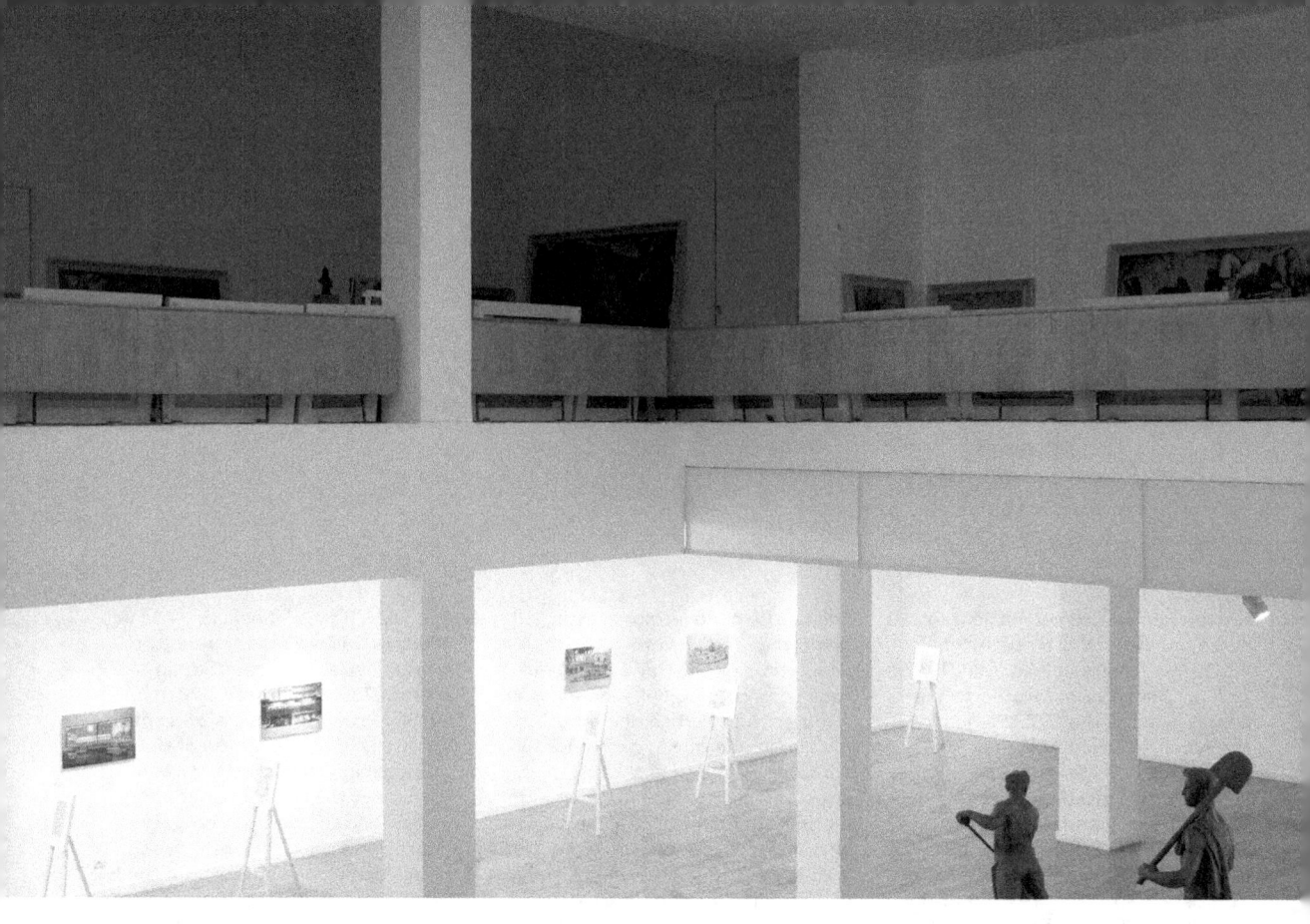

Exhibition view.

Pamje ekspozite.

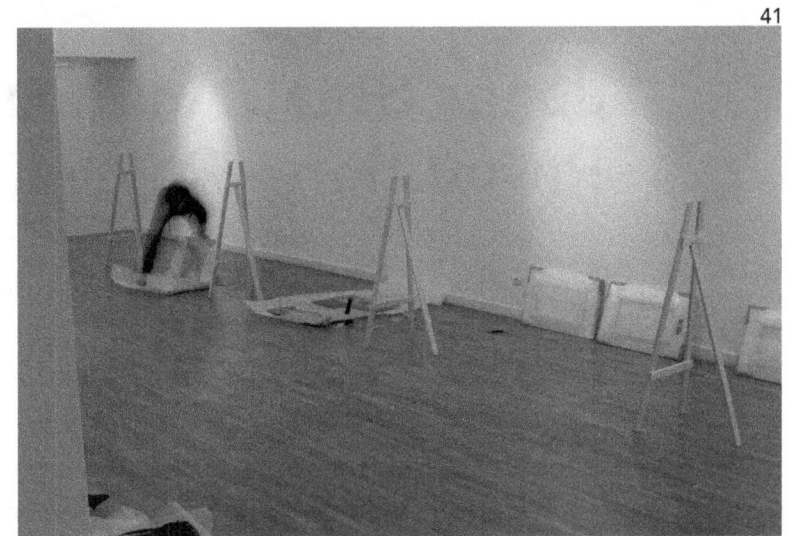

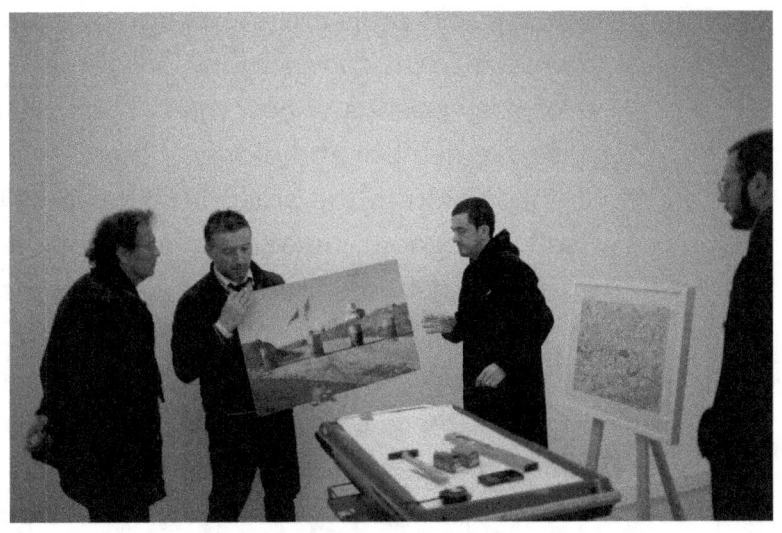

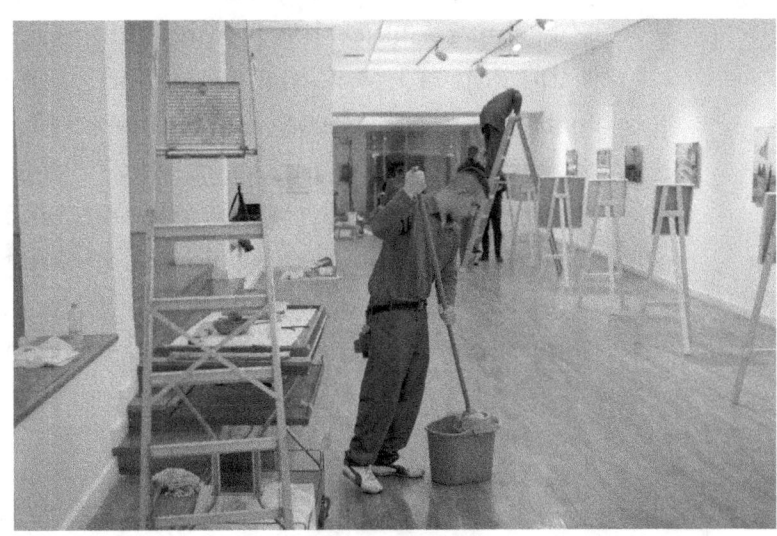

Jonas Staal: Anatomy of a Revolution – Rojava

This work of Jonas Staal draws on the documentation of his recent research in the autonomous Kurdish cantons of Rojava, in northern Syria, where he investigated the role of art in the current revolutionary struggle. These are pictures of the symbolic gestures that, in their execution and installation in public space, allow us to grasp the ways in which political missions and ideals are communicated in visual form, in which politics paints, draws, or sculpts, and in which a new political entity aims to institute and represent its legitimacy. Of particular interest in Staal's project is the image of a large-scale printer tasked with the permanent commemoration of the military conflict: churning out every day posters of new martyrs, barely keeping up with the history it is to remember and glorify.

According to the artist: "As the so-called Arab Spring manifested itself throughout the Middle-East, Syria fell into a bloody Civil War in 2012. Amidst this turmoil, inspired by the philosophy of the founder of the Kurdistan Worker's Party Abdullah Öcalan, Kurdish revolutionaries were able to take over three regions in the northern part of Syria. Together, these regions are now known as Rojava, meaning 'West,' referring to the Western part of Kurdistan. This takeover and the subsequent implementation of an alternative democratic system is declared to the world as the Rojava Revolution: a system based on secularism, gender-equality, self-government by cooperatives and councils and what the revolution has termed an 'ecology of freedom.' Most striking is the Rojava Revolution's rejection of the model of the nation-state. As the Kurdish peoples have suffered from a long history of what the movement calls "intracolonization," namely cultural oppression in Turkey, Iran, Iraq, and Syria, the revolutionaries decided that a new model was needed, one that would acknowledge the radical differentiated cultures, religions and ethnicities of the region. The photo series are glimpses into the foundations of this 'stateless democracy': from its people's parliaments, people's defense forces, educational institutions and monuments."

The many facets of the political, as much as visual, insurrection are installed in tandem with twelve drawings from the collection of the National Gallery of Arts, depicting a chapter of Albanian history in which a similar struggle was waged against a fascist, occupying force and the figure of the partisan–martyr became one of the embodiments of the post-war socialist state building project.

Jonas Staal: Anatomia e një revolucioni – Rojava. Kjo punë e Jonas Staal mbështetet në dokumentimin e udhëtimit të tij të fundit studimor në kantonet autonome kurde të Rojava-s, në veri të Sirisë, ku ai heton rolin e artit në luftën e tanishme revolucionare. Këto janë fotografi të gjesteve simbolike të cilat përmes ekzekutimit dhe instalimit të tyre në hapësirën publike na lejojë të kuptojmë mënyrat nëpërmjet të cilave misionet dhe idealet politike komunikohen në formë pamore, se si politika pikturon, vizaton apo gdhend, dhe se si një subjekt i ri politik synon të institucionalizojë dhe përfaqësojë legjitimitetin e vet. Me interes të veçantë në veprën e Jonas Staal është fotografia e një printeri të madh i ngarkuar me përkujtimin e vazhdueshëm të konfliktit ushtarak: prodhimin çdo ditë të fotove të dëshmorëve të rinj, duke përballuar me sforco ritmin e historisë të cilën duhet ta kujtojë e mbulojë me lavdi.

Artisti Staal thotë se: "Ndërsa e ashtuquajtura Pranvera Arabe përhapej në të gjithë Lindjen e Mesme, Siria u fut në një Luftë Civile të përgjakshme në vitin 2012. Në mes të kësaj trazire, revolucionarët kurdë të frymëzuar nga filozofia e themeluesit të Partisë Punëtore të Kurdistanit Abdullah Öcalan, arritën të marrin tre rajone në pjesën veriore të Sirisë. Së bashku këto rajone tani njihen si Rojava, që do të thotë 'Perëndim,' duke iu referuar pjesës perëndimore të Kurdistanit. Kjo ngjarje dhe implementimi i mëvonshëm i një sistemi alternativ demokratik i është prezantuar botës si Revolucioni Rojava: një sistem i bazuar në sekularizëm (laicizëm), barazinë gjinore, vetëqeverisjen nga ana e kooperativave dhe këshillave, si dhe në atë që revolucioni e quan 'ekologji të lirisë'. I habitshëm në këtë mes është refuzimi nga Revolucioni Rojava i modelit kombshtet. Duke qenë se si popull kurdët kanë vuajtur gjatë nga ajo që lëvizja kurde e quan "intrakolonizim", me fjalë të tjera një shtypje kulturore në Turqi, Siri, Irak dhe Iran, revolucionarët vendosën se ishte e nevojshme të krijohej një model i ri, një model i tillë që do të njohë diferencat radikale mes kulturave, feve dhe etnive të ndryshme të rajonit. Seria e fotove këtu janë shikime të shpejta në themelet e kësaj 'demokracie akoma pa shtet': që nga parlamentet e popullit, forcave të mbrojtjes popullore, institucioneve arsimore dhe monumenteve të saj."

Aspektet e shumta politike dhe pamore të Revolucionit Rojava janë instaluar krah dymbëdhjetë vizatimeve nga fondi i Galerisë Kombëtare të Arteve, të cilat përshkruajnë një kapitull të historisë shqiptare, gjatë së cilës një luftë e ngjashme u zhvillua kundër një force pushtuese fashiste dhe figura e partizanit martir u bë një nga mishërimet e projektit socialist të ndërtimit të shtetit të pasluftës.

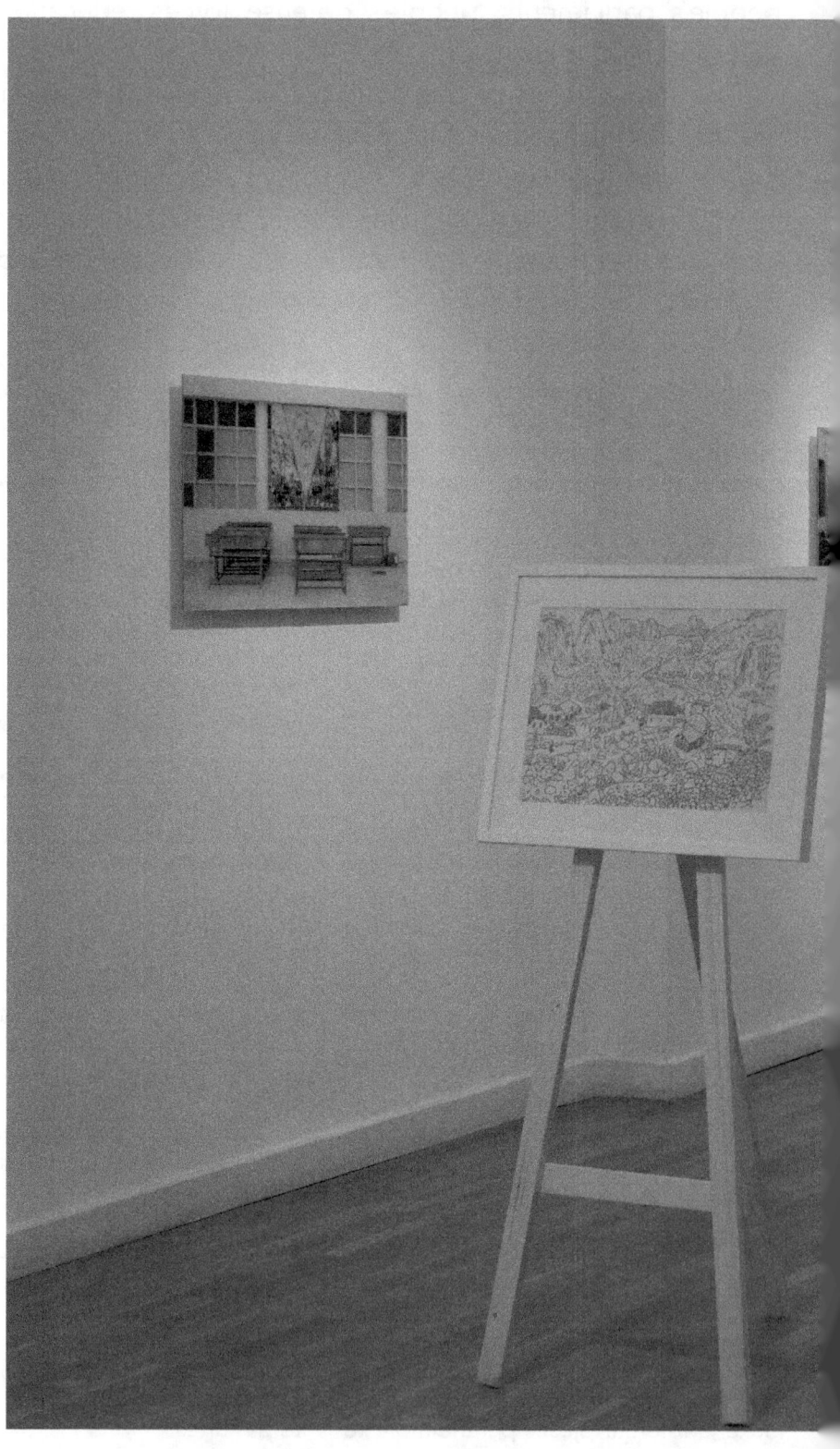

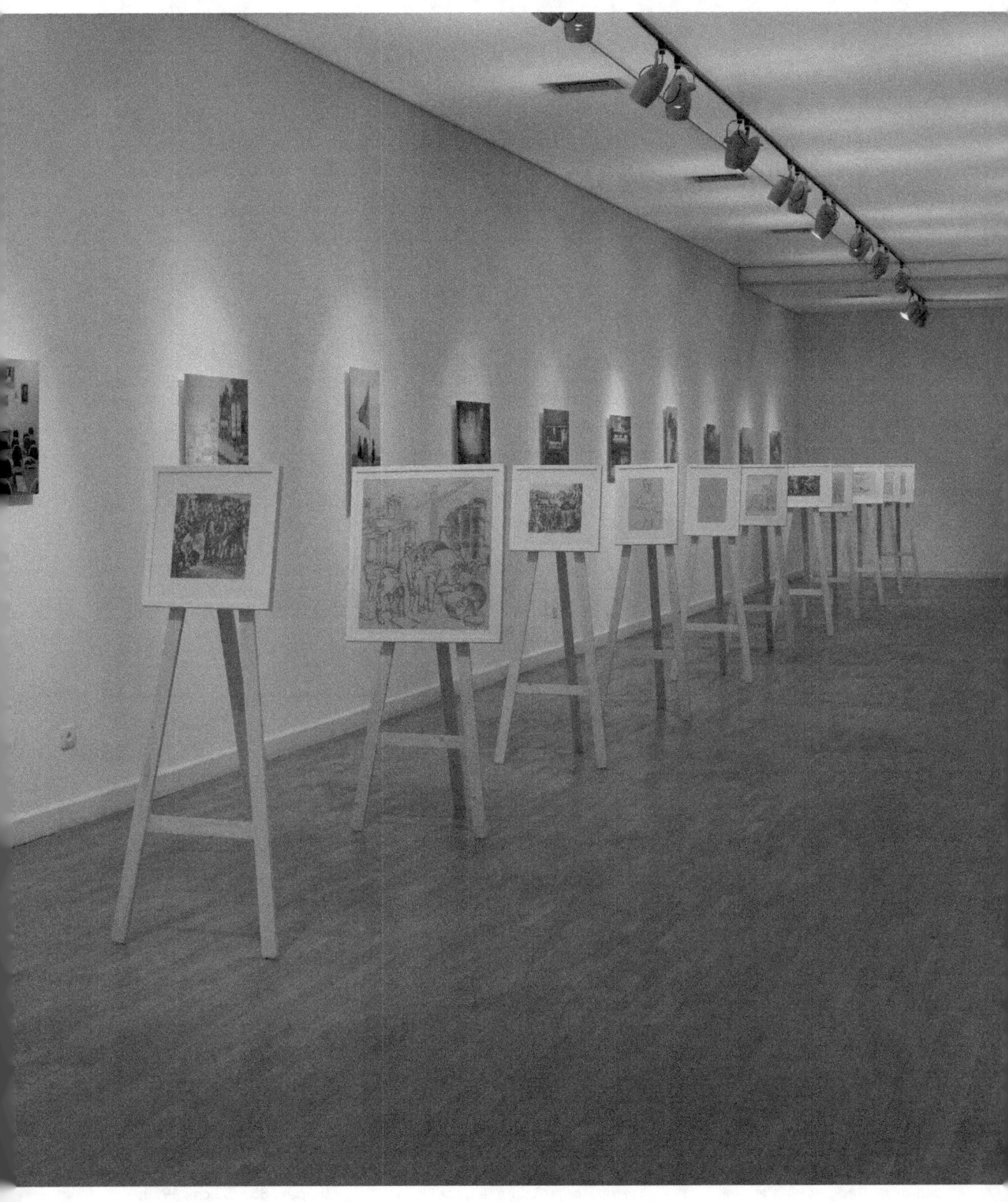

Jonas Staal, *Anatomy of a Revolution – Rojava*, 12 photographs accompanied by 12 works on paper, 2015.

Jonas Staal, *Anatomia e një revolucioni – Rojava*, 12 fotografi të shoqëruar nga 12 vepra në letër, 2015.

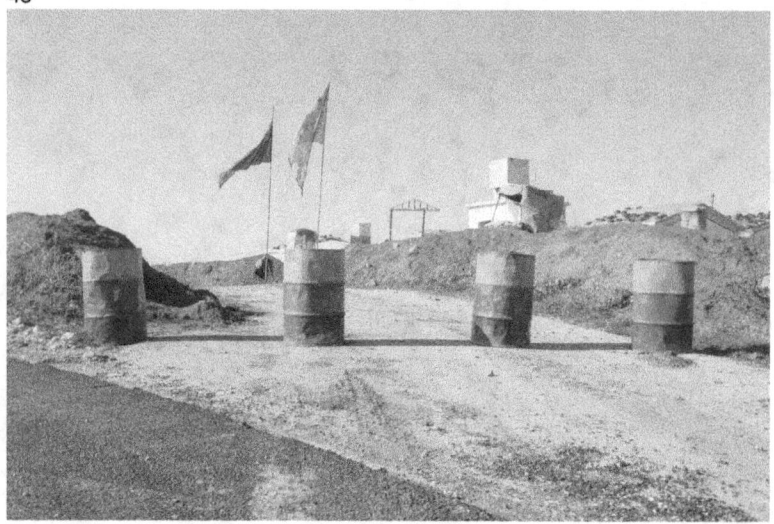

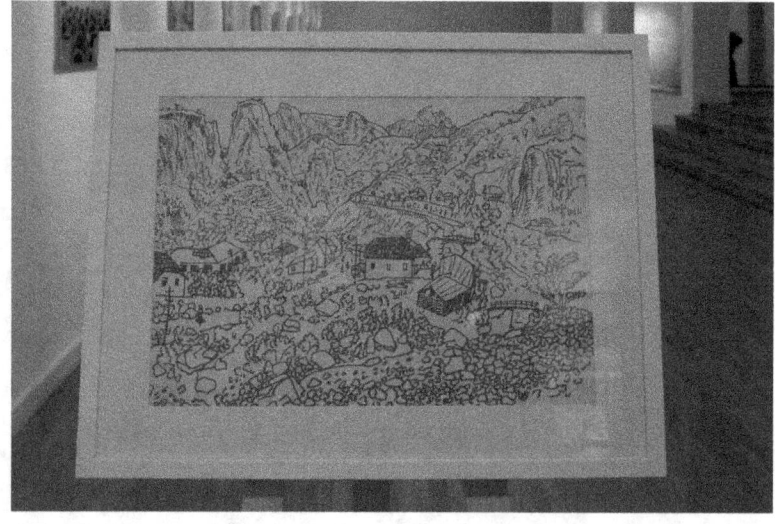

Entrance of a training camp of the self-organized people's armies People's Defense Forces (YPG) and Women's Defense Forces (YPJ) after crossing the border from Iraqi Kurdistan to Syrian Kurdistan into the autonomous canton of Cizîre.

Hyrja e një kampi trajnimi të ushtrive të vetë-organizuara të popullit, Forcave Popullore të Mbrojtjes (YPG), dhe Forcave Femërore të Mbrojtjes (YPJ), pas kalimit të kufirit nga rajoni Kurdistanit iraken në rajonin e Kurdistanit sirian, në kantonin autonom të Cizîre-s.

Sali Shijaku, *Mountain Landscape*, felt tip pen, 35 x 50 cm, 1973.

Sali Shijaku, *Peizazh nga malësia*, flamaster, 35 x 50 cm 1973.

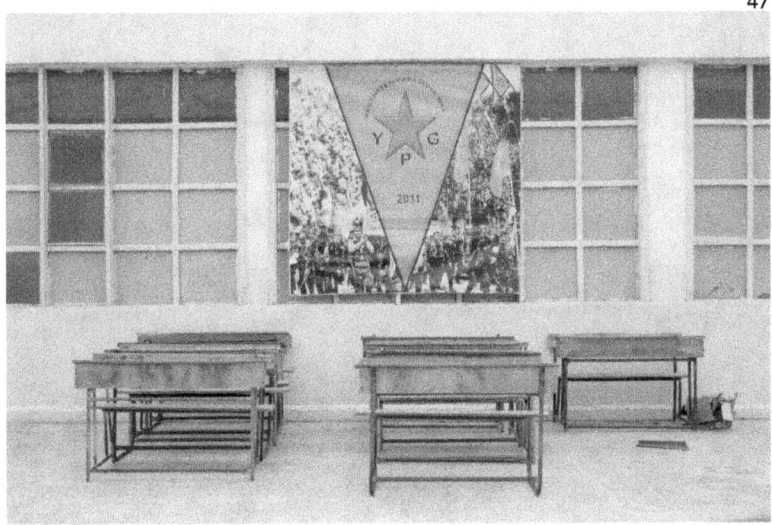

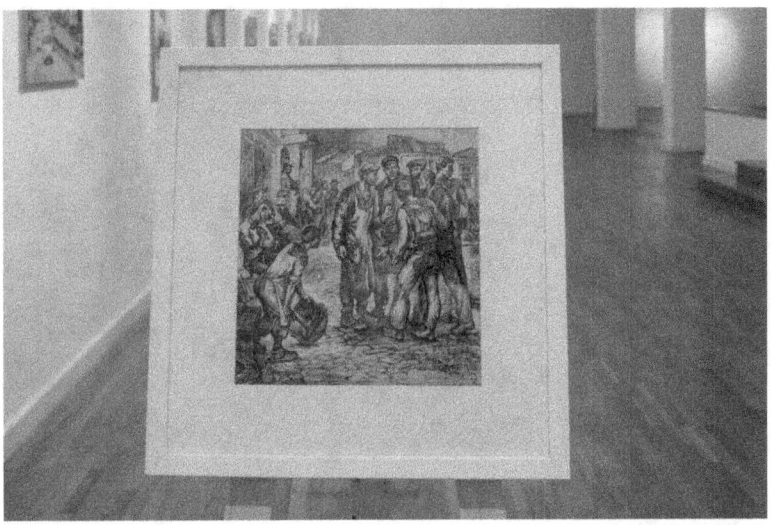

Classroom for ideological education
of the YPG.

Klasë për edukimin ideologjik të YPG.

Anastas Kostandini, *The Awakening
of the Workers*, pencil and ink, 22.5 x
27.2 cm, 1983.

Anastas Kostandini, *Zgjimi i
punëtorëve, laps dhe tush*, 22.5 x 27.2
cm, 1983.

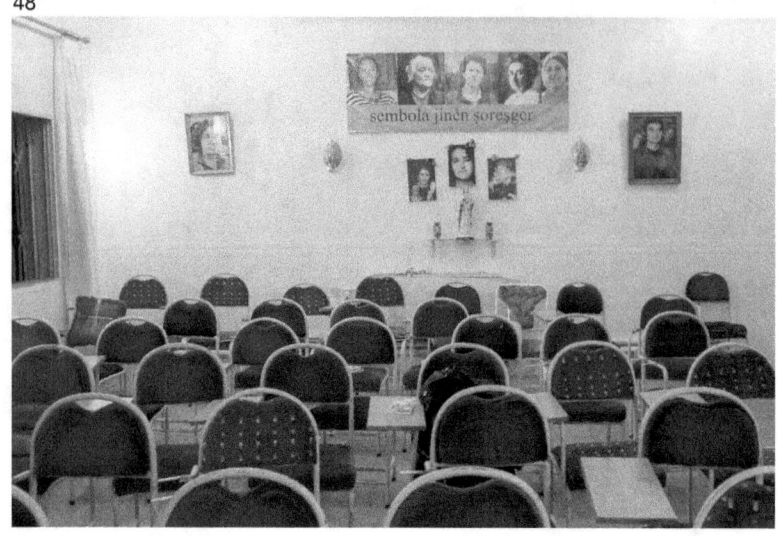

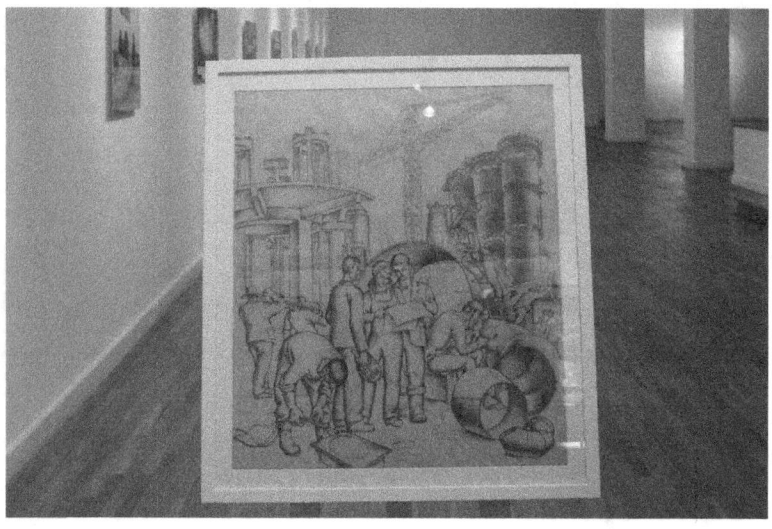

A classroom in the Women's Academy Star in Ramelan, displaying martyr portraits of women martyrs in the background. The slogan sembola jinên şoreşger means "symbols of women warriors," the portraits above depict revolutionaries Fidan Dogan, Clara Zetkin, Sakine Cansiz, Rosa Luxemburg, and Leyla Soylemez.

Një klasë në Akademinë Femërore të Yllit në Ramelan, ku shfaqen portrete martiresh të grave dëshmore në sfond. Slogani sembola jinên şoreşger përkthehet si "simbole të grave luftëtare". Portretet më sipër janë të revolucionarëve Fidan Dogan, Clara Zetkin, Sakine Cansiz, Rosa Luxemburg, dhe Leyla Soylemez.

Isuf Sulovari, *Sketch for At the Giant of the Metallurgy,* pencil, 59 x 52 cm, 1974.

Isuf Sulovari, *Në gjiganden e metallurgjikut – bocet,* laps, 59 x 52 cm, 1974.

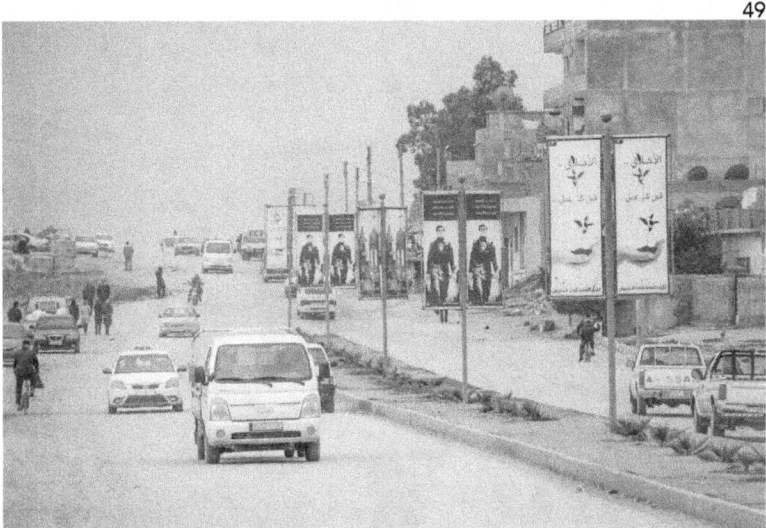

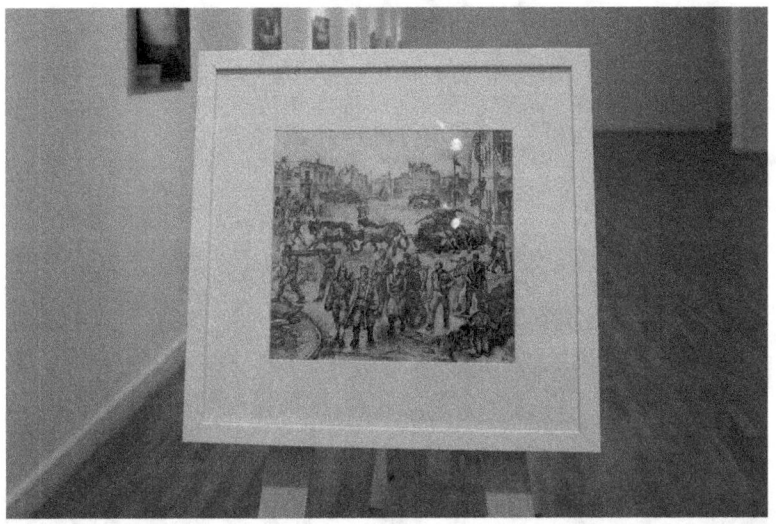

Posters of the YPJ on the streets of
Qamishli.

Pllakate të YPJ në rrugët e Qamishli-së.

Anastas Kostandini, *The Day of
Victory,* pencil and ink, 24.2 x 25.2
cm, 1983.

Anastas Kostandini, *Dita e fitores,* laps
dhe tush, 24.2 x 25.2 cm,1983.

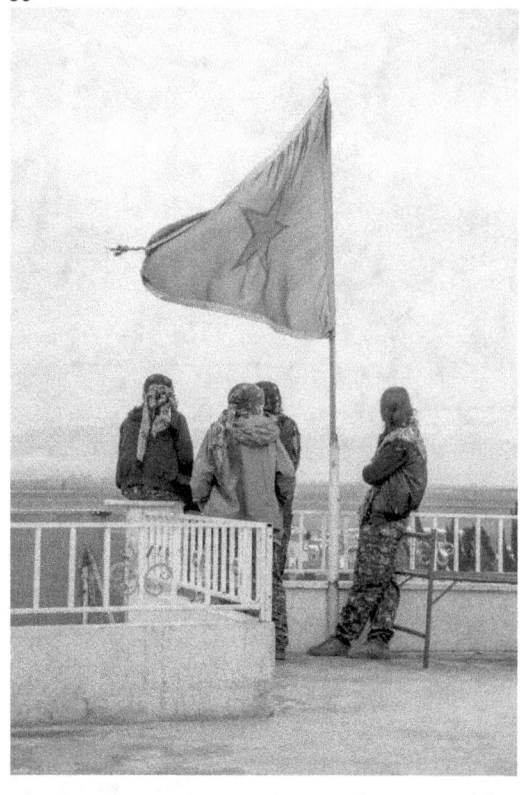

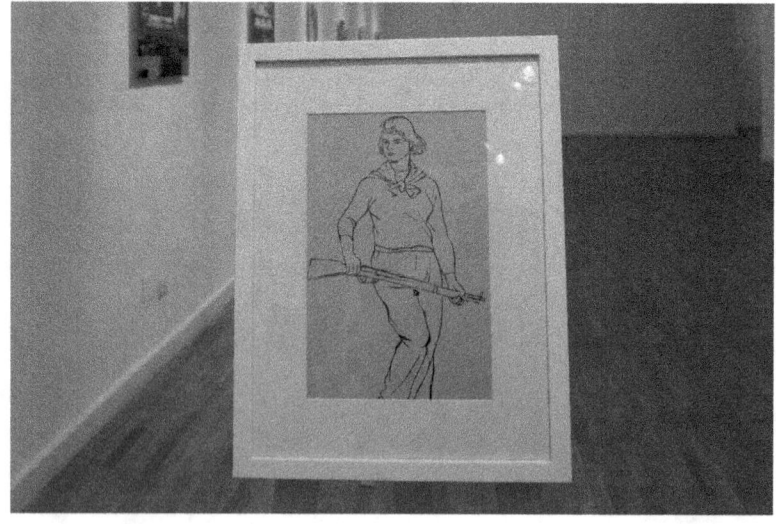

Special forces of the YPJ look over their training camp situated near Qamishli.

Forcat speciale të YPJ vështrojnë kampin e tyre të stërvitjes, që gjendet pranë Qamishli-së.

Isuf Sulovari, *Military Volunteer,* n.d., ink, private collection.

Isuf Sulovari, *Zboristja,* pa datë, tush, koleksion privat.

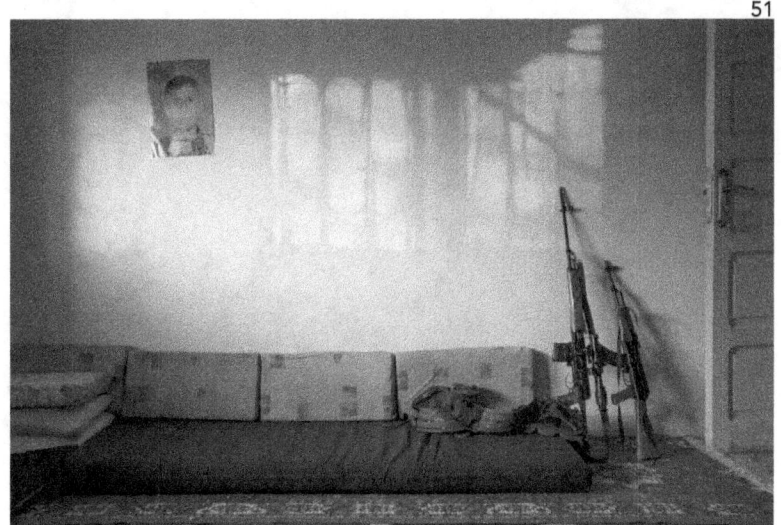

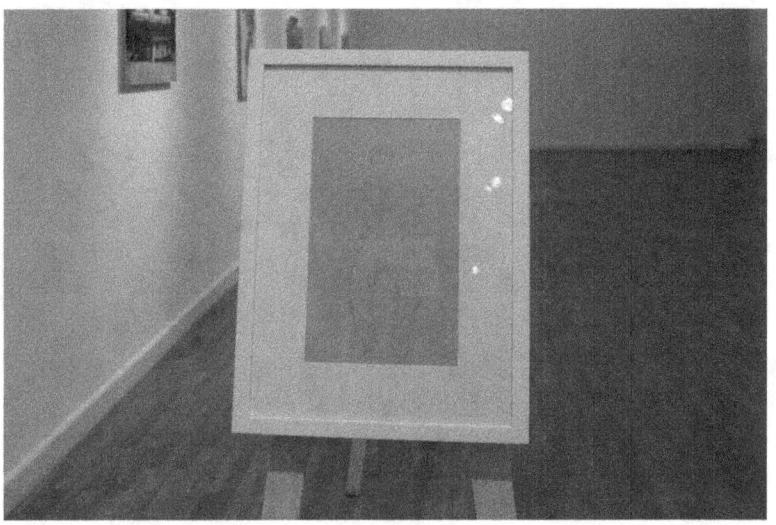

Living room in the headquarters of
the YPJ in Amuda.

Dhomë ndenjeje në komandën e YPJ
në Amuda.

Hasan Reçi, *The Soldier,* pencil, 30 x
18.7, acquired 1989.

Hasan Reçi, *Ushtari,* laps, 30 x 18.7 cm,
blerë 1989.

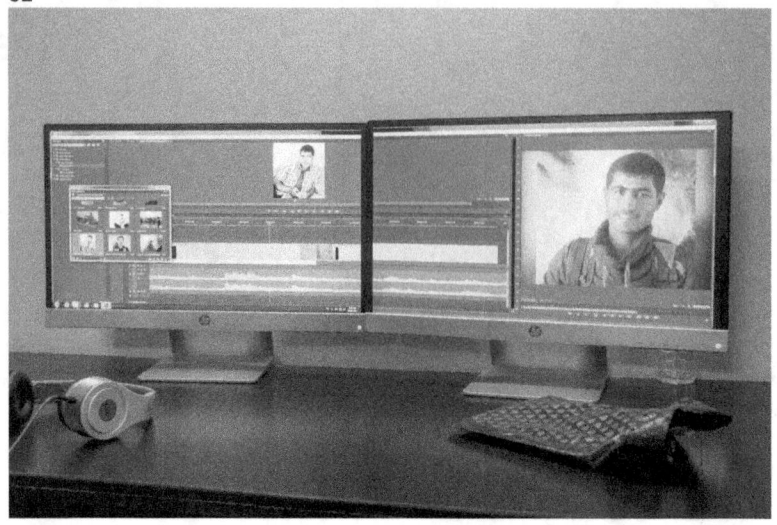

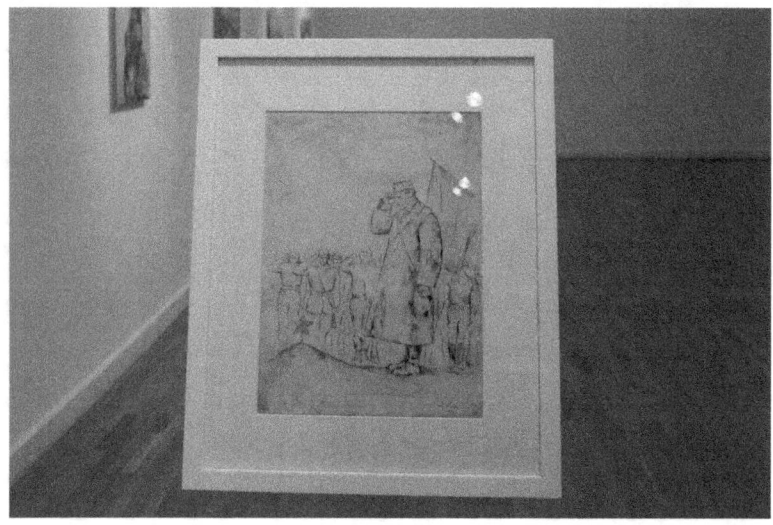

In the headquarters of Ronahi TV, the media station of the Rojava Revolution in Qamishli, a video is being edited commemorating a martyr of the People's Defense Forces (YPG).

Në studion e Ronahi TV, stacioni i medias i Revolucionit Rojava në Qamishli. Gjatë montazhit të një videoje në kujtim të një dëshmori të YPG.

Zef Shoshi, *Burial of the Comrade*, etch, 31.5 x 23.5 cm, 1973.

Zef Shoshi, *Varrimi i shokut*, gdhendje, 31.5 x 23.5 cm, 1973.

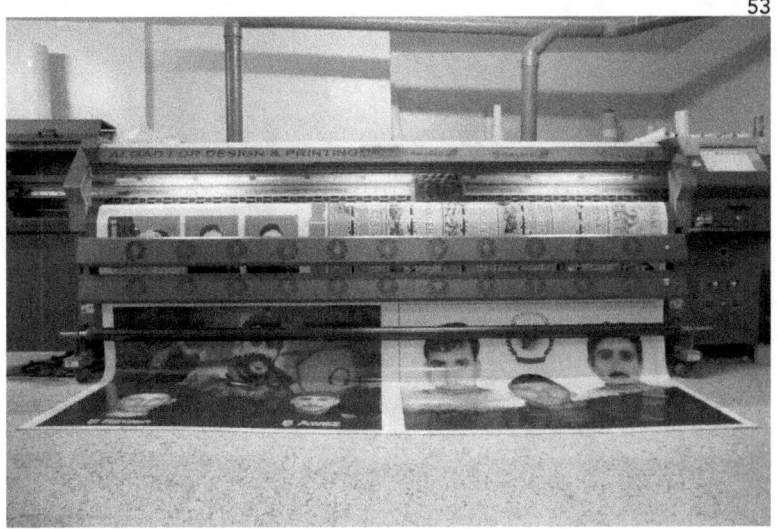

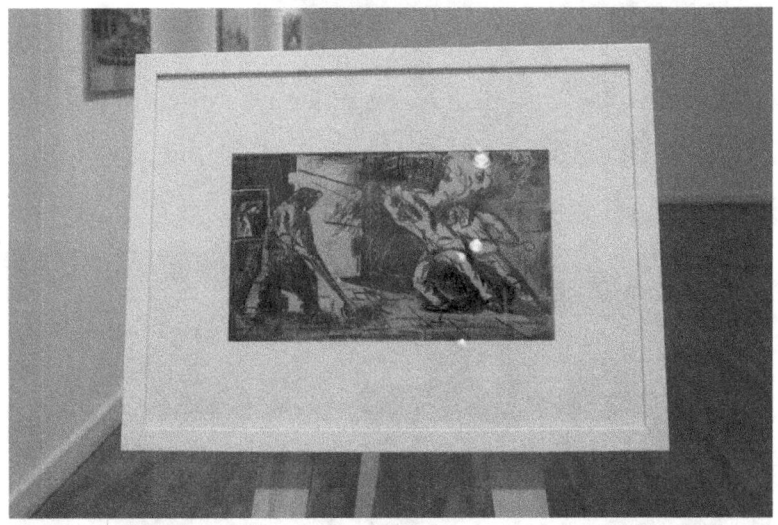

Printing house Algad in Qamishli produces the martyr images of the autonomous regions of Rojava.

Shtëpia botuese Algad në Qamishli prodhon imazhet e martirëve të rajoneve autonome të Rojava-s

Sali Shijaku, *In the Tractor Factory "Enver Hoxha,"* charcoal, 36.4 x 21.7 cm, acquired 1985.

Sali Shijaku, *Në kombinatin e autotraktorëve "Enver Hoxha"*, karbon, 36.4 x 21.7 cm, blerë 1985.

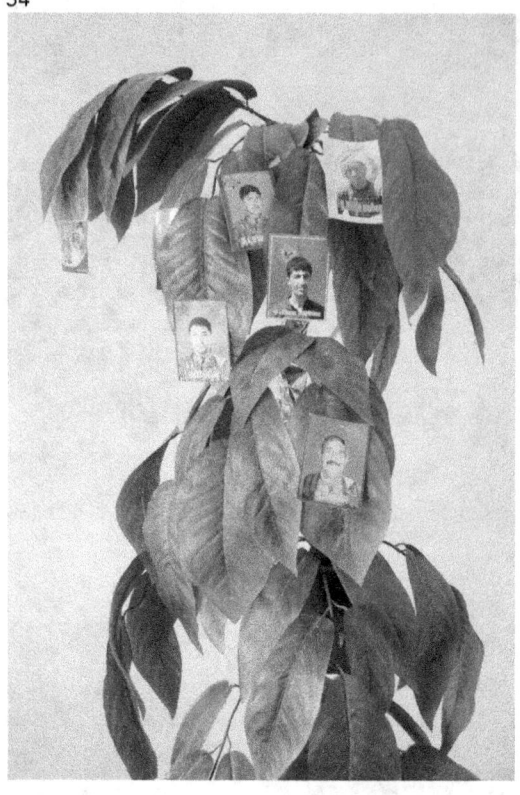

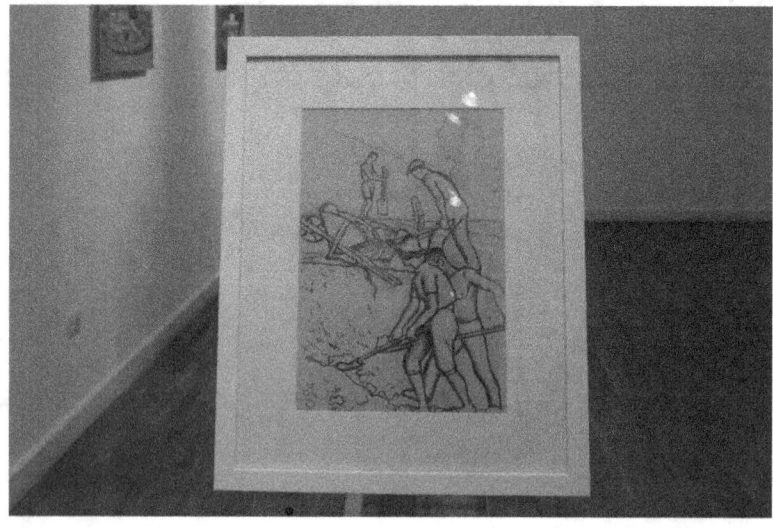

Plants in living rooms serves as commemorative objects of martyrs from the Rojava Revolution; each leaf carrying a single portrait, together forming the foundation of what the autonomous cantons have termed their "ecology of freedom."

Lulet në dhomat e ndenjes shërbejnë si objekte përkujtimore të dëshmorëve të Revolucionit Rojava; çdo gjethe mban një portret dhe së bashku formojnë themelin e asaj që kantonet autonome e kanë quajtur "ekologjia e lirisë".

Isuf Sulovari, *At the Railways*, pencil, 28.7 x 20.7 cm, n.d., private collection.

Isuf Sulovari, *Në hekurudhë*, laps, 28.7 x 20.7 cm, pa datë, koleksion privat.

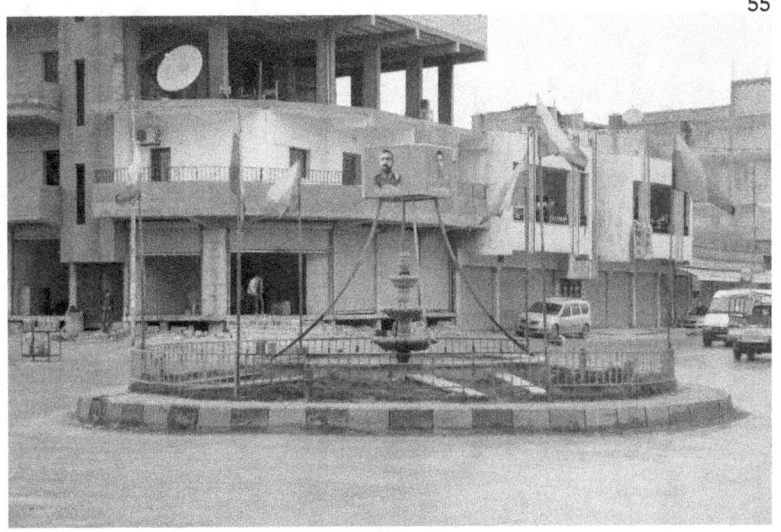

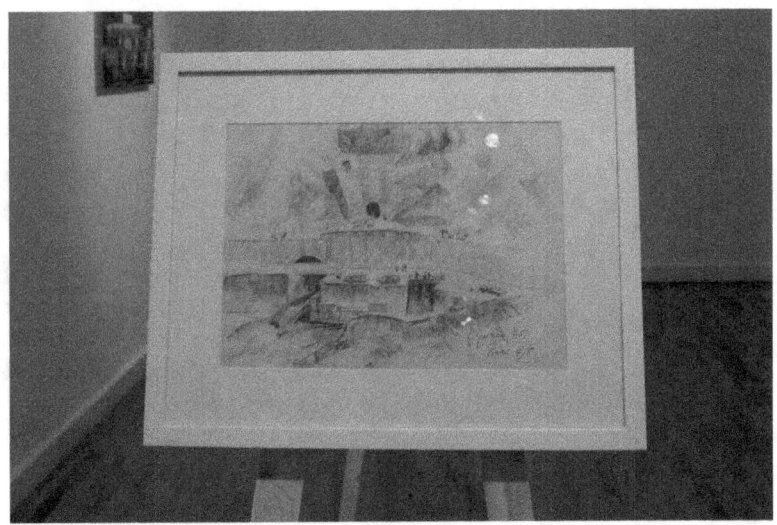

An old fountain of the Assad regime in Qamishli has been turned in to a monument to the Rojava Revolution, painted yellow-red-green – the colors of the flag of the independent cantons – carrying several martyr portraits of deceased revolutionaries from its defense forces.

Një shatërvan i vjetër i regjimit të Asadit në Qamishli është kthyer në një monument të Revolucionit Rojava, pikturuar me të verdhë-kuqe-jeshile – ngjyrat e flamurit të kantoneve të pavarura. Portrete të martirëve të vrarë revolucionarë, pjesë të forcave mbrojtëse.

Qamil Grezhda, *Fierza*, pencil, 25 x 34.7 cm, 1975.

Qamil Grezhda, *Fierza*, laps, 25 x 34.7 cm, 1975.

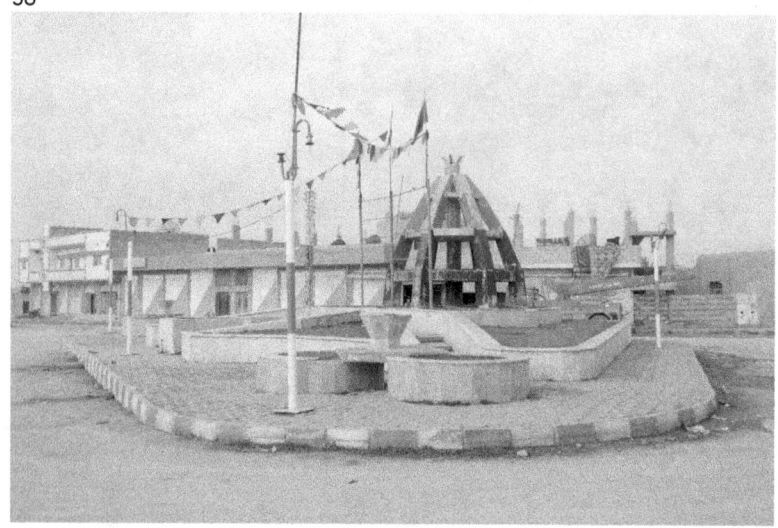

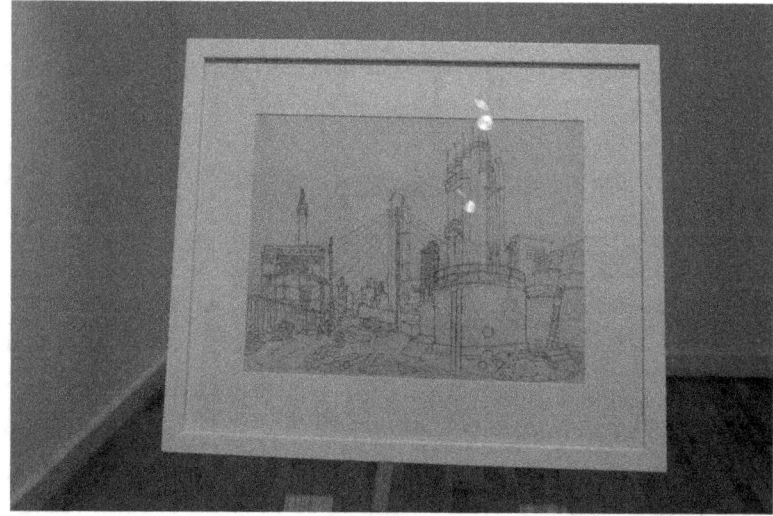

A sculpture of the Assad regime in Darbasiyah has been repainted in yellow-red-green – the colors of the flag of the independent cantons – and thus declared a monument for the Rojava Revolution.

Një skulpturë e regjimit të Asadit në Darbasiyah është rilyer me të verdhë-kuqe-jeshile - ngjyrat e flamurit të kantoneve të pavarura - dhe në këtë mënyrë është shpallur si monument për Revolucionin Rojava.

Isuf Sulovari, *From the Metal Factory*, pencil, n.d., private collection.

Isuf Sulovari, *Nga metalurgjiku*, laps, pa datë, koleksion privat.

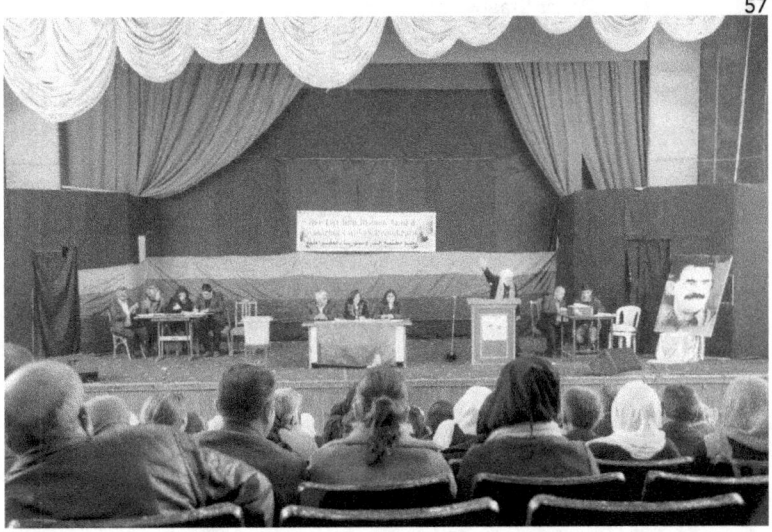

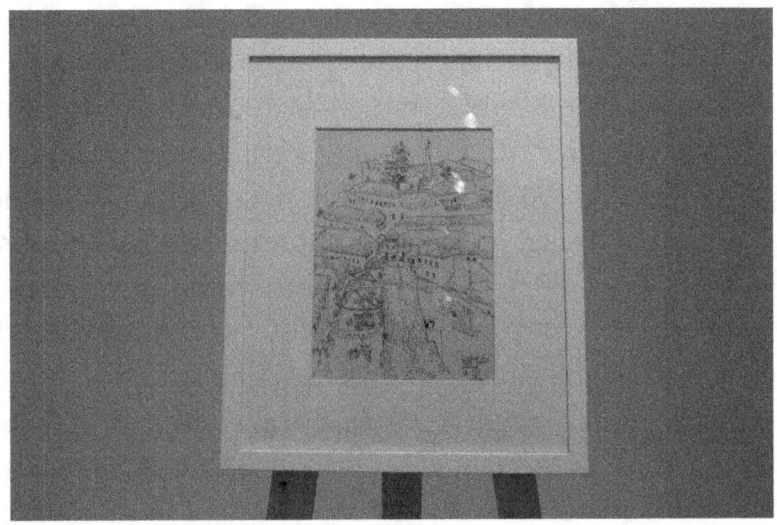

Candidates from neighborhood councils and cooperatives present themselves to become co-chair of the People's Council of the city of Qamishli. The slogan *Her Tist Jibo Jiyanek Azad û Avakirina Civakek Demokratîk* means "Everything for a Free Life and the Foundation of a Democratic Society." On the right, a portrait of the founder of the Kurdistan Worker's Party Abdullah Öcalan.

Kandidatët nga këshillat e lagjeve dhe kooperativave paraqesin veten që të bëhet bashkë-kryetarë të Këshillit Popullor të qytetit Qamishli. Slogani *Her Tist Jibo Jiyanek Azad û Avakirina Civakek Demokratîk* përkthehet si "Gjithçka për një Jetë në Liri dhe Themelimin e një Shoqërie Demokratike." Në të djathtë, një portret i themeluesit të Partisë Punëtore të Kurdistanit, Abdullah Öcalan.

Mumtas Dhrami, *Gjirokastër during the Folkloristic Festival*, ink, 27.8 x 20.7 cm, 1978.

Mumtas Dhrami, *Gjirokastra në ditët e Festivalit Folklorit*, tush, 27.8 x 20.7 cm, 1978.

Stateless Democracy

Bepey tazetirîn polîn, Kurdekan
Ser be regazî ballinden
Awetane leser parey zard û drawî
    mejû
Koçer in û be karwanî sefer da
    enesreynawe

According to recent classification
Kurds belong to the species of birds
Look at them. Here they are! On the
    slowly disappeared and torn
    pages of history
They are the migrants that are only
    recognized over the long
    distances their caravans travel

– Keyal Ahmed[1]

In one of the many streets of Qamishli, full of seemingly unfinished, concrete, and tarnished buildings, I'm guided down a small flight of stairs into a basement. Printing house Algad is stacked with machinery, some of which is reminiscent of a time when they were used for political posters stenciled by hand. In the neon-lit space I meet Yahiyu Abdullah, who is busy feeding data into a five-meter-wide plotter through a small built-in computer. A young boy is sitting in front of it, trying to keep up with the feed of images emerging from the printer, cutting out the pictures from the large, plasticized printed surface.

I recognize some of the imagery from the posters and banners on the streets: young men and women, surrounded by logos of their militia, each of them portrayed before they joined their comrades on one of the many battlefields of the region. They look straight into the lens, occasionally smiling or with a raised fist, but more often with a defiant look, calm, determined in their controlled anger. I observe the feed of silent gazes merging into each other.

Celebrated as heroes, the looks of these martyrs defy glorification. They belong to a collective body of resistance: the Rojava Revolution. And against the losses of this revolution, the printer runs: it is a feed of history being made at the very moment. The front line is only a few kilometers away, and here, in the basement, the printer runs against time; against forgetfulness.

1. The Rojava Revolution

We are in the independent canton Cizîre in Rojava, which means "west" and refers to the western part of Kurdistan. It's one out of three territories in the northern part of Syria which are currently under the control of a transitional, autonomous government consisting of all ethnic components in the region. The social movement of Rojava in the form of self-organized academies, cooperatives and peoples councils, is allied in the Movement for a Democratic Society (TEV–DEM) with the the prominent Democratic Unity Party (PYD) as its driving force. In order to secure a balanced political representation of the region, Kurds, Arabs and Assyrians, which form the largest communities in the region, are limited to a quota of 30 percent political representatives. Smaller communities are tied to a quota of 10 percent political representatives. Political representation thus attempts to reflect directly the diverse social texture of the region. The other two cantons are Afrin and Kobanê; the latter acquired fame as the most important front in the Kurdish resistance against the Islamic State. Whereas Cizîre borders on the east with Turkey and Iraq, Afrin and Kobanê border only with Turkey: from the Syrian side they are surrounded by forces of the Islamic State and the Assad regime.[2] They are thus territorially isolated. The total Kurdish territory is about two-thirds the size of Belgium, and according to recent estimates, the population has grown to a 4.6 million due to the many refugees from the Syrian civil war[3]; there are large-scale refugee camps such as Kampa Newroz that host, among others, Yazidi communities that the YPG and YPJ saved from massacre by the Islamic State.[4]

The Rojava Revolution runs parallel to what became known as the Arab Spring of 2012, although its roots in recent Syrian history go back to the 1960s, when Syrian Kurds were massively stripped of their citizenship.[5] An even more recent precedent for the Rojava Revolution was the Qamishli uprising in 2004, during which the ruling regime of Bashar al-Assad killed dozens of Kurds who displayed their flags and other signs of national and cultural identity. So when the Arab Spring hit Syria in 2012, they were ready. Dilar Dirik, academic and activist of the Kurdish Women Movement, describes the foundation of the

Rojava Revolution as follows:

> The Assad regime engaged in heavy clashes with the Free Syrian Army, the main opposition group, in areas like Damascus and Aleppo. As a result, the regime withdrew from the Kurdish areas in the northern part of the country, and the Kurds took their chance to take over: they at once seized control of the cities; they got rid of the institutions of the regime and established their own system. On July 19, 2012 this was declared as the Rojava Revolution.[6]

In early 2014, the Geneva II Conference on Syria was announced in an attempt to stabilize the Syrian war. Dirik recalls:

> The situation grew increasingly difficult, as the whole world was being dragged into the war: the US, Europe, Russia, the Gulf Countries, Turkey, Iran … It became something of a second Cold War. Assad fighting the rebels was just a microcosm of all the international interests that were invested in the region.[7]

In the context of this "second Cold War," representatives of the Rojava Revolution were not invited to join the convention, as the Turkish government was afraid of the effect Kurdish autonomy in Syria would have on the large – and historically severely repressed – Kurdish community and their revolutionary forces in Turkey, which are directly linked to those in Rojava. The Syrian Opposition Coalition was invited, but the Rojava Revolution refused to partake in this alliance, as they feel that Kurdish rights are not clearly acknowledged in coalition's political aims, and fear that the coalition is vulnerable to being used as a Western proxy. Instead, the three interlinked but independent cantons declared themselves fully autonomous. As Dirik points out, in the face of the states gathering in Geneva, the Rojava Revolution displayed an act of autonomy that took the form of "living without approval."[8]

Despite the fact that the Rojava Revolution is led by Kurds, the political institutions that they have developed resist an ethnic monopoly over the region. The three autonomous cantons of Rojava are founded on what on January 29, 2014 was officially announced as "The Social Contract" – in reference to Jean-Jacques Rousseau's famous text from 1762 – cowritten by all peoples living in the region: Kurds, Arabs, Assyrians, Chaldeans, Arameans, Turkmen, Armenians, and Chechens. Its opening lines state:

> In pursuit of freedom, justice, dignity and democracy and led by principles of equality and environmental sustainability, the Charter proclaims a new social contract, based upon mutual and peaceful coexistence and understanding between all strands of society. It protects fundamental human rights and liberties and reaffirms the peoples' right to self-determination. Under the Charter, we, the people of the Autonomous Regions, unite in the spirit of reconciliation, pluralism and democratic participation so that all may express themselves freely in public life.[9]

"The Social Contract" features a series of ideological principles that are fundamental to understanding the politics of the three autonomous cantons of Rojava. From the contract and related texts that I will discuss later in this essay, I have distilled the following six defining points:

The first is that of a radical secular politics, meaning that religious interests are separated fully from governance affairs.

The second is the requirement that presidencies over public institutions are always occupied by representatives of different ethnicities in order to avoid cultural hegemony.

The third is the principle of gender equality, enforcing a minimum of 40 percent participation of both women and men in political life, and the demand for co-presidencies of one woman and one man in all public institutions.

The fourth is that of communalist self-government, meaning that centralized structures of administration are reduced to the absolute minimum, whereas local councils and cooperatives that are self-governed are given maximum political agency.

The fifth is the principle of confederalism: the cantons are defined as "autonomous" because they are self-governed by their radically diverse communities. Most stunning is that rather than forming a "re-formist" attitude towards the nation-state and its politics of cultural unification and centralist administration, the Rojava Revolution rejects the model of the nation-state all together. The model of "democratic confederalism" and its aim of establishing "democratic autonomy" – two concepts central to the Rojava Revolution – strive to *practice democracy without the construct of the nation-state.*

The sixth is the principle of social ecology: the idea that the organization of power based on secularism, gender equality, communalist self-government, and confederalism represents an egalitarian model capable of self-rule without a dictatorship of minorities over majorities or the other way around. This last notion of social ecology attempts to define an understanding of power based on principles of coexistence and radical diversity, instead of unification and assimilation – it forms the fundament of the politics of the Rojava Revolution.

Whereas the world in 2012 was mainly concerned with toppling Assad, today its eyes have focused on the rise of the so-called Islamic State, which holds large pieces of territory under its control in both Syria and Iraq.[10] The rise of the Islamic State has allowed Assad to rebrand himself as a supposed "lesser evil" in a region over which the international community is clueless about how to maintain control. This situation, of course, is deeply tied to the history of colonialism and military intervention by that very same community: the history of the British mandate in Iraq, its instrumentalization in the Iran-Iraq War, the 2003 invasion of Iraq, the dismantling of Hussein's Sunni-led government in favor of the Shia majority, the CIA blacksites where Iraqi citizens were tortured and Islamic State militants recruited, and so on.[11]

The Islamic State stands in stark opposition to the only three-year-old Rojava Revolution and its stateless democracy. The Islamic State's ambition for an endlessly expanding caliphate – its *total state* – in its terrifying conquest and brutal patriarchal policies of cultural assimilation, subjection, and enslavement of women seems to form the bizarre mirror image of the total state of the security apparatus of the Coalition of the Willing's never-ending War on Terror and its radical and violent disregard for other states' and peoples sovereignty. Against the state terror of both Islamic State and the Coalition of the Willing, the Rojava Revolution forms an alternative that it has termed its "third way," in an echo of the project of Third Worldism, not as a source of tragedy to be scavenged by governments' oil, mineral, and state-building projects masked as "development," but as an actual, radically new political and internationalist – transnationalist – paradigm.[12]

Anthropologist and political activist David Graeber compares this ideological clash to the 1936 Spanish revolution in Catalonia: "If there is a parallel today to Franco's superficially devout, murderous Falangists, who would it be but Isis? If there is a parallel to the Mujeres Libres of Spain [the anarcho-feminist movement], who could it be but the courageous women defending the barricades in Kobane?"[13] Graeber rightfully points to a parallel with the anarchist, "libertarian-socialists" of Catalonia, who for two years were able to maintain a communalist autonomous region while squashed between the armies of Franco and the Soviets, which they both opposed while being severely critical of the Republican government.[14] In a similar manner, the Rojava Revolution and its coalition of multiethnic, multireligious peoples criticize the Western coalition as much as they resist Assad and the militants of the Islamic State. And in both revolutions – that of 1936 and that of 2012 – women militants, ideologues, and politicians formed a key role in redefining the revolutionary project. Rojava is the battlefield for the question of whether the very concept of democracy can be recuperated as a radical, emancipatory political and cultural practice. In order to understand why and how, we need to understand the specific anatomy of the revolution as it is found in the decades-long – if not centuries-long – struggle of the Kurds for their right to self-determination.

2. Anatomy of a Revolution

Kurdistan, which covers part of the Mesopotamian region, was divided in the seventeenth-century by the Ottoman and Persian Empire. In the early twentieth century the Ottoman Empire collapsed, and European governments and Mustafa Kemal Atatürk's army fought over the remainders. The subsequent Sykes-Picot Agreement drew harsh borders across the region, creating different spheres of influences controlled by the British and French colonial powers. This partition of the region after the First World War led to the fragmentation of the Kurds across four different states: Turkey, Syria, Iraq, and Iran.

The Kurds had hoped to gain cultural and political rights in the newly founded Republic of Turkey, but these were never granted. This denial was later repeated when the Kurds of Iran joined the 1979 revolution but were afterward confronted with a fatwa against them. In each of these states, under different conditions, the Kurds faced severe repression. While culturally acknowledged in Iran, political organization has continuously been punished by imprisonment and torture, if not outright murder; in Syria and Iraq, the Kurds were faced with the policies of forced Arabization of the Ba'athist regimes of Assad and Hussein. After the Ottoman Empire crumbled, the Turkish Republic took on the task of constructing its national identity, and thus erroneously designated the Kurds as "mountain Turks," repressing their language, culture, and all forms of political organization. From the very first Kurdish uprisings during the years 1925–38 in the southeastern part of the country, the Turkish Republic engaged in violent crackdowns buttressed by special terror laws that allowed all references to Kurdish language, culture, or history to be prosecuted as "separatism" and "terrorism." Kurdish uprisings were explained by the Turkish government in terms of economic deprivation and educational backwardness, never as a cultural and political resistance.

In the 1970s, the international rise of anticolonial resistance and socialist movements resonated with the Kurdish community. The fact that the Turkish left was unwilling to make Kurdish cultural and political rights a priority provided the foundation for the "largest people without a state" to imagine the establishment of an independent progressive nationalist state of their own. In the course of the '70s, the Kurdistan Revolutionaries group emerged from a fragmented left consisting of Kurdish Socialist, Maoist, and Leninist parties, and in 1978 it was officially declared the Kurdistan Workers Party (PKK). The first six key points of its founding manifesto were as follows:

a. Our era is the era of transition from capitalism to socialism and proletarian revolutions.

b. Kurdistan is an inter-state colony.

c. A national liberation struggle is an unavoidable duty in order to gain the freedom and independence of the Kurdish people.

d. The Kurdistan revolution shall be a *national and democratic* one, and the ultimate end would, in long term, be the *socialist revolution* with an uninterrupted transition to a "classless and non-exploitative" society.

e. The revolution's political objective is to establish an *independent, united and democratic Kurdistan.*

f. The revolution must be led by a revolutionary party of the proletariat which needs to be initiated by a "minority" composed of patriotic youth and intellectuals (enlightened) who are disassociated from material production.[15]

The founders and driving organizers of the PKK hailed from university circles, through which they had direct access to revolutionary liberationist theory. As Sakine Cansiz – one of the early PKK founders, who was shot dead in Paris on January 9, 2013 along with two other female Kurdish activists, Fidan Doğan and Leyla Şaylemez – recalled the years preceding the PKK:

In a short time, our movement became a political power, it went beyond a youth movement in '75, '76, and '77. At first, our movement had mainly an influence on the student youth movement, then the qualified and militant youth at schools and in all areas we were active in. It changed the environment at schools … We grounded our movement on ideological and political struggle and revolutionary violence. Necessary defense was actually a way of struggle that our movement [was] based on since the very beginning.[16]

The guiding force and most prominent representative of the PKK was Abdullah Öcalan, who had arrived in Ankara from a humble background at the edge of the Kurdish region in southeast Turkey. During his studies he became involved in Turkish and Kurdish leftist groups. In 1972, he was arrested for participating in a protest and imprisoned for several months. In prison, he was exposed to discussions with several key organizers of the revolutionary left, and once out, he worked toward the establishment of the PKK, which after its founding in 1978 soon became the leading revolutionary Kurdish party.

Only one year after founding the PKK, Öcalan moved to Syria, aware of a pending new military coup that would take place in 1980 as a response to the threat posed by the Kurdish leftist militants to the monocultural Turkish project, as well as in reaction to a devastating economic recession. While the military government engaged in a violent crackdown – arresting, torturing, and killing many of the members of Kurdish leftist factions – Öcalan established a safe haven for the PKK in Syria, building an international network in order to prepare his militia. The PKK cadre was trained by Yasir Arafat's Fatah, George Habash's Popular Front for the Liberation of Palestine, Samir Ghosheh's Palestinian Popular Struggle Front, and the Lebanese Communist Party in the basic techniques of guerrilla warfare. In 1984, Öcalan declared the party ready to reenter Turkish territory in order to establish a new revolutionary Kurdish government in the southeast. This was the beginning of the war between the PKK and the Turkish Republic, which would continue until the first substantial truce in 1999.[17]

The mountains of southeastern Turkey formed the perfect terrain for a guerrilla war, and from an elite cadre the PKK transformed into a mass movement. Many Kurds from rural areas joined as fighters or as civil militia that provided hiding places, food, and information. By 1992, "PKK rebels numbered about 10,000 total ... and they claimed to have about 60,000 armed civilian milis, about two thirds the strength of the Turkish soldiers normally stationed in the region (excluding police, special forces, and village guards)."[18] At this high point of the movement, it had established a parallel government including security forces, an information network, newspapers, a taxation system, training camps in neighboring states, and a well-organized diaspora.[19] The PKK had been transformed into a transnational movement.

Drawing from Leninist avant-garde theory, the cadres of the PKK had been structured rigorously and hierarchically. Öcalan's leadership was absolute, and militia members were prohibited from having any private property, engaging in any sexual relationships, and having partners or children. Under the conditions of harsh repression by the Turkish state, loyalty to the party and discipline in the ranks needed to be absolute.

This absolute loyalty and hierarchical structure, however, became mitigated by the internal rise of the Kurdish women's movement. Already within the original group of students that founded the PKK there had been important female members. According to Sakine Cansiz, the party had been "giving an ideological struggle from the very beginning against denial, social chauvinistic impression, primitive and nationalist approaches."[20] This related to the "feudal" conditions in which many Kurdish communities were forced to live and the nationalism of the Turkish Republic that kept Kurdish communities structurally underdeveloped. Women fighters standing equally amongst men became examples of self-determination and independence. For many young women, joining the PKK and its militant female ranks was a liberation.

According to many PKK members, the role of women in the movement became threatened in the years of the party's conversion to a mass movement, mainly due to men from rural areas joining the fight but refusing to recognize women as equals.[21] Due to the daily pressure of the war, the goal of female emancipation risked becoming a secondary issue. However, in the 1990s, the women of the PKK, encouraged by Öcalan, started to actively organize themselves in order to put their liberation from patriarchy within the party on the agenda – as a demand equally as important as the acknowledgment of Kurdish history, culture, and language. This development ran parallel to a series of crises within the PKK, partly due to Turkey's wish to get rid of the semiautonomous PKK region as soon as possible: "By 1995, Ankara was spending as much as $11 billion a year to fight the war ... Turkey also deployed some 220,000 troops in the region – tying up a quarter of NATO's second largest army in a domestic battle."[22] By the time Öcalan was captured by Turkey in 1999, the PKK was on the defensive and lost much of its territorial control. But the PKK's guerrilla war was only the first part of a liberation movement that would be prominently directed, ideologically and militarily, by its women's militia.

3. The Kurdish Women's Movement

Dilar Dirik describes how this parallel process of autonomous women's organizing against male patriarchy within the party informed the growing critique of the very aim of establishing a nation-state as such:

> The PKK experienced many ups and downs, related to the guerrilla resistance against the Turkish army, the fall of the Soviet Union, the collapse of many leftist liberational movements, and Öcalan's capture in Kenya on February 15, 1999, organized by the Turkish National Intelligence Organization in collaboration with the Central Intelligence Agency of the US. It was in this context in the course of the late nineties that the PKK began to theoretically deconstruct the state, fueled by the Kurdish Women's Movement, coming to the conclusion [that] it is inherently incompatible with democracy.[23]

What is crucial here is that through the newly emerging autonomous women's movement, the PKK, which started with the aim of creating an independent Kurdish nation-state, was forced into a structural self-critique. Although many of the young women had joined the PKK in order to escape being forced into servitude, they were confronted with similar power structures within the hierarchies of the PKK.[24] In response to this, Öcalan theoretically strengthened the coherence between the emerging autonomous organization of the women's movement, the PKK's opposition to colonialism and capitalism, and its claim from the first manifesto that its resistance would be dedicated to a classless society.[25] According to Öcalan:

> The male monopoly that has been maintained over the life and world of woman throughout history, is not unlike the monopoly chain that capital monopolies maintain over society. More importantly, it is the oldest powerful monopoly. We might draw more realistic conclusions if we evaluate woman's existence as the oldest colonial phenomenon. It may be more accurate to call women the oldest colonised people who have never become a nation. Family, in this social context, developed as man's small state. The family as an institution has been continuously perfected throughout the history of civilization, solely because of the reinforcement it provides to power and state apparatus.[26]

Öcalan's argumentation is a further development of the resistance against chauvinism-primitivism-nationalism that Cansiz regarded as the foundation of the PKK, but through the autonomous development of the women's movement this analysis is brought to its full consequence: not just in the rejection of the nation-state as such, but in a rejection of the very nature of the power structures that support the nation-state:

> Firstly, family is turned into a stem cell of state society by giving power to the family in the person of the male. Secondly, woman's unlimited and unpaid labour is secured. Thirdly, she raises children in order to meet population needs. Fourthly, as a role model she disseminates slavery and immorality to the whole society. Family, thus constituted, is the institution where dynastic ideology becomes functional.[27]

The critique by the women's movement thus brings Öcalan to redefine the relation between family, state, and capital, concluding that the underlying patriarchal model of power can never be fully liberatory – not just for women, but for any constituency that challenges its normative paradigm. What needs to be overcome is the very articulation of power structures underlying the national liberation struggle.[28]

Öcalan's attempt to define a new historiography that redefines the very nature of power is what finally brings him and his party to the total rejection of the nation-state project as a whole:

> The nation-state needed the bourgeoisie and the power of capital in order to replace the old feudal order and its ideology which rested on tribal structures and inherited rights by a new national ideology which united all tribes and clans under the roof of the nation. In this way, capitalism and nation-state became so closely linked to each other that neither could be imagined to exist without the other … It is often said that the nation-state is concerned with the fate of the common people. This is not true. Rather, it is the national governor of the worldwide capitalist system, a vassal of capitalist modernity which is more deeply entangled in the dominant structures of capital than we usually tend to assume: It is a colony of capital.[29]

Öcalan's thoughts on women's liberation and the autonomous women's movement redefined the foundations of the PKK struggle, providing the basis for what today, after many different name changes, is known as the Women's Communities of Kurdistan (KJK), founded in 2014. The KJK connected women's branches of political parties, cooperatives, and councils all over the region as well as internationally.

In prison, Öcalan's study was fueled by works such as that of philosopher Michel Foucault, but the most important influence was Murray Bookchin, from whom Öcalan distilled the key aspects of the new power paradigm he envisioned. As Bookchin writes:

> A free ecological society – as distinguished from one regulated by an authoritarian ecological elite or by the "free market" – can only be vast in terms of an ecologically confederal form of libertarian municipalism. When at length free communes replace the nation and confederal forms of organization replaces the state, humanity will have rid itself from nationalism.[30]

What Bookchin describes as an "ecological society" and "social ecology" is what Öcalan translates into the notion of an "ecology of freedom," a new power paradigm that would take the Kurdish women's movement's rejection of the nation-state as its primary point of departure.[31] Öcalan not only borrows this general paradigm of power from Bookchin, but also the foundational political principle of "communalism" (essentially decentralized communism, or communism without the state),[32] the organization model of "confederalism" (interrelated, coexisting, and mutually dependent but self-governed political entities), and the decision-making model of "direct democracy" (locally organized majority rule by confederal communities).[33] In 2005, Öcalan declared the conjunction of these concepts in the context of the Kurdish struggle as the project of "democratic confederalism."[34]

Essentially, Öcalan proposes a form of autonomy through practice, a series of interlinked structures of self-governance that operate independent of, but parallel to, existing states. The objective of the PKK thus switched from attaining recognition by Turkey and the international community, to self-recognition through practice.

While this theoretical shift was hard to communicate to the mass movement that had by now rallied behind the PKK[35] – thousands of whom had lost their lives in the exhausting years of guerrilla struggle driven by the ideal of an independent state – the solid, disciplined core of the movement and its absolute loyalty to its leader made it possible to reorient the struggle ideologically. The party itself started to restructure with an emphasis on autonomous democratic structures, and its affiliated political wings implemented so-called "co-presidencies" in the process: political positions, such as that of the mayor, were now required to have both a male and a female representative operating on the basis of absolute equality – a concrete achievement of the newly autonomously organized Kurdish women's movement.[36]

The fact that realizing this decentralized model of self-governance required highly disciplined, hierarchical, and militant cadres is not necessarily a paradox, but will possibly have to be explored as a prerequisite. The essential change was that the ideal of an ever-expanding cadre that would evolve into the leadership of an independent nation-state now became an instrument in service of a new emancipatory mass movement.[37] The full implementation of democratic confederalism and the practice of democratic autonomy would take hold with the start of the Rojava Revolution.

4. "Power is everywhere, but the state is not"

It's already evening when I visit the Star Academy in Ramelan, the ideological heart of the Rojava Revolution. The academy is organized by the Yekîtiya Star, the umbrella group of the women's movement in Rojava. I observe a silent classroom filled with young women soldiers and community organizers. The walls are covered with maps of Mesopotamia and Kurdistan, and images of past and present martyrs, including Arin Mirkan, who detonated herself to cover her retreating comrades and avoid capture by Islamic State militants. The images are organized around a small wooden shelf, on which a Maria figure is placed – one of the very rare religious objects in the radically secular iconography of the Rojava Revolution.

In the lecture of the teacher, Dorsin Akif, I recognize the basic terminology that drives the revolution: democratic confederalism, democratic autonomy, communalism, women's liberation, cooperatives, councils – key terms that have been repeated to me by student organizers, teachers, soldiers, politicians, farmers, judges, and artists during my days travelling throughout the canton. Akif's speech is only interrupted for a brief moment by the sound of shots and an explosion. Later on I am told that the Islamic State has moved within three kilometers of the school, but the students don't flinch for a moment. Their revolution takes place both in ideological education and armed struggle. After at least thirty days of ideological training, many of these young women will join the fight against the Islamic State, but not before they know what political model they are fighting for. When I speak with Akif after class, she says:

> Women have progressed much. For example, during the revolution of the French commune, women had a prominent role. Women led that revolution, but in the end: who remains without rights?

Women. The nation-state has organized itself as such that women rights are not recognized.[38]

In an extension of the rejection of the nation-state and its patriarchal foundations, the main task of the academy is to break the ties between the state and science, not in a rejection of science as such, but of the specific power structure underlying it. The alternative takes the form of "jineology," meaning "women's science," -*logy* referring to the Greek "logos" (knowledge) and *jin* referring to the Kurdish word for woman.

Journalist and representative of the women's movement Gönül Kaya writes that "in history, rulers and power holders have established their systems first in thought. As an extension of the patriarchal system, a field of social sciences has been created, which is male, class-specific, and sexist in character."[39] Based on this analysis, Kaya calls for a "women's paradigm," described as a rejection of the relation between the woman-object (slave) and the male-subject (master), which she considers inherently intertwined with modern science and which has in turn had a severe impact on social life, with nurture or domestic work – framed as part of feminine "nature" – not considered "labor," but instead articulated in terms of "service" to the masculine master.

Jineology rejects these "natures" as social constructs, but without rejecting the difference between the male and female subjects – what it rejects is the premise of the social construct that articulates differences in the context of patriarchal society. Jineology explores feminine, colonized history and science as knowledge that can sustain Rojava's "ecology of freedom," as Öcalan adapted Bookchin's concept of "social ecology." On the curriculum are not only the works of Öcalan and Bookchin, but also those of Foucault and Judith Butler, forming philosophical pillars in this political and scientific struggle. As Kaya writes:

Important tasks await us in the 21st century: the philosophical-theoretical and scientific framework of women's liberation, the historical development of women's liberation and resistance, mutual complementary dialogues within feminist, ecological, and democratic movements, the renewed description of all social institutions (e.g. family) according to liberationist principles ... The field of a new social science for all those circles that are not part of power and the state must be built. This is the task of all anti-colonialist, anti-capitalist, anti-power movements, individuals, women. We refer to these alternative social sciences as the sociology of freedom. Jineology can build and develop the ground base of these social sciences. It is a vanguard in this regard. It will both construct the sociology of freedom and be part of this sociology itself.[40]

Zîlan Diyar, a female guerrilla fighter, ironically comments on Western media outlets that, rather than exploring the ideological dimension of the struggle, "are so inspired by the clothes that the women are wearing, that they want to start a new fashion trend!"[41] Dilar Dirik considers this side-stepping of ideological struggle for the benefit of the orientalist, sensationalist imaginary as the very problem the Kurdish women's movement was founded to struggle against:

Rather than trying to understand the phenomenon in all its complexity, these articles often resort to sensationalist statements to exploit the audience's astonishment over the fact that "the poor women in the Middle East" could somehow be militants. Hence, instead of acknowledging the cultural revolution that the actions of these women constitute in an otherwise conservative, patriarchal society, many reporters fall for the same used-up categories: while state media, especially in Turkey and Iran, portray female guerrilla fighters as "evil terrorist prostitutes," family-hating, brainwashed sex toys of the male fighters, Western media often refers to these women as "oppressed victims looking for an escape from their backward culture," who would otherwise face a life full of honor killings and child marriage.[42]

In other words, the patriarchic, mediatized gaze claims that Kurdish women guerrillas are not truly fighting for a new definition of political power for women and men alike (i.e., women's liberation entails the liberation of men, albeit from themselves), but are "forced" to behave as such because their chances for a peaceful, "regular" household life are impossible (and supposedly, this is what they really desire). When considered from this perspective, patriarchy is thus essentially a mechanism of the status quo: even when we show that things can be different, it allows them to be interpreted to the contrary. This brings us back to Sakine Cansiz's description of the necessity of revolutionary violence as self-protection: this self-protection turns out to be as much about survival as it is about safeguarding the possibility for a political imaginary to become reality, which would otherwise be historically, politically, and culturally negated.

This is why the pillars of the autonomous cantons of Rojava enforce secular politics, gender equality through quotas, and the reduction of centralized structures to a minimum. These pillars are not derived from the model of the nation-state; they are the pillars of a new political imaginary that has yet to be developed in full, a political imaginary aimed at transforming our very practice and understanding of power through a history that the Star Academy is writing as we speak: "Power is everywhere, but the state is not everywhere. Power can operate in different ways."[43] Stateless democracy is based on the profound processes behind the Kurdish movement's decades of struggle and sacrifice, with women in front. This struggle has not only made it possible for power to operate in different ways; it has made *difference itself* possible.

5. Theater of the Stateless

In October 2014, artist Hito Steyerl – whose works *November* (2004) and *Lovely Andrea* (2007) are situated around her friend Andrea Wolf, a human rights activist and sociologist who became a PKK fighter and martyr after she was killed in 1998[44] – writes on the battles waged by the Rojava revolutionaries and the US air force against the Islamic State in the autonomous canton of Kobanê:

Turkish armed forces fire flares to add to the confusing scene of giant smoke plumes, ambulance horns, and faces illuminated by mobile phone screens. At the Cultural Center, a brilliant, all-female group of culture workers and municipality officials discusses the role of art with me. I plan to frame resident refugees observing F-16 jets circling above. What is the task of art in times of emergency?[45]

Interestingly enough, Abdullah Abdul, an artist who I meet in Amude, answers this question by returning to the history of the region. His small studio is located next to his house, where his young children are climbing on and off an enormous archive of objects – sculptures – lined up alongside his wall and floors. An unsuspecting visitor might think he had walked into an archeological exhibit. Instead, Abdul is creating a museum for a lost history: "Mesopotamia has a history of over five thousand years in which many peoples have lived here; there was a highly advanced civilization which was the source of world civilization."[46] Similar to the work that jineology does in recuperating a colonized science, Abdul is trying to retrieve the remnants of a colonized history of art and culture.

In the Mitra Hasake cultural center in Qamishli, among students practicing musical instruments and paintings mounted in the scarcely lit central hall, I have the chance to speak to Nesrin Botan, vocalist for the musical group Koma Botan – named after its founder, a musician who became a martyr in the armed struggle:

> We have an important role in the revolution … This revolution gives us the opportunity to express our culture, art, and folklore that used to be suppressed. We are now working hard for our culture and identity … Like a musician receives education from school, our fighters learn the art of fighting in the People's Defense Force (YPG). Like a teacher of art, our warriors show performance on the battlefield.[47]

Later on, in the guest house of the Democratic Unity Party (PYD), I see Botan appear in a music video on the Ronahi TV channel, the media outlet of the revolution which forms the permanent backdrop for those residing in the common room. Botan's video consists of a collage of film footage from PKK fighters as well as YPG and YPJ defense forces of Rojava surrounded by traditionally dressed singers; this is where both singer and soldier "show performance." I'm reminded of early media reports that repeatedly mentioned that fighters were singing in between their battles at the front.

The small cities and villages of concrete and brick buildings in the canton are separated by large swaths of farmland and oil fields, the jack pumps largely gone silent since the retreat of Assad, who took most of the crucial machinery for running them with him. The colors disrupting these sober landscapes are either those of the yellow, red, and green flag of the Rojava Revolution, or those of the martyr photos, which also display the names memorialized in the songs that fill the air wherever we go. Old monuments, fountains, and statues of Hafiz al-Assad, father of Bashar al-Assad, have been thrown off their pedestals. They have been repainted in the colors of Rojava, surrounded by flags of its defense forces and women's organizations, covered with martyr photos – all printed in a basement in Qamishli. These first monuments of the revolution bring a new memory into the public domain: that of those "performing" on the battlefield, the part of the collective revolutionary body that is re-inscribing its history – bloodily erased, repressed, blacklisted – into the imaginary of a radically new and different present.

When I attend the people's council of Qamishli, candidates are presenting themselves to obtain the position of new co-chair. Each of the city's neighborhood councils and cooperatives have brought their candidates forward. A long strip of yellow-red-green cloth serves as backdrop upon which is written: "Everything for a Free Life and the Foundation of a Democratic Society." In the front, the candidates enter and leave the stage, next to two tables with the elected selection committee keeping track of procedure. To the right of the stage is a photo of Öcalan on a modest, draped pedestal. But most importantly – as I realize while observing the packed space – the people's council is a *theater*. It is a theater of the stateless, where the Rojava Revolution is condensed down to its ultimate performance: the practice of self-governance, of self-determination, performing life without approval. In the face of our global crises in politics, the economy, and ecology, Rojava's stateless democracy proposes a political horizon that concerns us all.

What is the task of art in times of emergency? The artists and educators of Rojava seem to provide an answer. To write, imagine, and enact history according to the stateless – not only peoples *forced* into statelessness, but in the case of Rojava, those who have *decided to live without the state.*

This article originally appeared as Jonas Staal,"To Make a World, Part III: Stateless Democracy" in *e-flux journal* no. 63 (March 2015). The year-long Stateless Democracy research project conducted by New World Summit and New World Academy is being realized in collaboration with BAK, basis voor actuele kunst, Utrecht. I wish to thank the Democratic Unity Party (PYD), and its representatives Sheruan Hassan and Amina Osse in particular, for securing our travel and accomodations, and for facilitating the many interviews in Rojava. I thank the New World Summit research team – Younes Bouadi, Renée In der Maur, and documentary filmmaker Rens van Meegen – with whom I travelled to Rojava and who helped collect the necessary materials to understand the day-to-day practice of democratic confederalism. I further thank Dilar Dirik for her critical reflections on this essay, Vivian Ziherl for the many discussions on feminist politics, Mihnea Mircan for his call for workers to leave the studio and Vincent W. J. van Gerven Oei for his relentless editorial support. I would also like to thank Urok Shirhan for helping me understand that internationalism means there are no "others"; rather, there are mechanisms of separation – inside and outside of ourselves – that need to be overcome in order to recognize this. I hope this essay contributes to that process.

1.   Keyal Ahmed, "Benderî Bermûda" (1999).
2.   Solid data regarding the changing territorial constellation of the war is generally hard to find due to its daily developments. This Wikipedia map was recommended to us by one of Rojava's administrators.
3.   "Rojava's population has nearly doubled to about 4.6 million. The newcomers are Sunni and Shia Syrian Arabs who have fled the scorched wasteland that Assad has made of his country. They are also Orthodox Assyrian Christians, Chaldean Catholics, and others, from out of the jihadist dystopia that has taken up so much of the space where Assad's police state used to be." Terry Glavin, "In Iraq and Syria, it's too little too late," *Ottawa Citizen,* Nov. 14, 2014.
4.   "The unexpected and quick defeat of the Kurdish peshmerga forces in Sinjar, which was until recently populated mainly by followers of the ancient Yazidi Mesopotamian faith, prompted the Syrian Kurdish People's Protection Units (YPG) to jump into the scene … 'After IS stormed Sinjar and the peshmerga withdrew from there, a security vacuum emerged and the Yazidis faced the threat of a huge massacre. So, we decided to move in,' said Redur Khalil, YPG's spokesman … The YPG and PKK have even formed a special force, the Sinjar Defense Units, to defend Sinjar." Mohammed Sali, "PKK forces impress in fight against Islamic State," *Al-Monitor,* Sept. 1, 2014
5.   "In the 1960s, some 120,000 Syrian Kurds were stripped of their citizenship, forcing them to live in a sort of grey zone where they could not own property, were banned from

certain professions, could not own cars, and could not get passports to leave the country. Syria also banned Kurdish political parties and put limits, similar to its neighbor Turkey, on Kurdish-language publications and education." Aliza Marcus, *Blood and Belief: The PKK and the Kurdish Fight for Independence* (New York: NYU Press, 2007), 61.

6. Interview conducted with Dilar Dirik in De Balie, Amsterdam on Oct. 22, 2014.

7. Ibid.

8. Ibid.

9. "The Social Contract," January 29, 2014.

10. Exactly how much territory and how to define this in terms of monopolized violence – implied by the term "state" – is highly contested. The *New York Times* created this "visual guide to the crisis in Iraq and Syria" in an attempt to provide data on the origins of Islamic State fighters as well as the areas currently under their control.

11. A relevant article reconstructing the rise of the Islamic State consists of interviews with a senior official militant – nom de guerre Abu Ahmed – who was imprisoned in the US-led Camp Bucca, where the current leader of the IS, Abu Bakr al-Baghdadi, was incarcerated as well, and where the main recruitment of his cadre took place. See Martin Chulov, "Isis: The Inside Story," *The Guardian*, Dec. 11, 2014.

12. Curator Vivian Ziherl speaks of the term of "Thirld Worldism" as a history that has to be continuously rewritten, thus questioning dominant linear – modernist – narratives that laid the foundation for colonization as such. One such attempt at an alternative historical exploration of Third Worldism can be found in Vijay Prashad, *The Darker Nations: A People's History of the Third World* (New York: The New Press, 2007).

13. David Graeber, "Why is the world ignoring the revolutionary Kurds in Syria?," *The Guardian*, Oct. 8, 2014. See also "No. This is a genuine revolution," David Graeber interviewed by Pinar Öğünç about his

travel to Rojava, ZNET, Dec. 26, 2014.

14. On the 1936 Spanish revolution, see Murray Bookchin, *To Remember Spain: The Anarchist and Syndicalist Revolution of 1936* (San Francisco: AK Press, 1994); for a more extensive historical examination of the concept of libertarian socialism, see *Libertarian Socialism: Politics in Black and Red*, eds. Alex Prichard, Ruth Kinna, Saku Pinta, David Berry (New York: Palgrave MacMillan, 2012).

15. Amil Kemal Özcan, *Turkey's Kurds: A Theoretical Analysis of the pkk and Abdullah Öcalan* (New York: Routledge, 2006), 87.

16. "The PKK Foundation in Sakine Cansiz's words," written on November 25, 1978.

17. This truce was far from permanent, and in fact marked the beginning of the dominance of armed struggle in the Kurdish liberational movement: "At the start of June 2004, KONGRA-GEL [the organizational name of the PKK at the time] declared the undeclared five-year unilateral cease-fire 'obsolete' as they claimed that Turkey's military operations against the limited remaining guerrilla forces within the borders had been accelerated since early spring. In fact, there existed no five-year ceasefire but an end to the 'armed struggle'."Amil Kemal Özcan, Turkey's Kurds: A Theoretical Analysis of the PKK and Abdullah Öcalan (New York: Routledge, 2006), 214.

18. Marcus, Blood and Belief, 179.

19. Ibid., 230.

20. "The PKK Foundation in Sakine Cansiz's words."

21. Abdullah Öcalan recalls: "Young women fighters in particular, whose participation should have been understood as an important enrichment of the movement, were treated disparagingly as a burden, punished for their love of freedom and forced into the most primitive patriarchal relationships." A. Öcalan, Prison Writings II: The PKK and the Kurdish Question in the 21st Century (London: Transmedia Publishing, 2011), chapter "The PKK."

22. Marcus, Blood and Belief, 249.

23. 25 Interview conducted with

Dilar Dirik in De Balie, Amsterdam on October 22, 2014.

24. 26 Kurdish Women's Movement representative Fadile Yıldırım recalled on this issue that "the enemy is not just outside, we also have an enemy inside … The Kurdish women's freedom movement started inside the national liberation movement." Fadile Yıldırım, "Women and Democracy: The Kurdish Question and Beyond," lecture at the first New World Summit, May 4, 2013, Sophiensaele, Berlin.

25. 27 Öcalan's most elaborate attempt to articulate a social, historical, cultural, and political analysis of the roots of the Kurdish Question – narrating the birth of subsequent tribalism, statism, capitalism, and patriarchy – in order to provide a viable scenario for an autonomous and democratic Kurdish movement can be found in his *Prison Writings: The Roots of Civilisation* (London: Transmedia Publishing, 2007).

26. Abdullah Öcalan, *Liberating Life: Woman's Revolution* (Cologne: International Initiative Edition/Neuss: Mesopotamian Publishers, 2013), 35.

27. Ibid., 36.

28. See Ahmet Hamdi Akkaya and Joost Jongerden, "Reassembling the Political: The PKK and the project of Radical Democracy," *European Journal of Turkish Studies* 14 (2012).

29. Abdullah Öcalan, *Democratic Confederalism* (London: Transmedia Publishing, 2011), 10.

30. Murray Bookchin, *The Next Revolution: Popular Assemblies and the Promise of Direct Democracy* (New York: Verso Books, 2015), 138.

31. Bookchin's most elaborate description of the ecological society is to be found in T*he Ecology of Freedom: The Emergence and Dissolution of Hierarchy* (Palo Alto: Cheshire Books, 1982). Janet Biehl, a long-time collaborator with Bookchin, reported on the exchange between Öcalan and Bookchin during the conference "Challenging Capitalist Modernity," Feb. 3–5, 2012, Hamburg. See J. Biehl, "Bookchin, Öcalan, and the Dialectics of

Democracy," *New Compass,* Feb. 16, 2012.

32. Bookchin defines this concept as follows: "Communalism draws on the best of the older Left ideologies … From Marxism, it draws the basic project of formulating a rationally systematic and coherent socialism that integrates philosophy, history, economics, and politics … From anarchism, it draws its commitment to antistatism and confederalism, as well as the recognition that hierarchy is a basic problem that can be overcome only by a libertarian socialist society." Ibid., 15.

33. On the relation between confederalism and participatory democracy Bookchin writes: "A confederalist view involves a clear distinction between policymaking and the coordination and execution of adopted policies. Policymaking is exclusively the right of popular community assemblies based on the practices of participatory democracy. Administration and coordination are the responsibility of confederal councils which become the means for interlinking villages, towns, neighborhoods, and cities into confederal networks." Ibid., 75.

34. 36 Marlies Casier and Joost Jongerden distinguish three interrelated projects: "A democratic republic, democratic autonomy and democratic confederalism. The democratic republic seeks to redefine the Republic of Turkey, by disassociating democracy from nationalism; democratic autonomy refers to the right of people to decide on their own priorities and policies, to determine their own future; and the project for democratic confederalism is to serve as a model for self-government, its concrete realization sought through the political organization of society at four different levels, namely, communes in villages and districts, the organization of social groups (such as women and youth), organization on the basis of cultural and religious identities, and civil society organizations.," "Understanding Today's Kurdish movement: Leftist Heritage, Martyrdom, Democracy, and Gender," *European Journal of Kurdish Studies* 14 (2012).

35. Amil Kemal Özcan attributes the capacity of the PKK to communicate Öcalan's new ideas of radical democracy to its policies of "micro-education" – a tireless if necessary one-to-one model of communication with its constituency. Further, Özcan states that "the PKK-led 'cause' of the Kurdish populace in the Republic of Turkey is not a national one but an archetype of 'identity liberation movement' for which a nation-state is not sine qua non but a forthcoming peril. It is thus, in spite of Öcalan's bold 'surrender' (the total abandonment of aims and objectives of a classical nationalist movement such as independence, federalism or semi-autonomous rule, the unkind and undisguised opposition to the Kurdish autonomization in northern Iraq), that the undeniable majority of the Kurdish masses continue to back the PKK – under any name – and the 'president Öcalan.'" Amil Kemal Özcan, *Turkey's Kurds: A Theoretical Analysis of the PKK and Abdullah Öcalan* (New York: Routledge, 2006), 219.

36. "Since 2005, the PKK and all affiliated organizations have been restructured on the basis of this project under the name of KCK (Association of Communities in Kurdistan-Koma Civakên Kurdistan) which is a societal organization presented as an alternative to the nation-state. The KCK has aimed to organize itself from the bottom to the top in the form of assemblies. 'KCK is a movement which struggles for establishing its own democracy, neither ground on the existing nation-states nor see them as the obstacle.' In its status, called KCK Contract, its main aim is defined as struggling for the expansion of radical democracy which is based upon peoples' democratic organizations and decision-making power." Ahmet Hamdi Akkaya and Joost Jongerden, "Reassembling the Political: The PKK and the project of Radical Democracy," *European Journal of Turkish Studies* 14 (2012).

37. "In the light of lessons we have learned from the latest international experiences, not being a party force which stands completely above the people but which becomes the servant of the people, and not being a dysfunctional assembly but an innovation of an assembly which is functioning and determining everything is the most fundamental – and distinguishing – task that we will fulfil for socialism. The success that we achieve in this respect will at the same time be the success of socialism." From a speech by Öcalan in 1995, quoted in Amil Kemal Özcan, *Turkey's Kurds,* 140.

38. Interview with Dorsin Akif conducted in the Star Academy in Ramelan on Dec. 23, 2014.

39. Gönül Kaya, "Why Jineology? Re-Constructing the Sciences towards a Communal and Free Life", *Kurdish Question,* Dec. 28, 2014: http://kurdishquestion.com/index.php/kurdistan/north-kurdistan/why-jineology.htm

40. Ibid. For a critical account, see Janet Biehl, "Impressions of Rojava: a report from the revolution," *ROAR Magazine,* Dec. 16, 2014; and J. Biehl, *Rethinking Ecofeminist Politics* (Boston: South End Press, 1991), 29.

41. Zîlan Diyar, "The Whole World is Talking About Us, Kurdish Women," *Kurdish Question.*

42. Dilar Dirik, "The Representation of Kurdish Women Fighters in the Media," *Kurdish Question.*

43. Janet Biehl, "Revolutionary Education: Two Academies in Rojava," *Ecology or Catastrophe,* Feb. 7, 2015.

44. Pablo Lafuente, "For a Populist Cinema: On Hito Steyerl's November and Lovely Andrea," *Afterall* 19 (Autumn/Winter 2008).

45. Hito Steyerl, "Kobanê Is Not Falling," *e-flux,* Oct. 10, 2014.

46. Interview with Abdullah Abdul conducted in the artist's studio in Amude, Dec. 18, 2014.

47. Interview with Nesrin Botan conducted in the Mitra Hasake Cultural Center, Dec. 20, 2014.

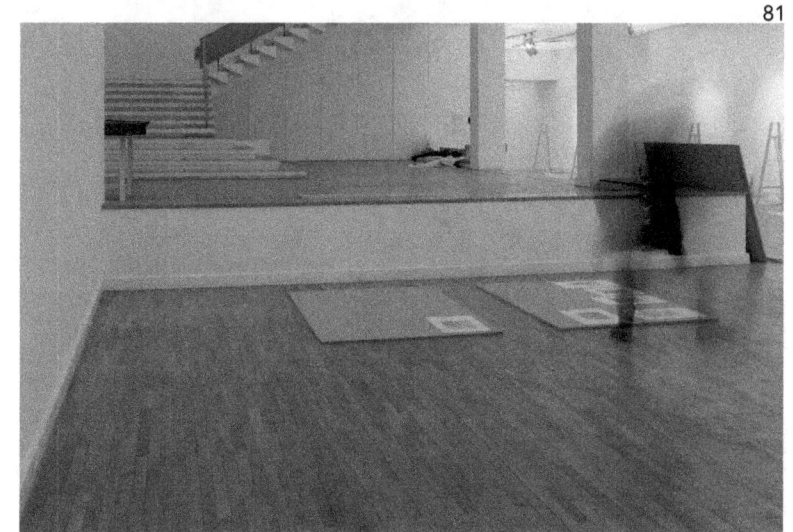

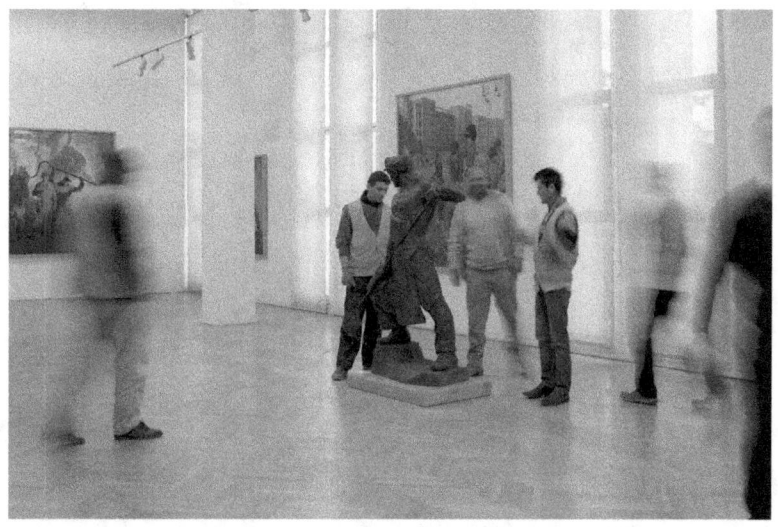

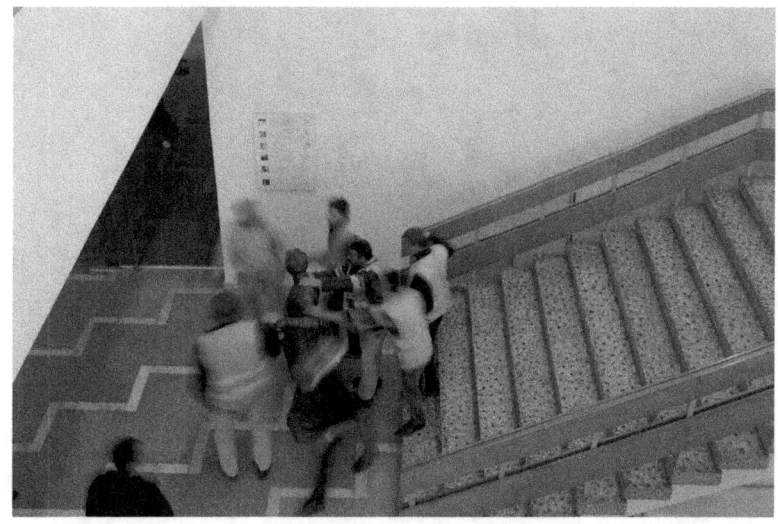

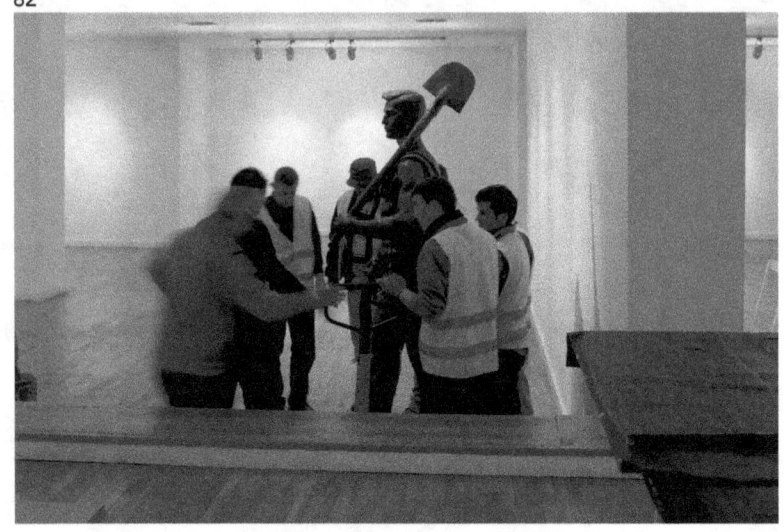

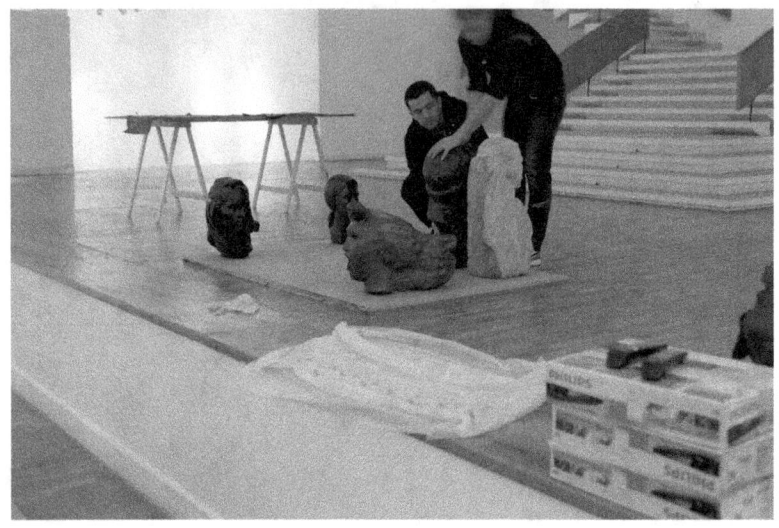

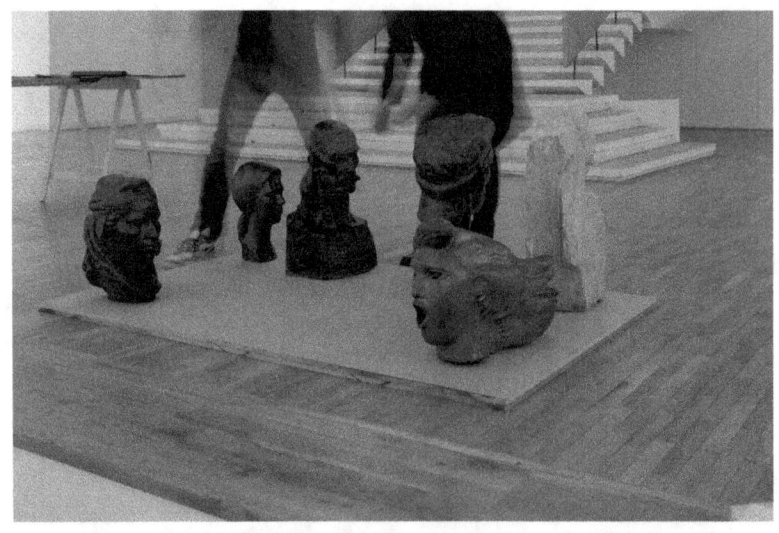

Ciprian Mureşan: Dead Weights

The work is an idiosyncratic engraving press, that collapses sculptural volume and mass, form and gravity. Selected bronze sculptures from the National Gallery of Arts collection are installed to weigh down on their makeshift pedestals: sheets of MDF, between which damp engravings by Mureşan both dry and hide. Pressure and invisibility become interchangeable forces of image-making, while sculptures are both displayed and functionally reduced to their gravitational pull. Between these regimes where images can exist and create meaning, the thing-ness of sculptural volumes and the invisible engravings "privatize" the space of the museum, transform what should be been a transparent look at a moment in the evolution of Albanian sculptural style into a personal laboratory, an *ersatz* studio installed at the center of the gallery. The sculptures are not installed as elements in a discussion of style and its evolutions, but as instruments in the 'live' making of a yet-invisible project by the artist.

Ciprian Mureşan: Pesha të rënda. Vepra është një proces krejtësisht personal gdhendjeje, që përzien në një vëllimin skulpturor dhe masën, formën dhe gravitetin. Skulpturat e zgjedhura nga fondi i Galerisë Kombëtare të Arteve janë instaluar për të peshuar mbi piedestalet e tyre të improvizuara me fletë druri MDF, mes të cilave njëkohësisht edhe thahen, edhe fshihen gravura akoma të njoma nga Mureşan. Rëndesa dhe padukshmëria bëhen forcat shkëmbyeshme imazh-krijuese, ndërsa skulpturat edhe ekspozohen edhe reduktohen funksionalisht te tërheqja e tyre gravitacionale. Mes këtyre regjistrave ku imazhet mund të ekzistojnë dhe krijojnë kuptim, gjëjësia e vëllime skulpturore dhe gravurat e padukshme e "privatizojnë" hapësirën e galerisë, duke transformuar atë çka duhej të ishte një vështrim transparent në një moment të evolucionit të stilit skulpturor shqiptar, në një laborator personal, në një studio artisti të instaluar në qendër të galerisë. Skulpturat nuk janë instaluar si elemente për një diskutim mbi stilin dhe zhvillimet e tij, por si instrumenta në krijimin aktual të një projekti ende të padukshëm nga artisti.

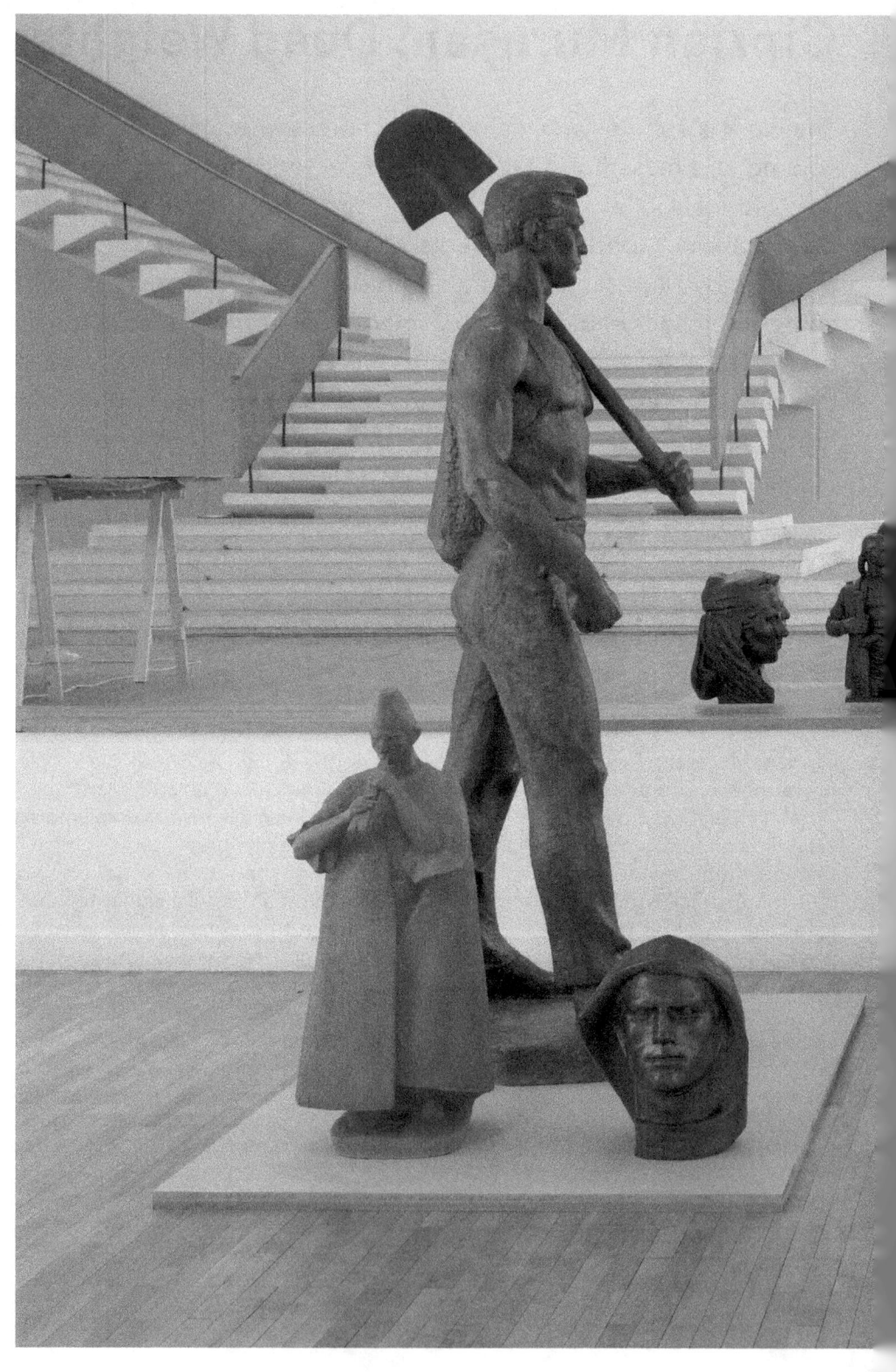

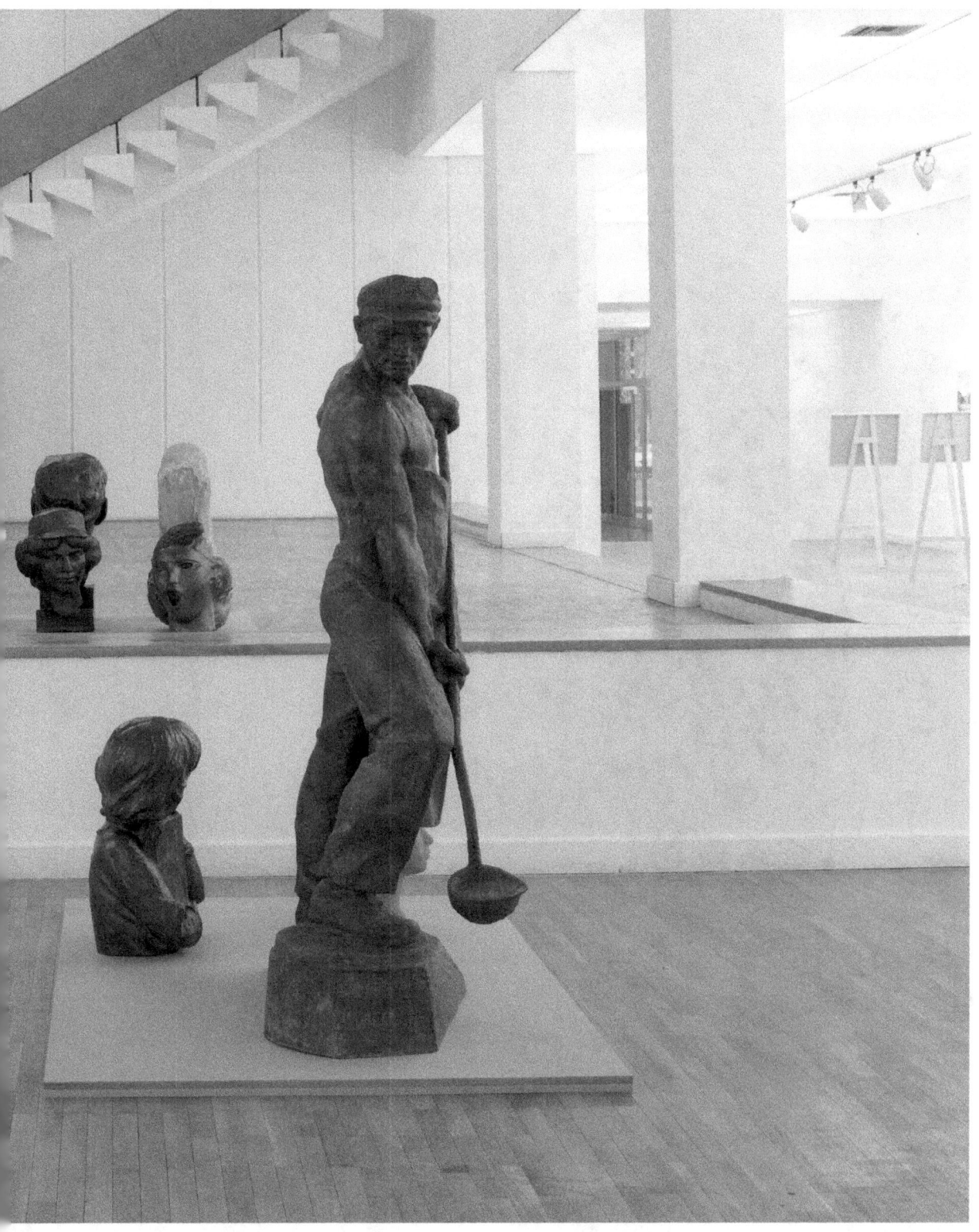

Ciprian Mureşan, *Dead Weights,*
mixed media, National Gallery of
Arts, Tirana, Albania, 2015.

Ciprian Mureşan, *Pesha të rënda,*
media e përzier, Galeria Kombëtare e
Arteve, Tiranë, Shqipëri, 2015.

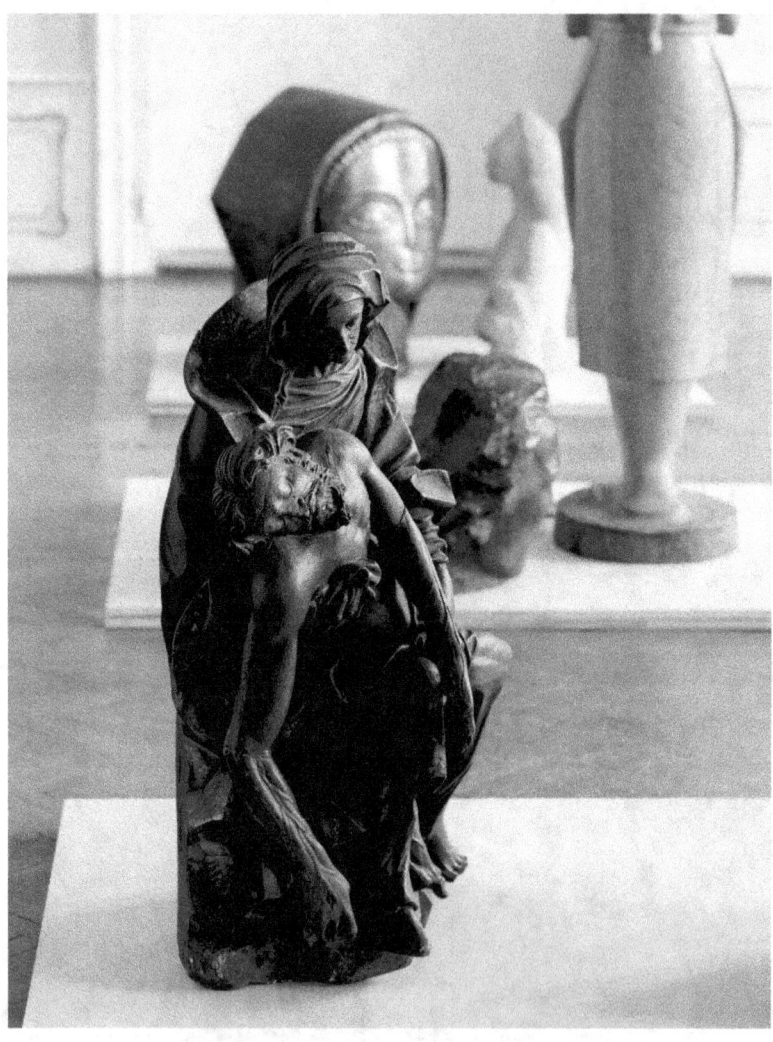

Ciprian Mureşan, *Dead Weights*, mixed media, Art Museum of Cluj-Napoca, 2012.

Ciprian Mureşan, *Pesha të rënda*, media e përzier, Muzeu i Artit i Cluj-Napoca-s, 2012.

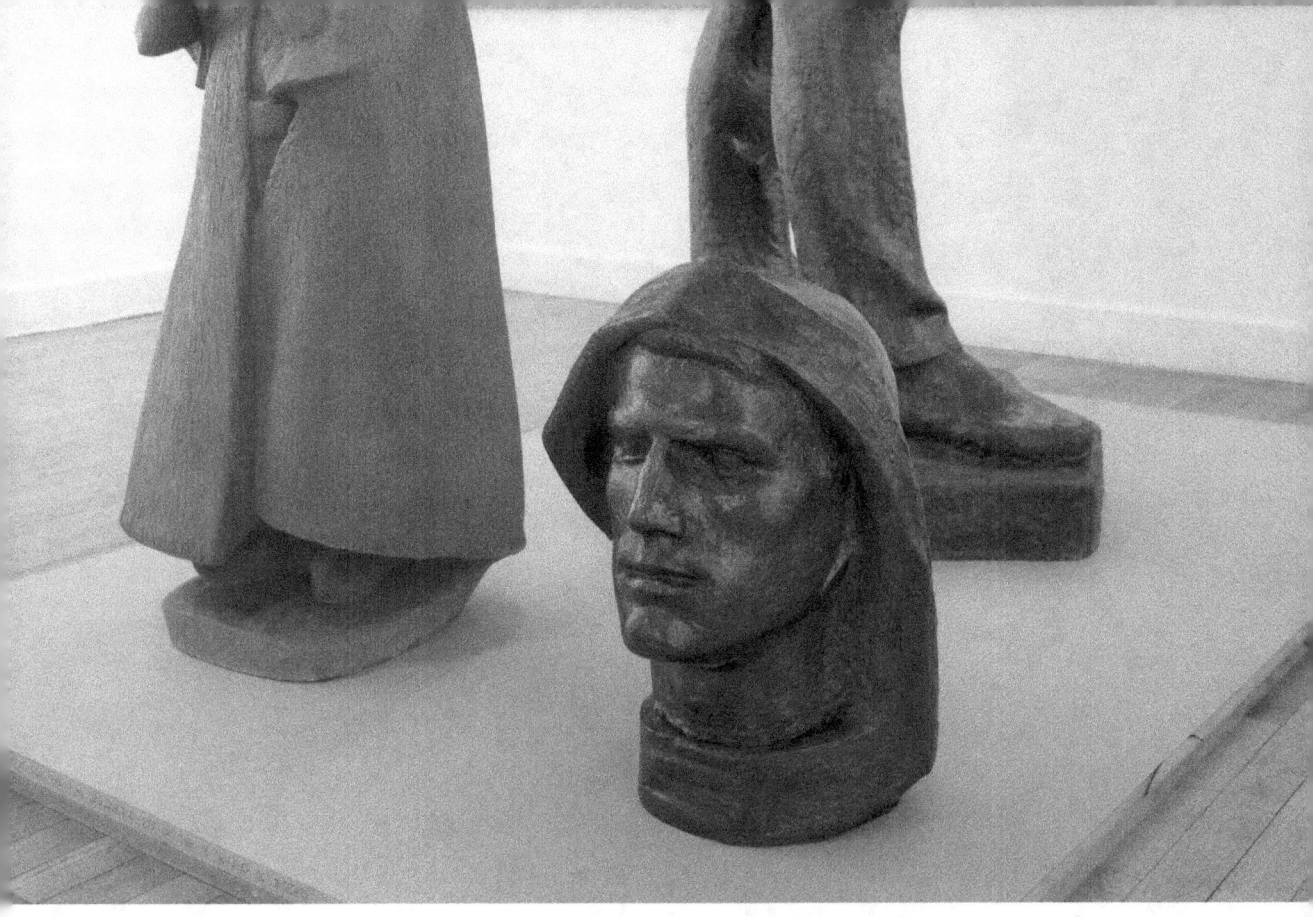

Detail of *Dead Weights:*

Detaj i *Peshave të rënda:*

Fuat Dushku, Portret of an Oil
Worker, bronze, acquired 1980.

Fuat Dushku, *Portret naftëtari*, bronz,
blerë 1980.

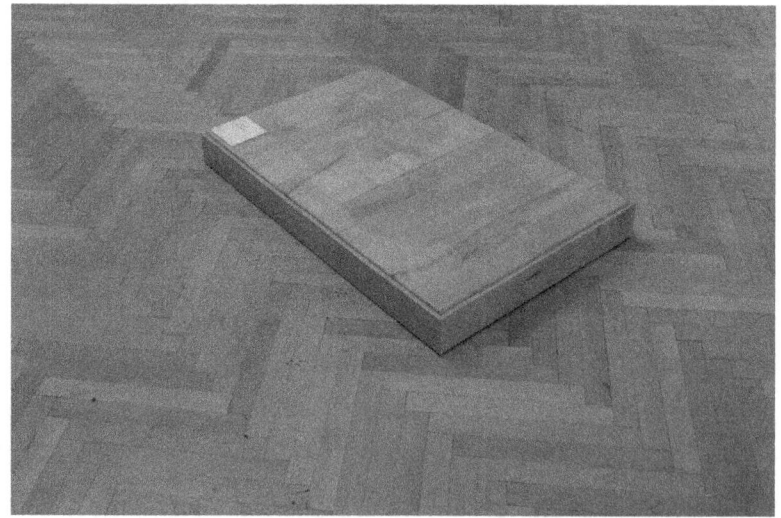

Empty pedestal of the *Metal Worker*.

Piedestali bosh i *Metalurgut*.

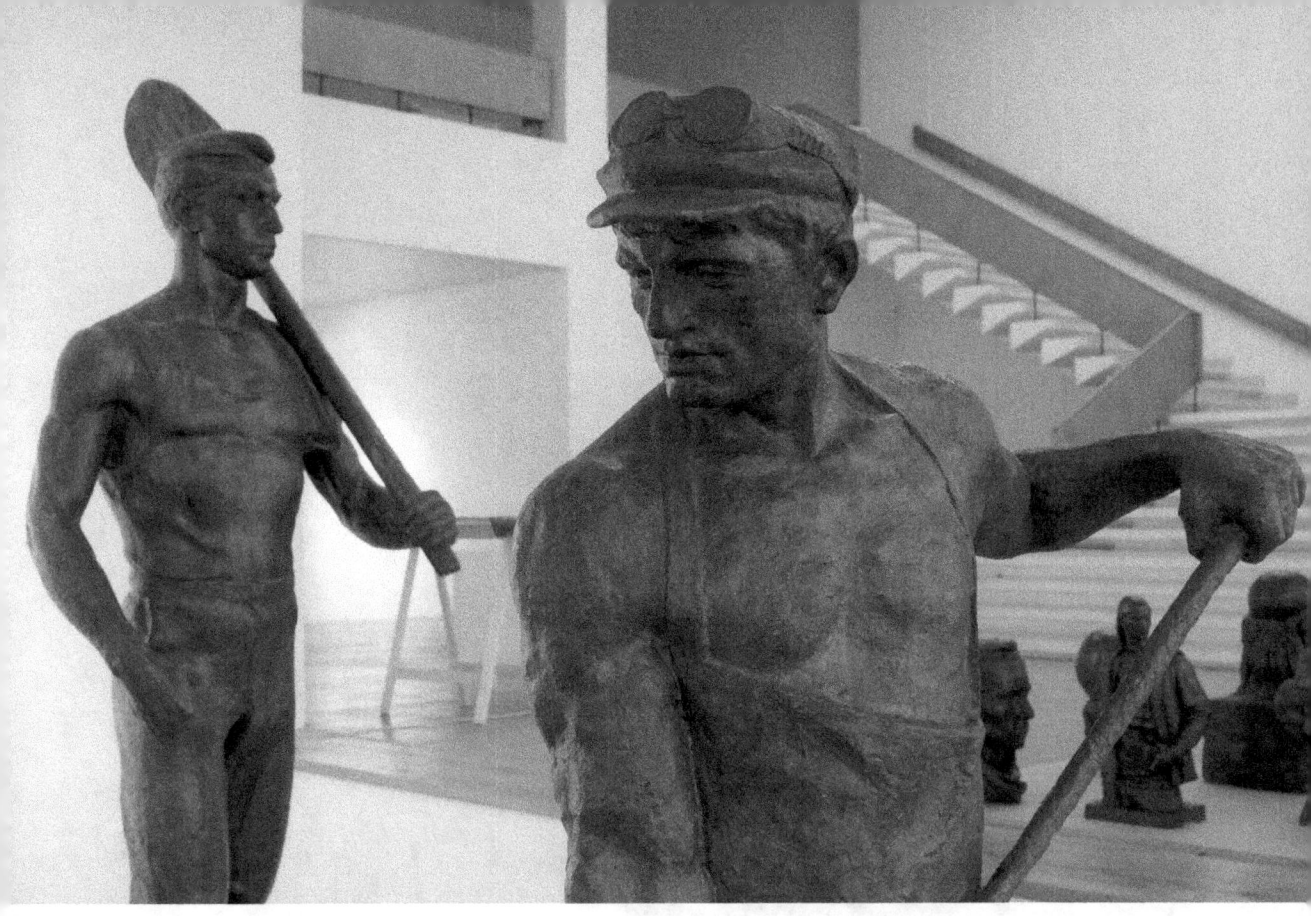

Detail of *Dead Weights:*

Detaj i *Peshave të rënda:*

Fuat Dushku, *Metal Worker*, bronze,
acquired 1980.

Fuat Dushku, *Metalurgu*, bronz, blerë
1980.

90

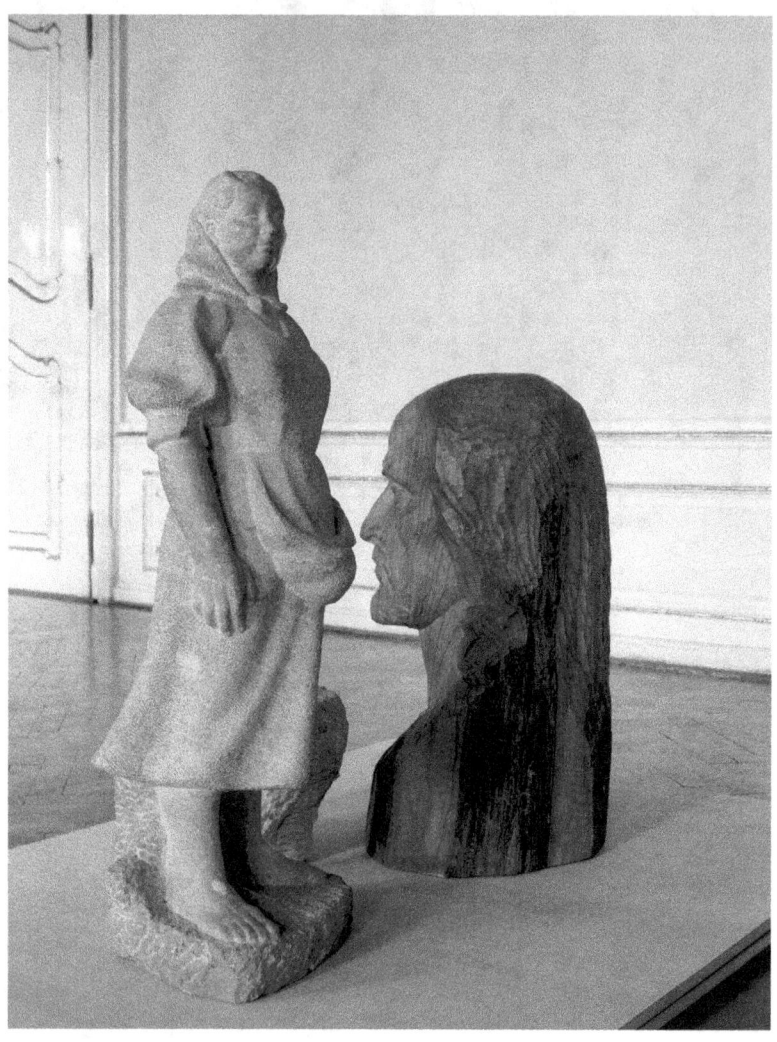

Ciprian Mureşan, *Dead Weights*,
mixed media, Art Museum of Cluj-
Napoca, 2012.

Ciprian Mureşan, *Pesha të rënda*,
media e përzier, Muzeu i Artit i Cluj-
Napoca-s, 2012.

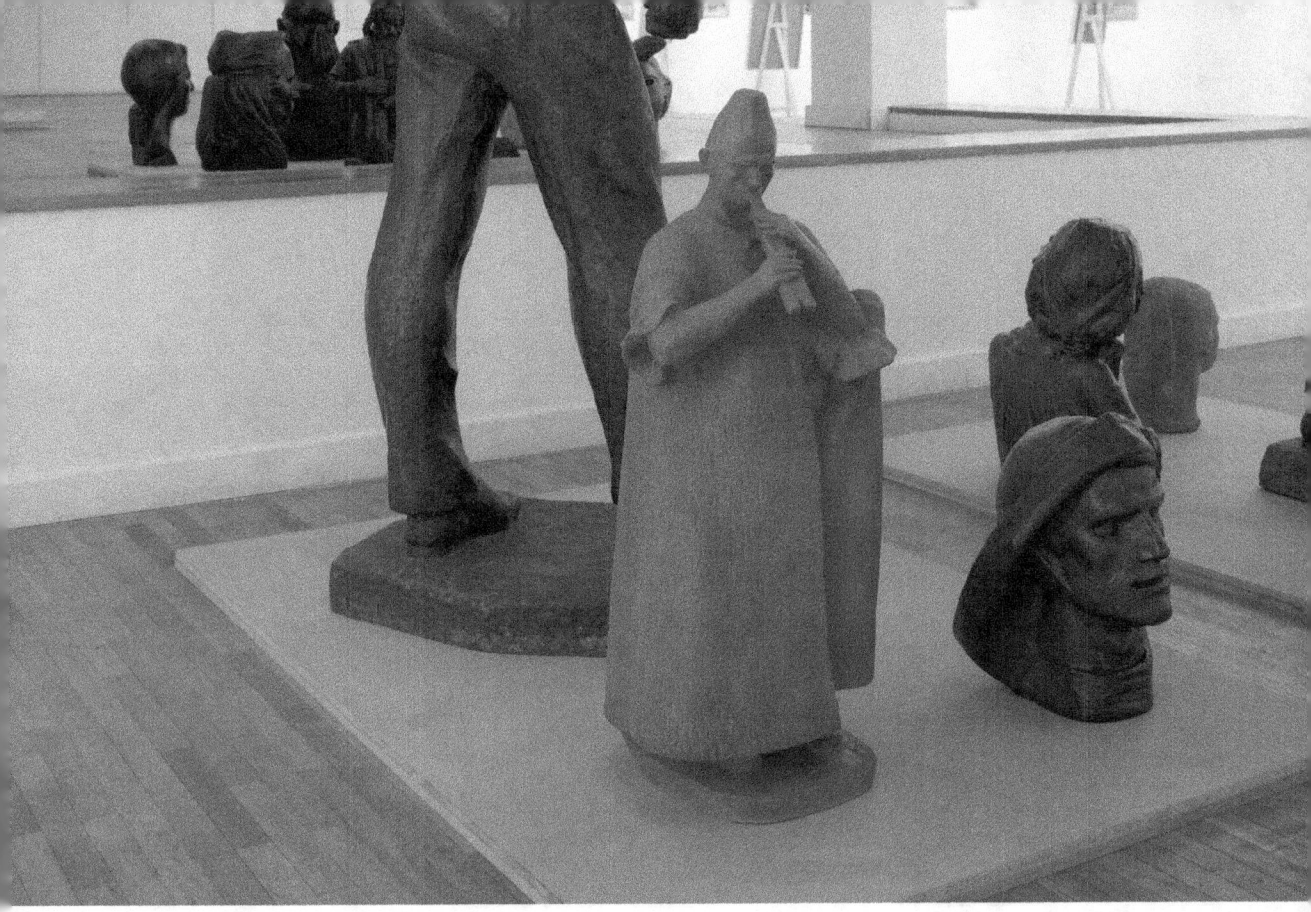

Detail of *Dead Weights:*

Dushku, *Flute Player (Shepherd Janino),* terra cotta, acquired 1986.

Detaj i *Peshave të rënda:*

Fuat Dushku, *Fyelltari, bariu "Janino",* baltë, bletë 1986.

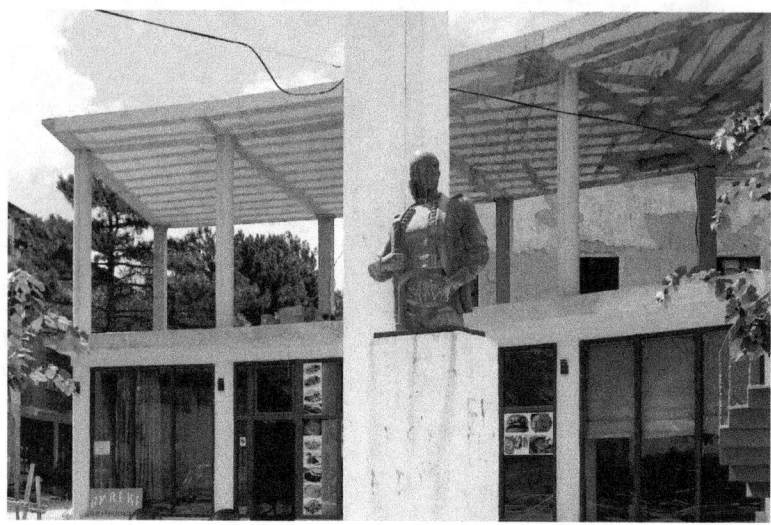

Kristaq Rama, *Bust of People's Heroine Qerime Shota Galica*, bronze, Kukës, 1968 (ALS–554).

Kristaq Rama, *Busti i Heroines së Popullit Qerime Shota Galica*, bronz, Kukës, 1968 (ALS–554).

Detail of *Dead Weights:*

Detaj i *Peshave të rënda:*

Kristaq Rama, *Girl from Dropull*, bronze, acquired 1977.

Kristaq Rama, *Dropullitja*, bronz, blerë 1977.

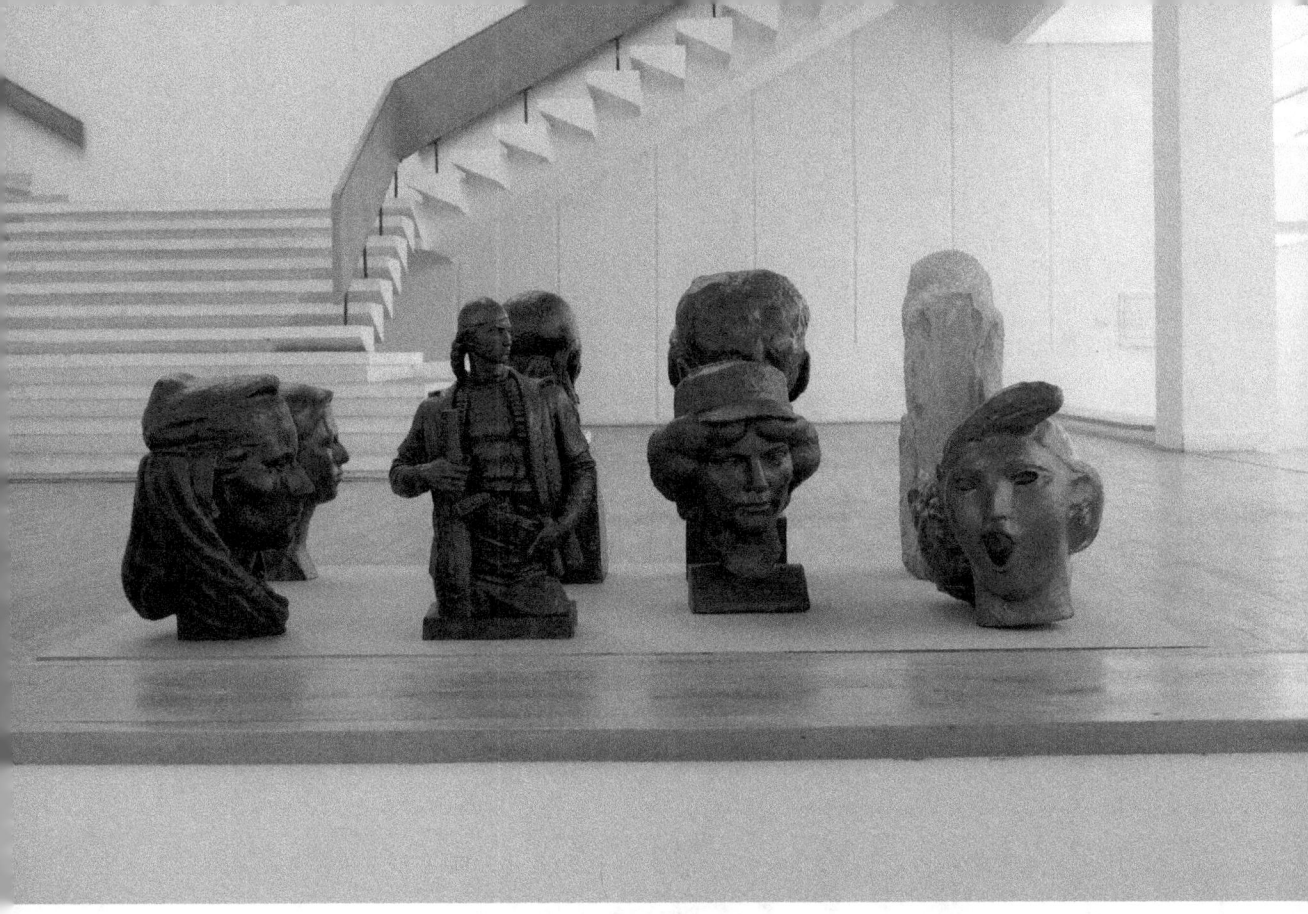

Kristaq Rama, *Shote Galica*, bronze, acquired 1984.

Mumtas Dhrami, *Girl with Braids*, bronze, acquired 1983.

Thoma Thomai, *Singing Girl*, bronze, 1971.

Kristaq Rama, *Shote Galica*, bronz, blerë 1984.

Mumtas Dhrami, *Vajza me kordele*, bronz, blerë 1983.

Thoma Thomai, *Vajza që këndon*, bronz, 1971.

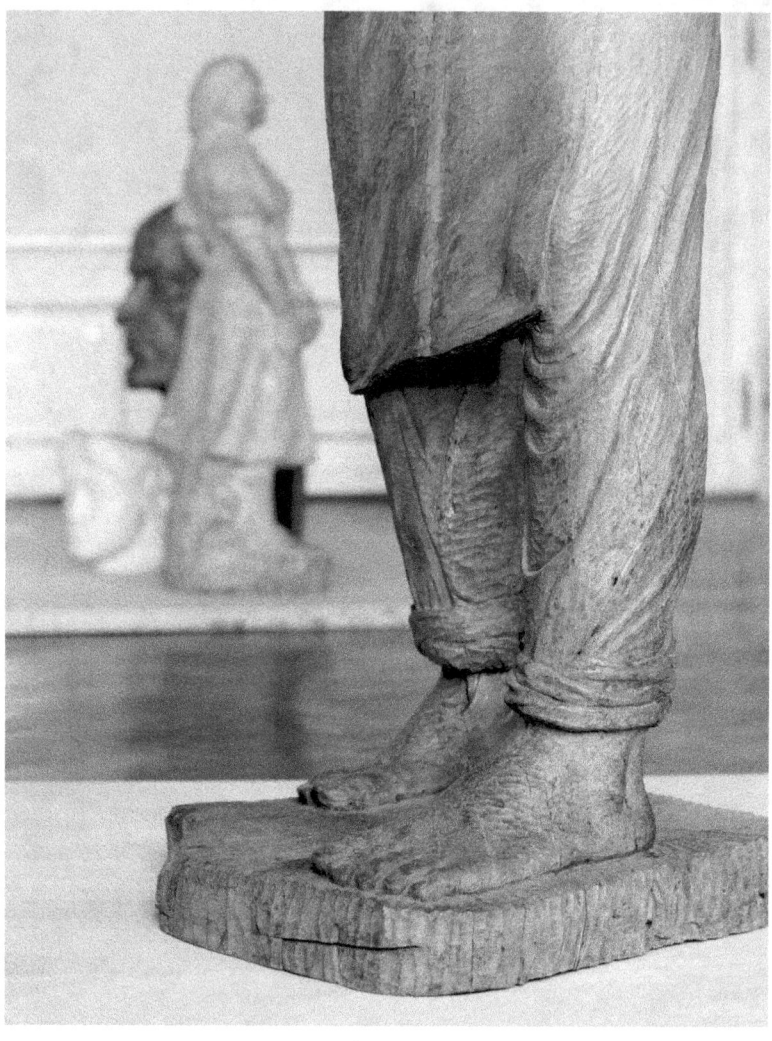

Ciprian Mureşan, *Dead Weights*,
mixed media, Art Museum of Cluj-
Napoca, 2012.

Ciprian Mureşan, *Pesha të rënda*,
media e përzier, Muzeu i Artit i Cluj-
Napoca-s, 2012.

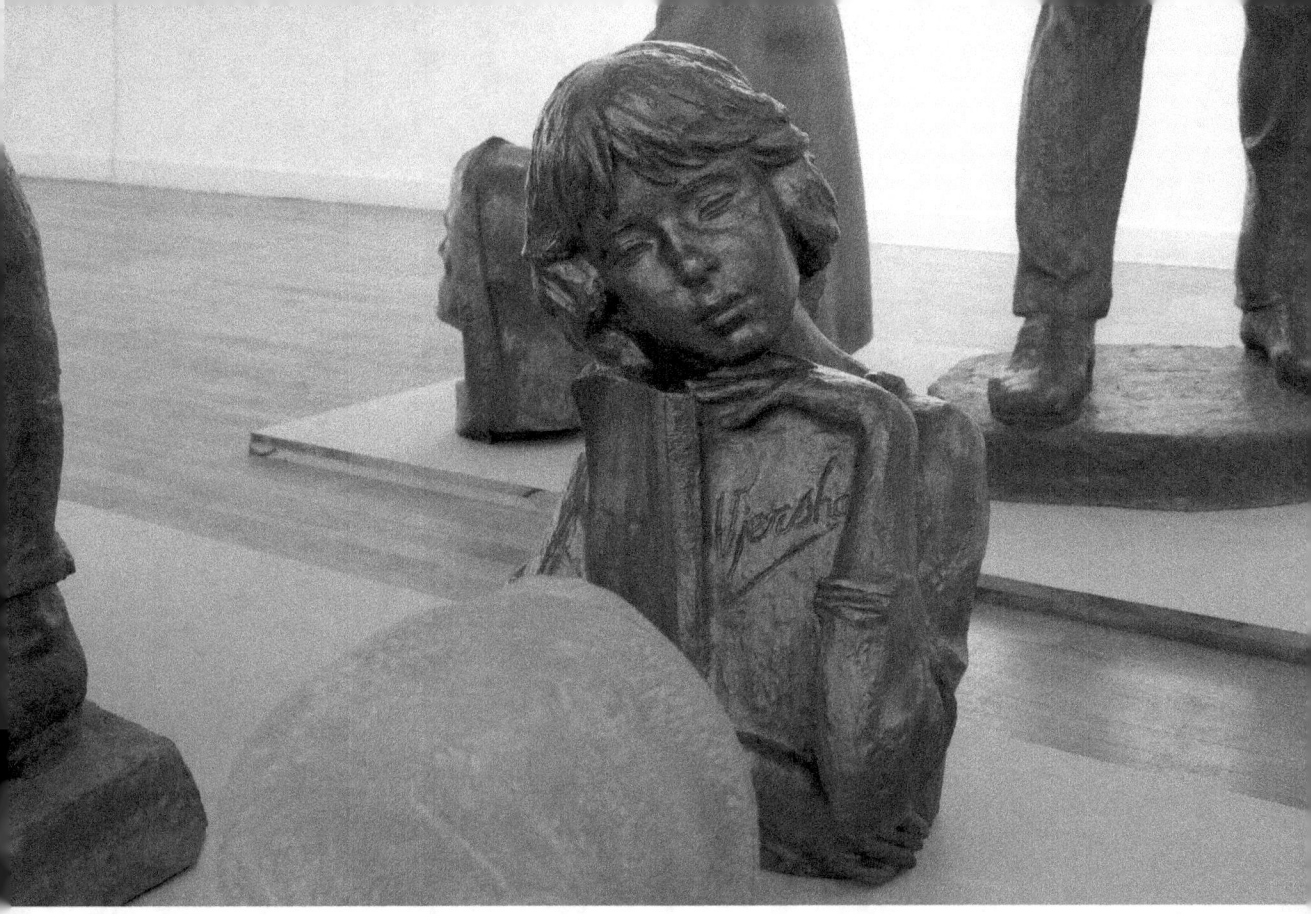

Detail of *Dead Weights:*

Detaj i *Peshave të rënda:*

Kujtim Qamo, *Book Lover*, bronze, acquired 1986.

Kujtim Qamo, *Mikja e librit*, bronz, blerë 1986.

Detail of *Dead Weights:*

Detaj i *Peshave të rënda:*

Nelo Lukaçi, *Woman from Mirditë,* stone, acquired 1967.

Nelo Lukaçi, *Mirditorja,* gur, blerë 1967.

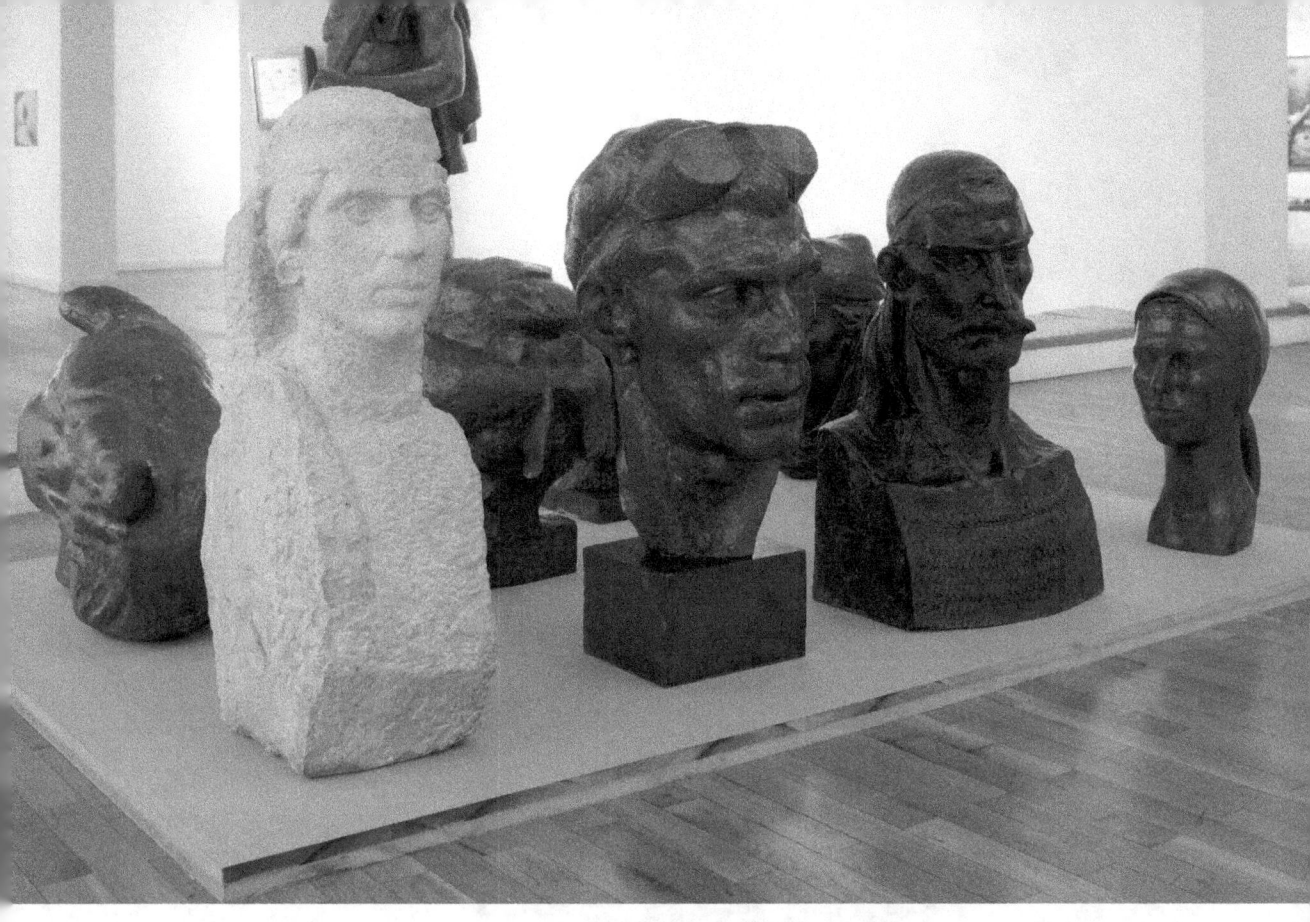

Mumtas Dhrami, *Foundry Worker,*
bronze, acquired 1972.

Mumtas Dhrami, *Fonditori,* bronz,
blerë 1972.

Sotir Kosta, *Lekë Dukagjini,* bronze,
acquired 1973.

Sotir Kosta, *Lekë Dukagjini,* bronz,
blerë 1973.

Thoma Thomai, *Porcelain Factory
Worker,* bronze, 1970.

Thoma Thomai, *Punëtorja e Porcelanit,*
bronz, 1970.

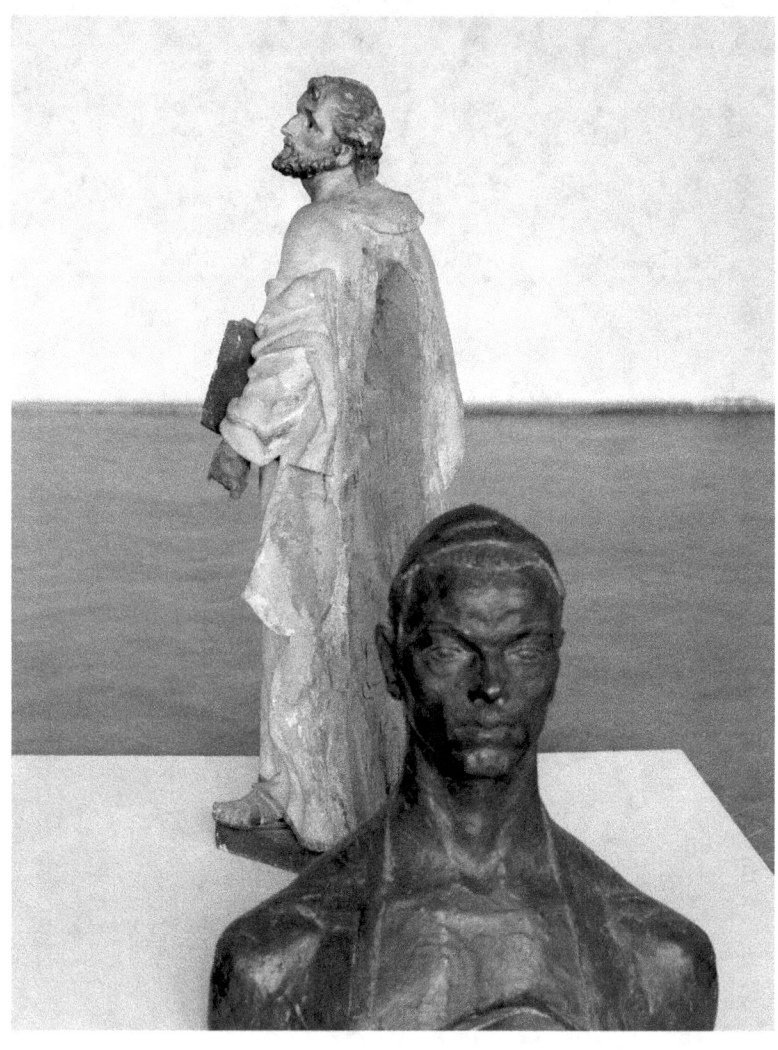

Ciprian Mureşan, *Dead Weights*, mixed media, Art Museum of Cluj-Napoca, 2012.

Ciprian Mureşan, *Pesha të rënda*, media e përzier, Muzeu i Artit i Cluj-Napoca-s, 2012.

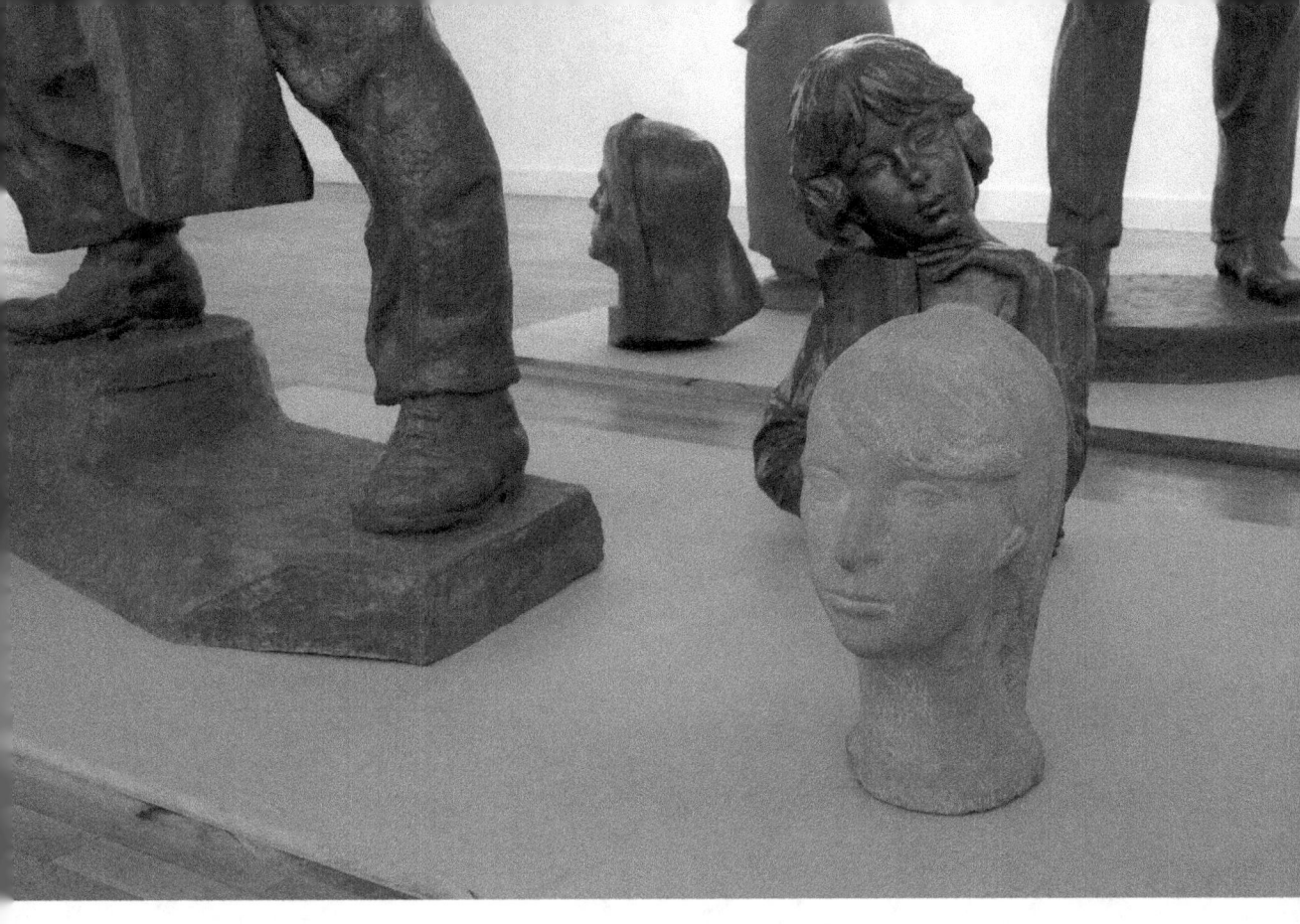

Detail of *Dead Weights:*

Thoma Thomai, *Worker,* stone,
1983–4

Detaj e *Peshave të rënda:*

Thoma Thomai, *Punëtorja,* gur, 1983–4

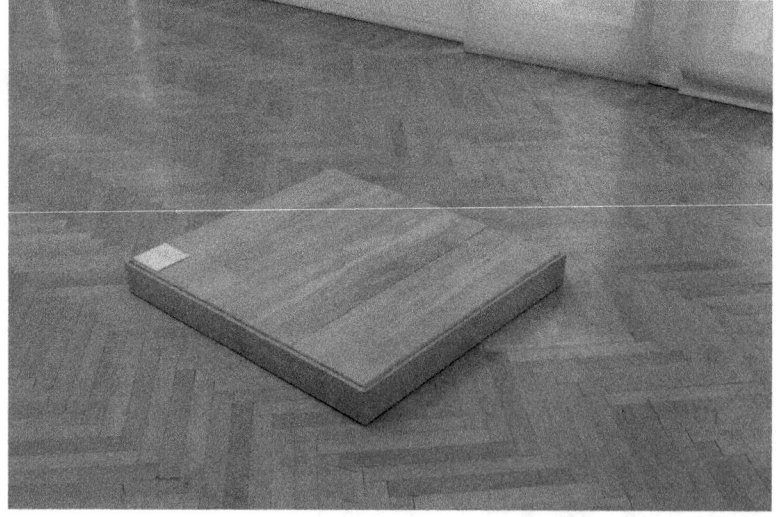

Empty pedestal of *The Contemporary
of the Republic.*

Piedestali bosh i *Versnikut të
Republikës.*

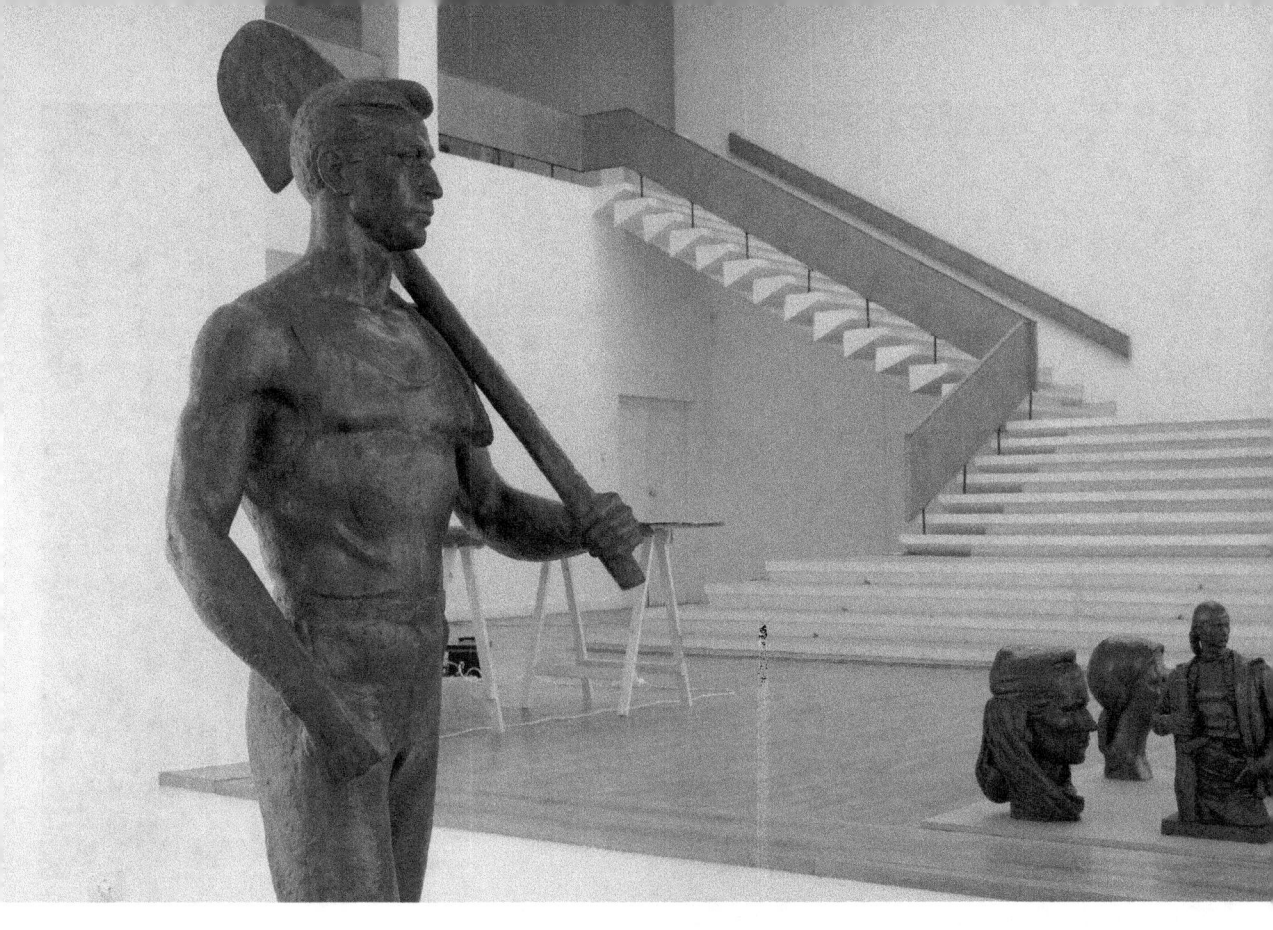

Detail of *Dead Weights:*

Kristaq Rama, *The Contemporary of the Republic,* bronze, acquired 1964

Detaj e *Peshave të rënda:*

Kristaq Rama, *Vërsniku i Republikës,* bronz, blerë 1964

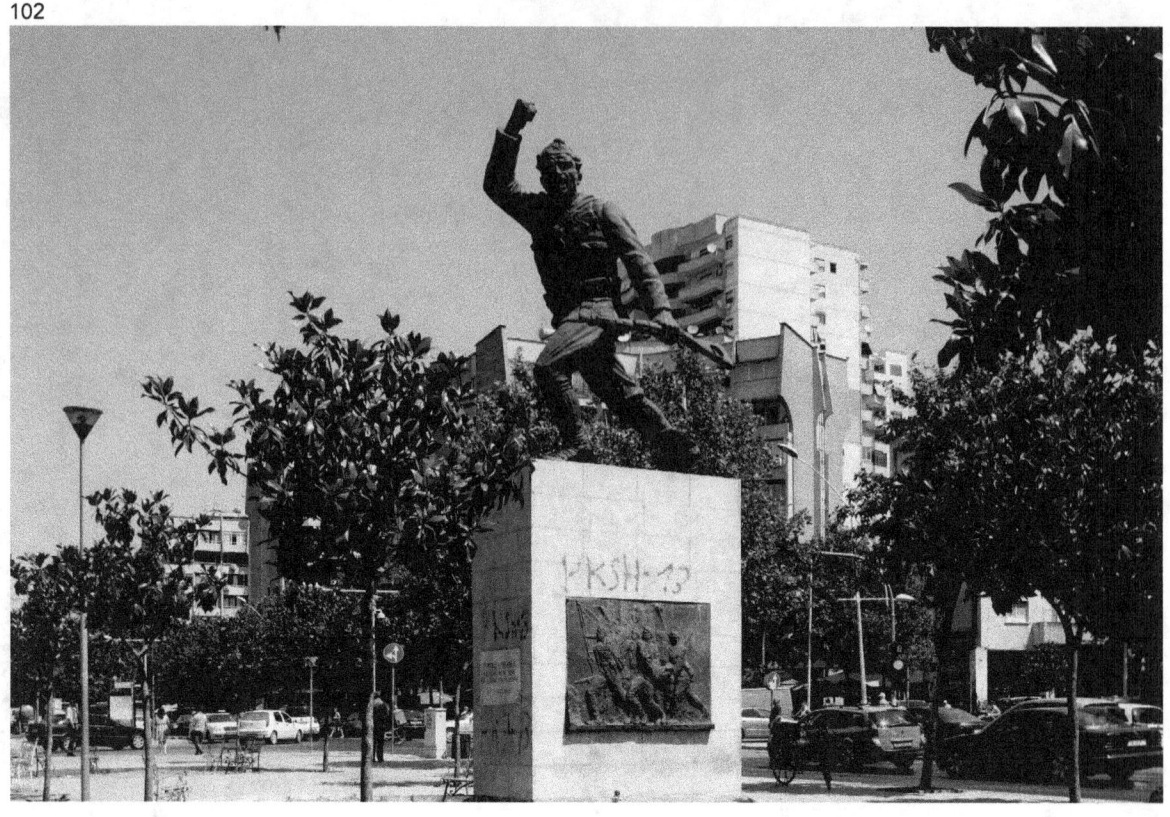

Andrea Mandro, *Liberating Partisan*,
bronze, 1946–9 (ALS–1).

Andrea Mandro, *Partizani çlirimtar*,
bronz, 1946–9 (ALS–1).

Një kohë e shkuar në themel të kohës sonë

Në kohët që jetojnë për shqiptarët e sotëm, askush nuk e di se kur kalojnë pranë shtatoreve të mëdha prej bronxi apo betoni, ato janë artefakte të një drejtimi artistik që i referohet skulpturës së realizmit socialist. Kjo sepse asnjë rradhë nuk shkruhet për to në tekste shkollor dhe, nëse është shkruar ndonjë libër arti, numri i pakët i lexuesve nuk merret në konsideratë si njohje apo dije rreth arsyeve: pse ato shtatore u krijuan dhe pse duhet të jenë sot në hapësirat urbane apo rurale, në hapësirat muzeore apo institucionale administrative të Shqipërisë së sotme?

Rrjedhat e historisë së artit informojnë se kohët njëqindvjeçare lidhen dhe arsyetohen me dhe pas njëra-tjetrën. Në fund të një mbylljeje dyzetvjeçare politike dhe kulturore nuk do vononte që ligjet e historisë të binin mbi artin shqiptar dhe ta përfshinin zhvillimin apo dekadencat e tij në vrullin e ideve bashkëkohore kuratoriale. Në forma krejt të natyrshme, kësi ide, janë një pasqyrim dijesh, janë një vëzhgim esencial mbi ritmet e trysnisë që ushtron imazhi artistik mbi formimin e një brezi njerëzor, i cili mund të ngadalsojë apo të shpejtojë transformimin, për mirë apo për keq, të standardeve të jetesës dhe të nivelit të lirive individuale në një shoqëri të caktuar.

Një nga idetë e ekspozitës së ndërtuar nga kuratori Mihnea Mircan "Punëtorët dalin nga studioja. Duke mos parë më realizëm socialist" është se:

Kjo ekspozitë është një përpjekje për të hedhur dritë mbi fragmente të veçanta të fondit të Galerisë Kombëtare të Arteve në Tiranë…

Mendoj se këtu nis një arsyetim i shëndetshëm, që orienton në vijim t'i kushtohet vëmendje të gjitha modeleve të trashëguara të artit në kohën e komunizmit. Rimarrja e tyre në konsideratë dhe vlerësimi i tyre real mbështetur në kohën diktatoriale të krijimit, zbulon lidhjen e heshtur me atë segment evident të artit bashkëkohor që referohet, mbështetet dhe ideologjizohet nga politikat e sotme.

Skulptura e realizmit socialist në Shqipëri nis asokohe kur Partia Komuniste Shqiptare u njësua me republikën, shtetin, kulturën dhe kur në sheshin qëndror të Tiranës zuri vend monumenti "Partizani çlirimtar", krijuar në vitet 1946–9, nga skulptori Andrea Mano. Natyrshëm, arti i realizmit socialist shqiptar u bë pjesë e realizmit socialist, si lëvizje artistike masive në strukturat e arteve postmoderne të historisë së vet dhe asaj botërore.

Artistët e realizmit socialist dolën nga gjiri i asaj pjese të shoqërisë që e kishin lidhur jetën me partinë në pushtet dhe kuratorët e tij me ata njerëz që e kishin lidhur jetën me ideologjinë e diktaturës së proletariatit. Ideologjia e ngriti klasën e tij deri në lartësinë e pushtetit të vendimmarrjes dhe të orientuesve ideo-estetikë në brendësitë e studiove të artistëve të popullit.

Pikturat dhe skulpturat e krijuara mbanin në sipërfaqet dhe volumet e tyre jo vetëm imazhin heroik të njeriut të ri, por edhe vullnetin e vetëm kuratorial të formimit të një arti uniform të realizmit socialist. Dhe në vitet 1960 realizmi socialist shqiptar ishte i gatshëm dhe solli për gati tridhjetë vite me radhë pushtetin e imazhit tek masat popullore dhe jo askurr emocionin natyral të veprës së artit.

Idetë e reja që lëvrohen nga kuratorë ndërkombëtarë dhe që vijnë nga kombe të Evropës Lindore, të cilët u çliruan por edhe u pushtuan "miqësisht" nga kultura komuniste kërkojnë të rianalizojnë funksionimin e mjediseve figurative ideologjike të krijuara gjatë gjysmës së dytë të shek. XX në këndvështrime të reja të artit bashkëkohor.

Kuratorë të tillë, janë disa herë më të afërt me këto mjedise, janë disa herë më të ndjeshëm dhe disa herë më kreativ për të rivitalizuar modelin e propagandës së një arti ideologjik, që lind në funksion të një politike të vetme. Ata janë llogjik në krahasimin e artit të diktaturës komuniste me *një art praktikash të angazhuara të artit bashkëkohor në shërbim të regjimeve të ndryshme të bashkëbisedimit politik*, siç Mircan e cilëson botën e sotme politike në konceptin e ekspozitës "Punëtorët dalin nga studioja. Duke mos parë më realizmin socialist".

Thënë thjeshtë: arti i realizmit socialist në shërbim të diktaturës së proletariatit i lind e drejta të hyjë në bashkëbisedim pohues apo kontradiktash me të gjithë artin e zhvilluar që nga koha e pas rënies së Murit të Berlinit e deri në ditët e sotme.

Fillimet e skulpturës shqiptare të realizmit socialist janë derivat i modeleve të shkollës romane dhe helene të artit akademik, që vazhdonin të shfaqeshin në gjysmën e parë të shek. XX. Skulptorët Odhise Paskali, me kulturë klasike italiane dhe Janaq Paço, me një të tillë greke, sollën performanca skulpturore akademike vetjake, të cilat nuk kishin asnjë bazament të trashëguar skulpturor stilistik e historik në Shqipëri. Skulptura realiste në Shqipëri është produkt kreativ i kahut të individëve intelektualë evropiano-perëndimor dhe aspak i zhvillimit tradicional të një mjedisi skulpturor të mëparshëm gjatë shek. xix. Modelet e para të kësaj skulpture, që ata sollën përmes një krijimtarie me burim të importuar nga neoklasicizmat, ishin subjekte historike natyrale vendase me një frymë kombëtare. Kjo i bën këto modele të mos kenë brenda tyre forcën e jehonës gjithëpërfshirëse.

Nga "Punëtorët dalin nga studio. Duke mos parë më realizëm socialist" u dëshmua se është hera e parë që veprat e skulpturës dhe pikturës së realizmit socialist të fondit të GKA u vendosën në marrëdhënie ekspozimi me vepra të artit bashkëkohor të aristëve të huaj. Skulpturat e zgjedhura u ekspozuan jo në arsyen pse u krijuan, jo në arsyen e vlerësimit të artit të artistit, por për të treguar qëllimin dhe misionin e realizmit socialist, që mbeti një qëllim i parealizuar dhe një mision në tentativë. Veprat e tij u bënë mjete të ekzekutimit të një mendimi të fortë, debatues dhe të vëmendjes ndaj pyetjes:

Mënyrat që po përdor apo dhe përvojat që po kalon arti bashkëkohor janë tejkalim, kundërshtim, rebelim ndaj realizmit socialist si pjesë e artit postmodern, kanë një qëllim të ri apo janë një vijim i shtuar në arsye të lidhjes së ngushtë e të nëndheshme të artit në shërbim të panoramës politike, dhe se kjo e fundit, po i vesh artit bashkëkohor një robërim të ri teknologjiko-ideologjik dhe po i jep atij funksione shërbimi për politikën që ekziston si ideologji jo-independente?

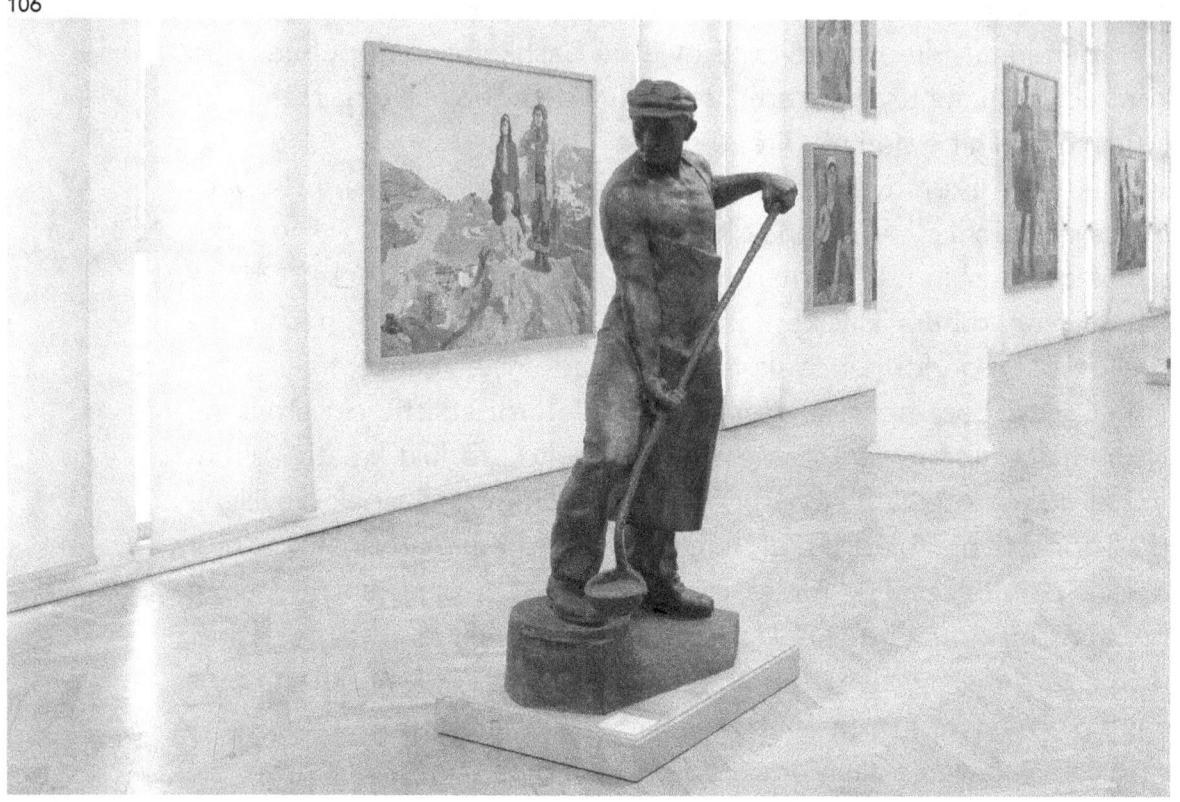

Ritmet për të zhvilluar skulpturën në Shqipërinë politike të shekullit xx u nxitën në mënyrë drejtuese nga ideologjia dhe në mënyrë organizuese nga artistët aktiv të Lidhjes së Shkrimtarëve dhe Artistëve të Shqipërisë. Në këtë mënyrë asokohe kupola politike krijoi brenda strukturës së vet kupolën artistike dhe bashkë krijuan artistë jo të lirë, që realizonin skulptura të komanduara në shërbim të realizmit socialist apo artit jo të pavarur. Arti u vesh me ideologji, e cila u paraqit në formën e pesë parimeve bazë të socializmit politik. Parimet socialiste të huazuara në këndvështrimin e kulturës sovjetike mbi artin, i'u bashkangjitën stilit realist. Në Shqipëri u importua në vitet 1950 të shek. xx, realizmi socialist sovjetik i viti 1932, i cili u instrukturua në institutet e artit rus të Leningradit dhe të Moskës, si dhe në institutet aplikative të artit në vendet ish-komuniste të Evropës Lindore. Artistët shqiptarë të realizmit socialist studjuan në vitet 1950–60 në këto shkolla, të cilat morën përsipër të aftësojnë artistët shqiptarë. Ata në vitet 1970 formuan ikonografinë e veçantë të realizmit socialist të artit shqiptar. Në skulpturë u glorifikua figura e punëtorit dhe iu servir

Fuat Dushku, *Metal Worker*, bronze, acquired 1980.

Fuat Dushku, *Metalurgu*, bronz, blerë 1980.

masës/popullit si makinahero, si "Njeriu i Ri", i cili nuk i ngjante askujt, por duhej imituar nga të gjithë. Njëkohësisht, bota komuniste dhe arti duhej të befasonin dhe mrekullonin popullin me *punën* dhe për këtë krijuan skenën e madhe të saj. Atje populli duhej të gjente burimin e vetëm të kënaqësisë. Puna u respektua si mjedisi ku shpenzohej koha e jetës, mbisundonte dinjiteti komunist dhe kryhej formimi kulturor. Liria artistike dhe jeta e skulptorit zhvillohej në këtë skenë të madhe të punës e të edukimit, në të cilën artisti përmes kontrollit dhe vetkontrollit e brendashkruante hapësirën e studjos së tij.

Kjo është përpjekja e suksesshme e kësaj ekspozite, ku natyrshëm një vend shërbimi dhe mbështetës ishte skulptura e realizmit socialist, që ruhet me fanatizëm dhe respekt në GKA.

Skulpturat në bronz dhe simbolike të Njeriut të Ri, skulpturat e punëtorëve, skulpturat që u kryen në frymëzimin e entuziasmit socialist dhe kanë si subjekte koka njerëzore apo buste në akte të ndryshme, vijnë nga ajo kohë dhe rievokojnë sistemin e krijimit artistik, zbulojnë kufizimet në tema, tregojnë mbi një sistem stilistikor të kufizuar në mjete shprehëse, rrëfejnë rreth mangësisë dhe rregullave të lirisë së krijimit, si dhe janë dëshmi e dëshirës apo dhe vullnetit të artistit, për të qenë pjesë e kryerjes së artit të realizmit socialist, i cili tentoi me urdhëra dhe parime të vërtetësojë realitetin e kohës, por nuk bëri gjë tjetër vetëm se solli figura të cunguara dhe statike të atij realiteti të modeluar politikisht, të cunguar ideologjikisht, zbrazur nga emocionet e pasura individuale dhe të frikësuar nga shumëllojshmëria e bukurisë së lirive vetjake. Politikat komuniste krijuan artin në shërbim e tyre, e ngurtësuan pavarësinë dhe lirinë artistike, duke mbivlerësuar gjuhën kolektive krijuese. Të gjitha këto bënë që skulptura shqiptare të jetë e standardizuar në një lloj pasqyrimi, të jetë e pakët në individualitete të shquara krijuese, të rritej forcërisht imitimi i skulptorëve të rinj ndaj produktit të artistëve të viteve 1960, si dhe në arsyetimin e sotëm kemi një histori të trashëguar të skulpturës monumentale, të kavaletit dhe të eksterierit tipike të realizmit socialist shqiptar.

Ekzistenca e tyre është një libër i madh me figura, që dëshmon mirë e bukur jetën e përfunduar të një perandorie të vogël diktatoriale në Ballkan. Ajo ishte e pajisur me kanone figurative komuniste, të cilat

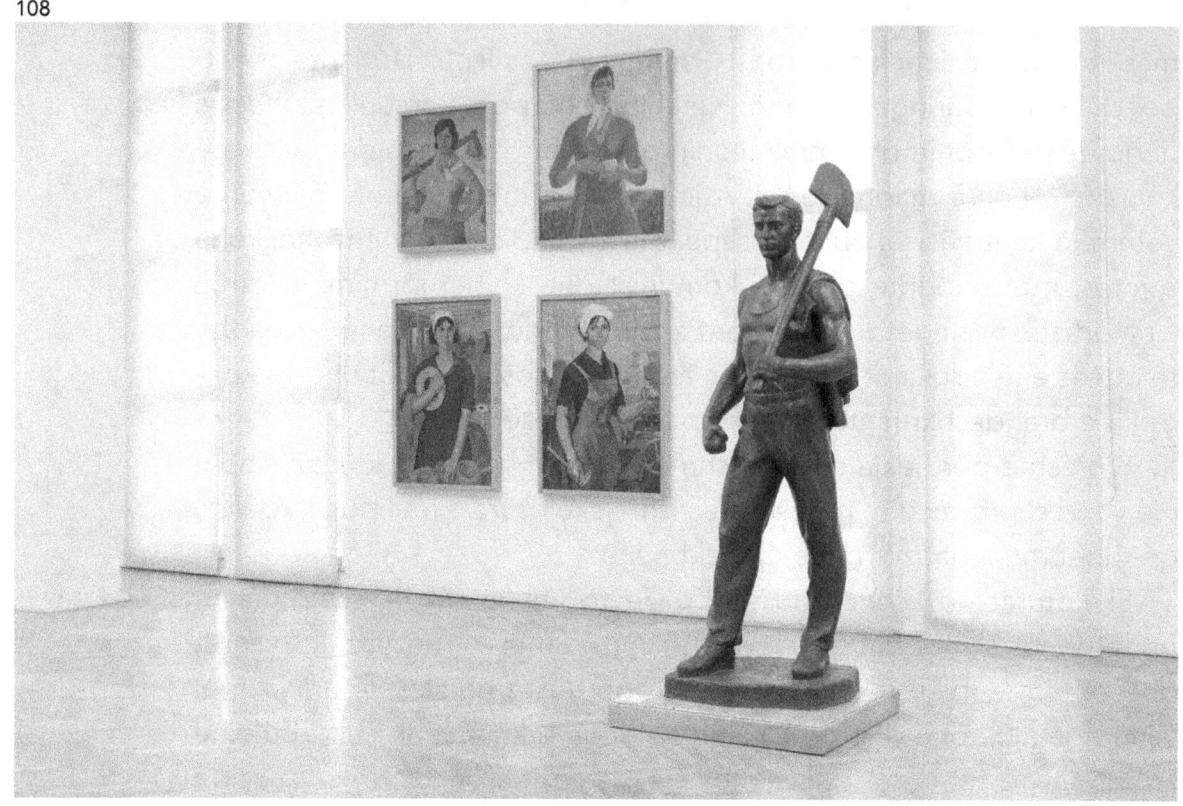

formonin imazhin e trupit të njeriut të ri dhe psikologjinë patologjike të frymës pozante të entuziasmit të rremë, që injektohej nga idioma "lart frymën revolucionare", pjellë e mendjeve dominuese për lavdi dhe nderim ndaj udhëheqësit komunist, që funksiononte në emër të shërbimit ndaj popullit dhe për popullin në shoqërinë socialiste.

Gjithësisht artefaktet e skulpturës së realizmit socialist në Shqpëri ishin krijim në shërbim të praktikave ideologjike në çdo anë të jetës së organizuar e kontrolluar. Shtatoret, bustet, lapidarët, monumentet, portretet ishin modele jofrymëzuese, por modele të kujtesës urdhërore mbi popullsinë. Në mënyrë të drejtëpërdrejtë ata i kujtonin njerëzve se jetonin "me heroizëm" në komunizëm dhe kjo ishte reale. Se jetonin në sistemin me mirëqenien më të lartë dhe kjo ishte e gënjështërt. Atyre iu ishte thënë se ishin njerëzit e rinj, qeniet më sublime e të lumtura të botës dhe kjo ishte joreale.

Kjo e bën idenë kuratoriale të Mihnea Mircan shumë të fortë, dinjitoze dhe të na rikujtojë kujtesën e ushtruar të artefakteve komuniste mbi punëtorët e tradhëtuar. Shoqëritë e sotme kapitaliste edhe me

Kristaq Rama, *The Contemporary of the Republic*, bronze, acquired 1964.

Kristaq Rama, *Vërsniku i Republikës*, bronz, blerë 1964.

artin e tyre na kujtojnë se shoqëritë komuniste dhe arti i tyre kanë mbetur evident me peshën e rëndë të imazheve të realizmit socialist në hapësirën njerëzore. Ata kanë një trysni të pashoqe dhe shtyhen për të bërë pjesë në shoqërinë pasmoderne të mileniumit të III dhe këtë po ia mundëson në një formë apo në një tjetër globalizmi si një proces dhunues dhe uniform, si një megamakinë edhe më e madhe se megamakina ideologjike e shoqërive komuniste.

A nuk janë shpesh herë veprat e artit konceptual të prezan-tuara ndërkombëtarisht një referim ironik i materialit figurativ dhe ideologjik të megamakinës artistike kombëtare të vendeve ish-komuniste? Përse?

Sepse pesha e tyre është e rëndë, historia që mbartin është e pashmangshme, krijimtaria artistike është irealitet në realitetin e epokës postmoderne.

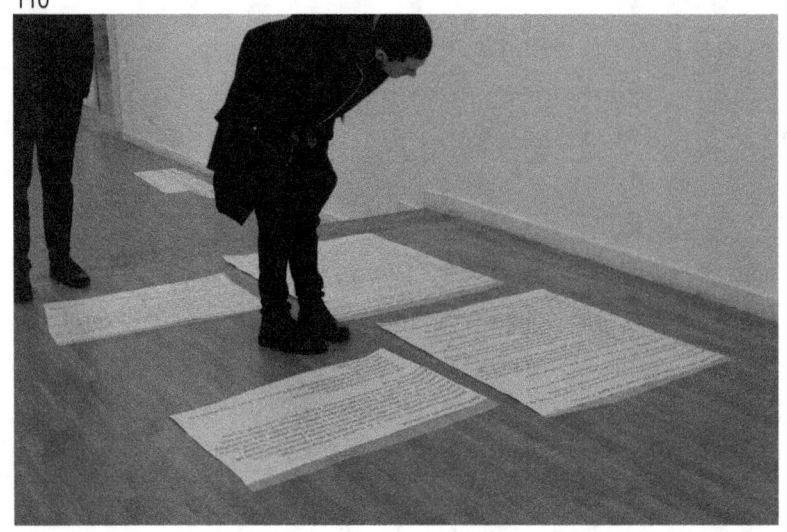

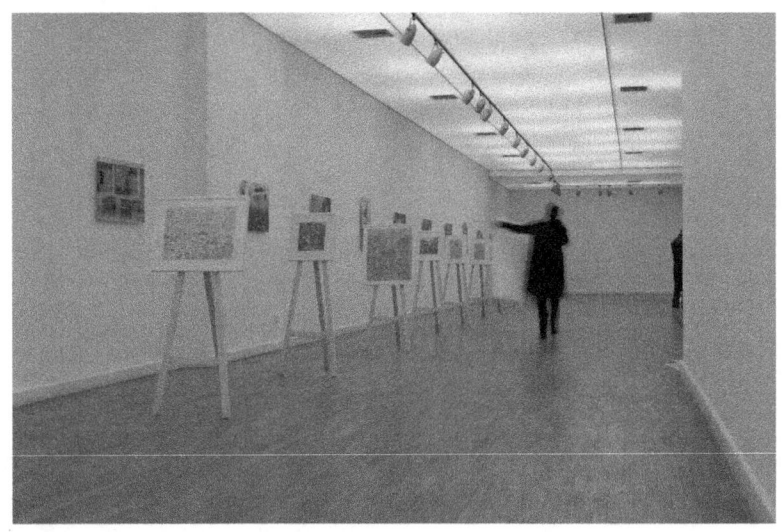

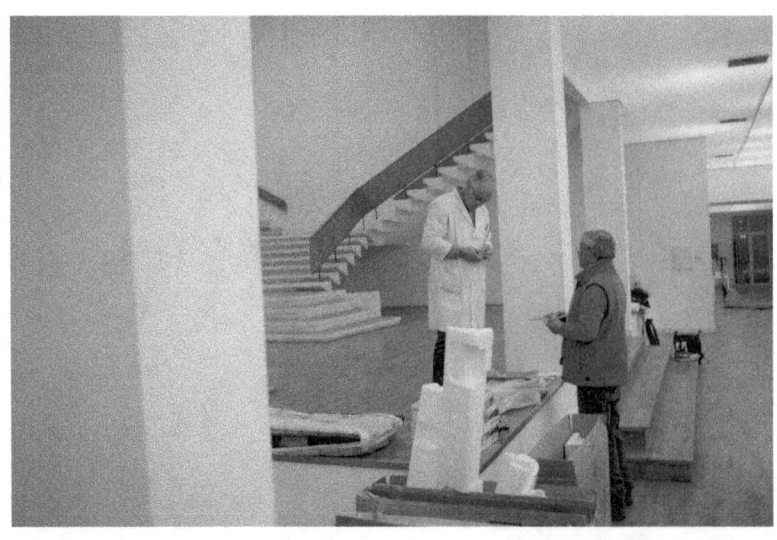

Irwin

In 1992, in Ljubljana, Slovenia, the artist collective IRWIN, the music band Laibach and the Scipion Nasice theatre company, previously united under the heading Neue Slowenische Kunst, merged to become the NSK State in Time. The manifesto of this transformation describes the State as an infinite political entity without physical boundaries, an abstract organism, a Suprematist body "ever-inspired by the moment of grace of its becoming," "manifesting itself in time yet at the same time transcending time." The initiative was a response to the contemporaneous nationalist furore in Yugoslavia and an attempt to imagine alternatives to dire political circumstances. Irwin proceeded to create the spectral, artistically-edited double of a process of national autonomy. But this ghostly double was to lead a strangely real life: during the 1990s, the largest number of nsk passports were issued in Sarajevo at the end of the war (1995).

The project developed by setting up temporary embassies and consulates, the NSK Folk Art Museum peacekeeping regiments, post offices, and by continuing to issue passports to whoever applied to become a citizen of the state. Starting in 2004, this pattern changed dramatically as the NSK passport website was flooded by thousands of citizenship applications from Nigeria and neighbouring countries. Applicants were attempting to acquire NSK State passports in the belief that these would enable them to travel to Europe, move to Slovenia or to the country of nsk. Instead of rejecting this as a parasitical outgrowth of the original project, Irwin continued to print the passports, while engaging with the prospective citizens and advising them on the goals and uses of the State in Time. However, to a significant extent, the project had been re-scripted and taken over by other actors, hijacked or hacked by motivations very different from the ones on which it had been premised. An exhibition, preceded by elaborate research and an extensive PR and communication campaign, that the artists presented in Lagos in 2010 attempted to map out these questions in dialogue with local NSK passport applicants: a different view of the contemporary world emerges from those hours of interviews, a version of the present commensurate and alien at the same time. How does one think, work and make (state) art in the service of a non-existent country?

Irwin. Në vitin 1992, në Lubjanë, Slloveni, kolektivi artistik Irwin, grupi muzikor Laibach dhe kompania teatrore Scipion Nasice, të bashkuar më parë nën titullin Neue Slowenische Kunst, u shkrinë për t'u bërë Shteti NSK në Kohë. Manifesti i këtij transformimi e përshkruan këtë Shtet si një entitet të pakufishëm politik, pa kufij fizikë, një organizëm abstrakt, një trup Suprematist "frymëzuar pambarimisht nga momenti i pafundëm amëshues i ardhjes së tij në jetë", i cili "shfaqet në kohë e në të njëjtën kohë e tejkalon atë". Iniciativa ishte një kundërpërgjigje ndaj shpërthimeve të njëkohëshme nacionaliste në Jugosllavi dhe një përpjekje për të imagjinuar alternativa ndaj rrethanave të tmerrshme politike. Irwin vazhdoi duke krijuar një dublazh spektral, të redaktueshëm artistikisht, të një procesi autonomie kombëtare. Por ky dublazh fantazmagorik pati një jetë çuditërisht të vërtetë: gjatë viteve 1990-të, numri më i madh i pasaportave NSK janë lëshuar në Sarajevë në fund të luftës (1995).

Projekti vazhdoi duke ngritur ambasada dhe konsullata të përkohshme, ngritjen e Muzeut NSK për Artin Folklorik regjimente paqeruajtëse, zyra postare, dhe duke vazhduar të lëshojë pasaporta për cilindo që aplikonte për t'u bërë një qytetar i këtij shteti. Duke filluar nga 2004 ky model ndryshoi në mënyrë dramatike pasi websajti i pasaportave të shtetit nsk u përmbyt nga mijëra aplikacione nënshtetësie nga Nigeria dhe vendet fqinje. Aplikantët përpiqeshin të merrnin pasaporta të shtetit nsk me besimin se këto do ti mundësonin udhëtimin për në Evropë, lëvizjen në Slloveni apo në vetë Shtetin NSK. Në vend që të hidhte poshtë këtë fenomen si një zgjatim parazitar të projektit fillestar, Irwin vazhdoi të prodhonte pasaporta, ndërsa angazhohej me qytetarët e ardhshëm duke i këshilluar ata për qëllimet dhe përdorimet e Shtetit në Kohë. Megjithatë, projekti tashmë ish rishkruar në një masë të konsiderueshme dhe përvetësuar, rrëmbyer ose hakeruar nga aktorë të tjerë për motive shumë të ndryshme nga ato për të cilat kish nisur. Një ekspozitë që artistët paraqitën në Lagos në 2010, paraprirë nga hulumtime të thella dhe një fushatë e vazhdueshme publicitare, u përpoq ti japë përgjigje këtyre pyetjeve në dialog me aplikantët lokalë mbajtës të pasaportave NSK; nga ato orë të gjata me intervista shfaqet një pikëpamje e ndryshme mbi botën bashkëkohore, një version mbi tashmen sa i matshëm aq dhe i huaj në të njëjtën kohë. Si mendon, si punon dhe si prodhon art (shtetëror) dikush në shërbim të një vendi jo-ekzistent?

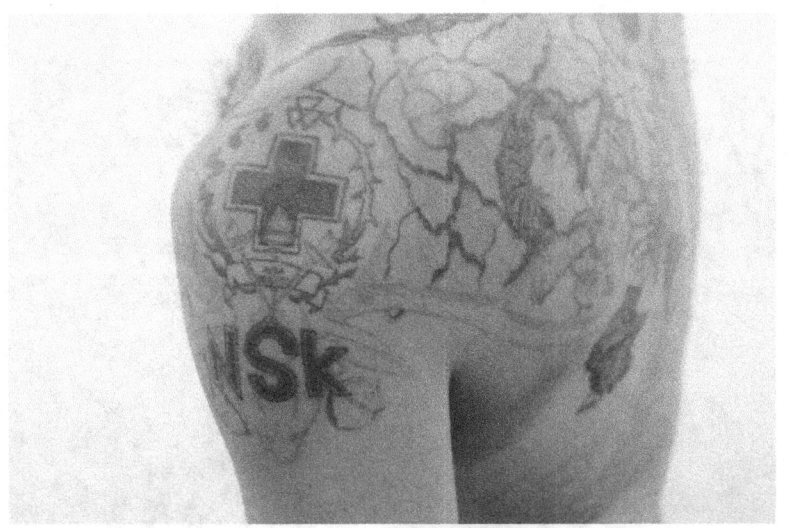

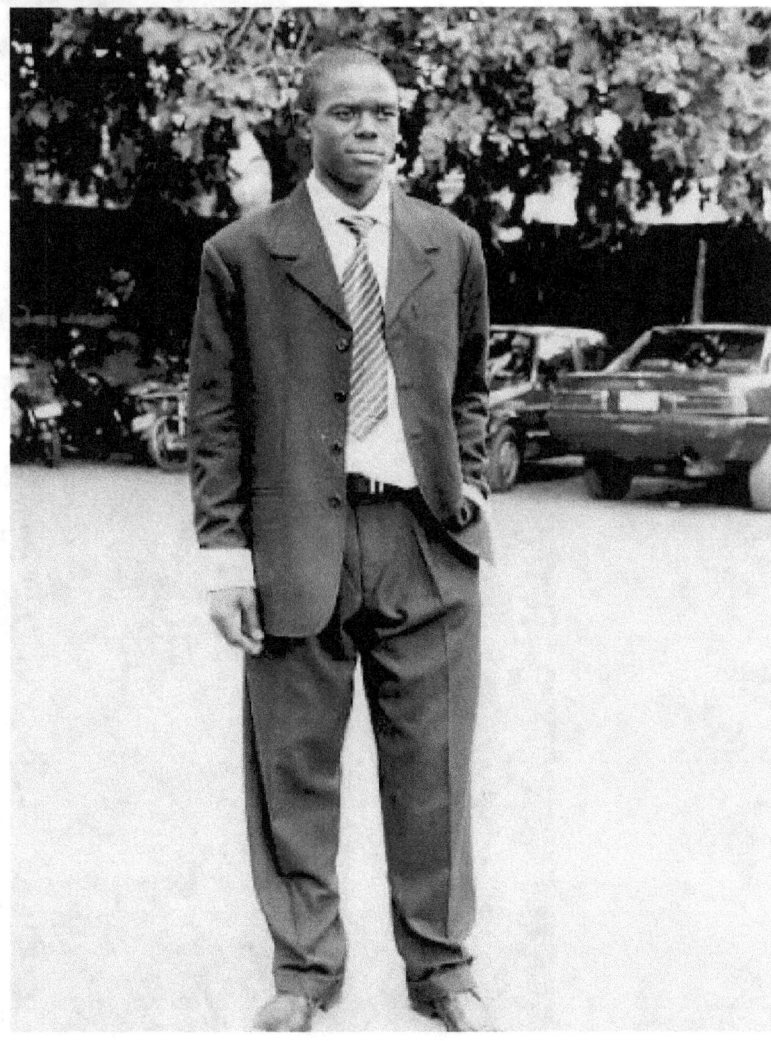

IRWIN, NSK *State Folk Art Archive*, digital slideshow, 2009–ongoing:

IRWIN, *Arkivi i Shtetit NSK për atin folklorik*, slideshow dixhital, 2009–në vazhdim:

Danaja, *Tattoo*, 2010.

Danaja, *Tatuazh*, 2010.

Christain Nnoruga, NSK *Citizen*, 2009.

Christain Nnoruga, *Qytetar i Shtetit NSK*, 2009.

IRWIN, *Manifestoes of the State in Time*, wall texts, 2010

IRWIN, *Manifeste të Shtetit në Kohë*, tekste në mur, 2010

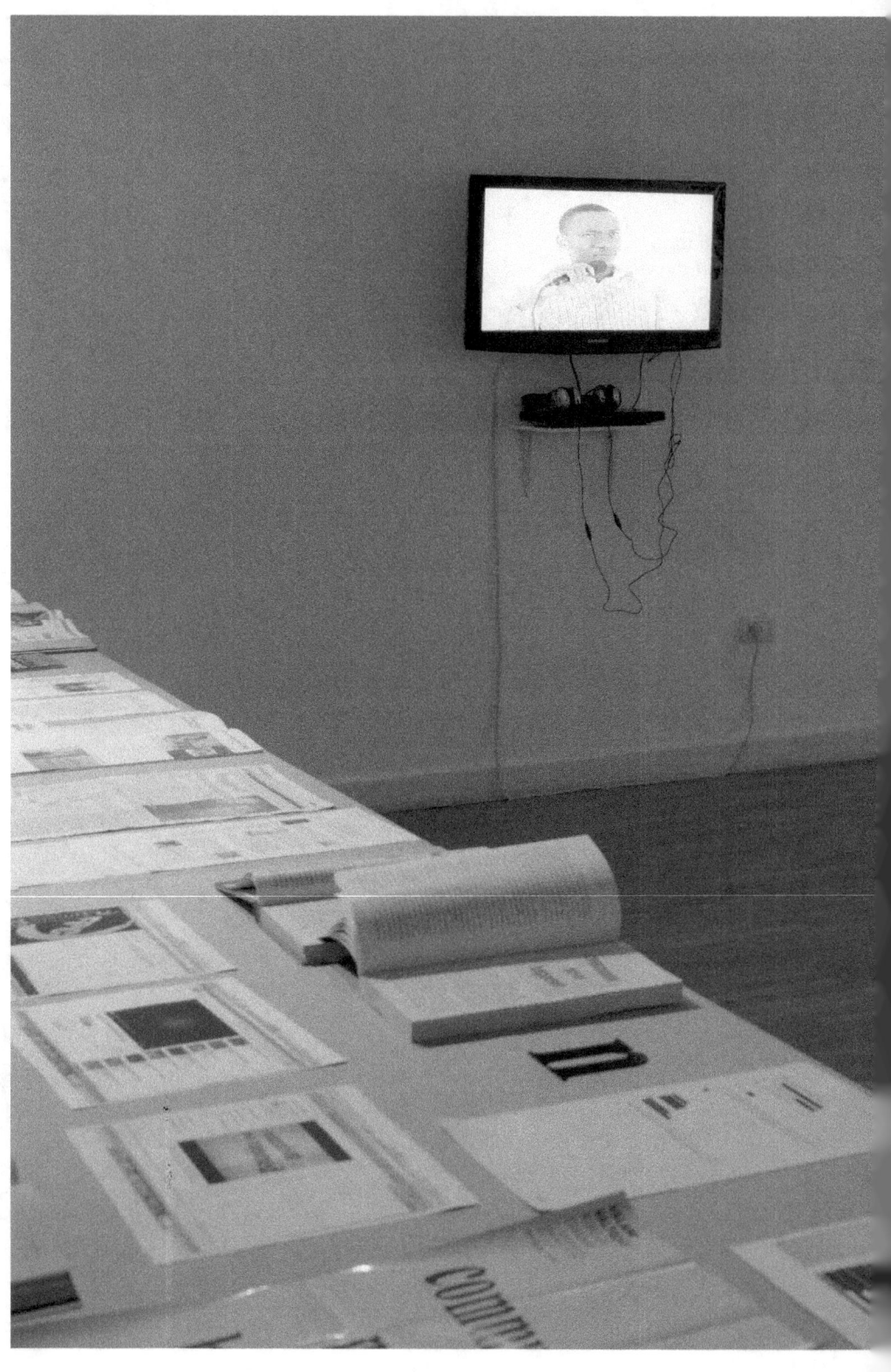

IRWIN, NSK *Lagos Interviews*, video, 46',
2010

IRWIN, *Intervista në Lagos të Shtetit NSK*,
video, 46', 2010

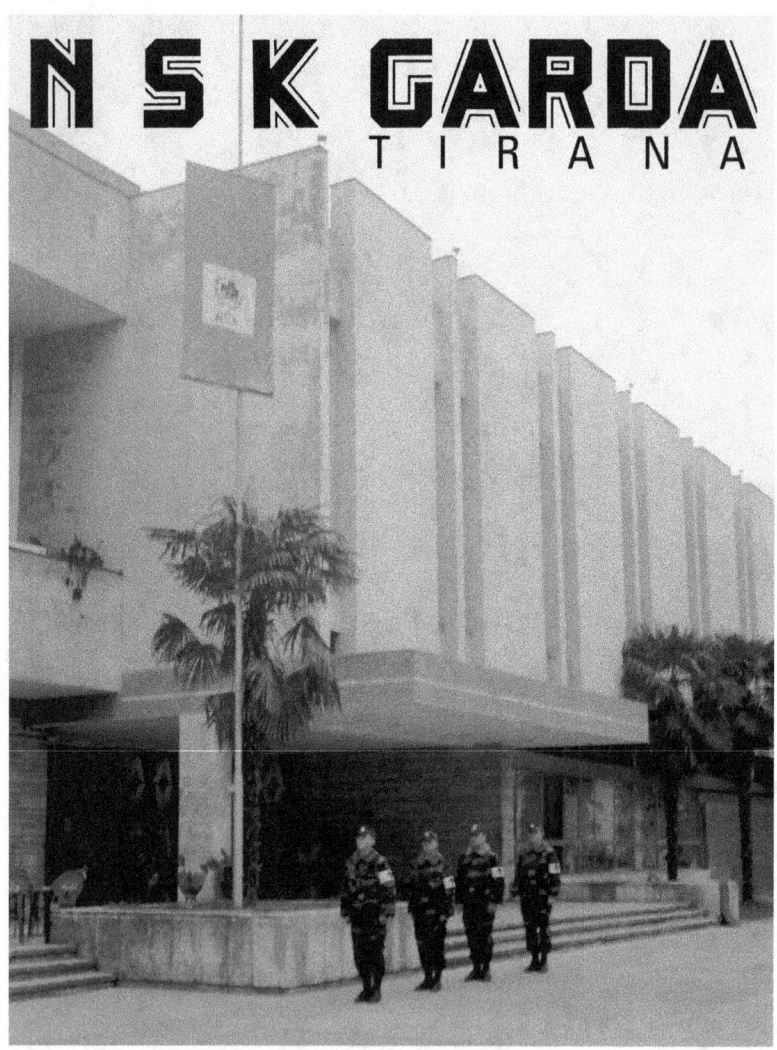

IRWIN in collaboration with the Albanian Army, NSK *Garda Tirana*, National Gallery of Arts, Dec. 21, 1998, iris print, 140 x 100 cm.

IRWIN në bashkëpunim me Forcat të Armatosura të Shqipërisë, NSK *Garda Tirana*, Galeria Kombëtare e Arteve, 21 dhjetor 1998, stampim iris, 140 x 100 cm.

The Nigerian Connection: On NSK Passports as Escape and Entry Vehicles

In late July 2010, Borut Vogelnik and Miran Mohar (two members of the IRWIN group and representatives of the NSK State in Time) and my-self (curator, artistic director of Hartware MedienKunstVerein [HMKV], and diplomat of the NSK State in Time) set out on a trip to Lagos, Nigeria. Invited by the Centre of Contemporary Art (CCA) Lagos, and supported by the Goethe- Institute, we travelled to West Africa for the first time. Our reasons were diplomatic.

For some time the NSK *Država v času* (NSK State in Time), a state without territory founded in 1991 as an artistic response to the in-dependence of Slovenia and to the subsequent war(s) in the former Yugoslavia, had been receiving a substantial number of requests for citizenship, especially from Nigeria. In 2006–7 the requests came in the form of e-mails and telephone calls to individual representatives and diplomats of the NSK State in Time, and to representatives of the Republic of Slovenia. This produced a general feeling of panic among us. What was going on? Why were Nigerian citizens suddenly so des-perate to get NSK passports – and even to actually use them for trav-el? Was it possible that the Nigerian applicants took the concept of the NSK State in Time more seriously than its founders, i.e., that they "overidentified" with it – an artistic/political strategy developed to perfection by Laibach/NSK in 1980s Yugoslavia?[1] What if the Nigerians who already possessed an NSK passport took the promise of the pass-port seriously and *really* started travelling with it? What if they got into serious trouble at the border, possibly leading to arrest? Border au-thorities would treat the NSK passport as either a fake document or an authentic document (i.e., a real passport). Either way, using it might be considered a criminal act, in the first case because forged documents are illegal and in the second because carrying two passports could, at times, create problems for Nigerian citizens.[2]

Noticing the rising number of requests from Nigeria after 2006, the Republic of Slovenia urged the artists to post information on the NSK website saying that "NSK citizenship does not equal Slovenian citizenship" and that an "NSK passport does not allow its holder to enter the Schengen zone." However, posting this information did not remedy the situation. The demand for NSK passports kept rising.

From Dortmund to Lagos

In April 2009, HMKV, located in Dortmund, Germany, participated in an exchange program organized by the Goethe-Institute called Cultural Managers from Africa in Cultural Institutions in Germany. For two weeks Hansi Loren Momodu, curatorial assistant at CCA Lagos, was a guest at HMKV's offices, observing the practical work of operating a German Kunstverein, especially in the area of media-based artistic practices. The Goethe-Institute has always been keen on follow-up projects (a kind of sustainability!) so at the end of Hansi's stay we thought about possibilities for future cooperation. I said that, unfortunately, I had no links to Nigeria or to any other African country. But as soon as I said this, I realized it wasn't true. There was indeed something that connected me to Nigeria – if only indirectly.

I told Hansi in detail about NSK's "immaterial state." In addition to its temporary embassies and consulates materializing from time to time in various places, the NSK State in Time issues passports as a "confirmation of temporal space" (NSK), which can be obtained by any person irrespective of citizenship or nationality. I told her that these passports were printed by the same printing house as the real Slovenian passports, and that they were hugely popular, especially among Nigerians. Holding one quarter of all NSK passports issued since 1991, Nigerians represent the largest single group of citizens of the NSK State. I also told her that the state's founding artists were extremely worried that people might use the NSK passport in ways that were never intended, such as trying to leave Africa and come to Europe. I also explained that we constantly received e-mails and telephone calls from Nigerians asking for information on how to organize a trip to the NSK State in Time, and where to go and whom to contact once they arrived. Finally, I told her that the state's founding artists were afraid that the NSK passports were traded on the black market and that people paid horrendous sums to shady middlemen who promised that the passport provided entry into the First World. What a crushing disappointment it would be when they found out this wasn't true! So, Hansi and I agreed that it was time for the state's founding artists to travel to Nigeria and see the situation for themselves – and, if necessary, to inform the unsuspecting Nigerians about the true nature of the NSK passport.

"Be home before sunset": Lagos, Nigeria

I arrived at Murtala Mohammed International Airport in Lagos just over a year later, at eight o'clock in the evening. It was pitch dark. A city of over twenty million inhabitants in one of the most oil-rich countries in the world had no street lights. As I learned later, Lagos is a megalopolis without a functioning electricity network. Eddy, who would be our driver for the entire week, was waiting for me at the airport. He welcomed me warmly. As we drove along the highway from the airport to the city center, pedestrians constantly crossed the street in total darkness, suddenly looming up in front of our car illuminated only by the headlights. At one point Eddy said, "See the big cars on the side of the street?" Tank-like armoured vehicles stood half-covered at intervals of 300 meters. "Police" Eddy said. "Some years ago it was normal to get robbed on the street leading from Lagos airport to downtown. Things have gotten much better lately." I was very happy to hear this, although it took me a moment to realize the significance of what he had said.

Miran Mohar and Borut Vogelnik from IRWIN had arrived a few days earlier and had already familiarized themselves with the surroundings.[3] They had begun conducting interviews with Nigerian NSK passport holders and applicants at the CCA Lagos. The CCA is a truly amazing place – virtually the only site for contemporary art in the entire city of Lagos. It exists thanks to the initiative of a single woman, Bisi Silva, who not only raises the funds to run the center but who also donated all of her own books, transforming the upper floor into a small public library focussing on contemporary art and theory. The lower floor is usually used for exhibitions and workshops.

The event entitled *Towards a Double Consciousness: nsk Passport Project* took place at the CCA July 26–31, 2010. It consisted of screenings, lectures, and panel discussions. The final panel discussion addressed the NSK State's "Nigerian connection" and the significance that the state had taken on in the contemporary Nigerian consciousness.[4] The announcement and outline for this discussion read:

> Since the initial presentations around the world in the 1990s of State in Time, the project is currently receiving a substantial number of requests for citizenship to the NSK State from Africa, especially from Nigeria. This has resulted in many Nigerians assuming a dual identity as holders of NSK and Nigerian passports. In view of these new developments, IRWIN conducted interviews with African/ NSK citizens living in London, to ascertain their reasons for applying. Could it be in support of the initial artistic purpose of NSK? Do they see it as an avenue with which to move from one territory to another? Or is it for other socio-political reasons? Towards a Double Consciousness: NSK Passport Project will allow further debate on both the artistic and political implications of the NSK State in Time action, offering an examination of their original artistic interventions within the Nigerian context … *Towards a Double Consciousness* attempts to interrogate the way in which artists propose and individuals search for alternative – real or fictional – possibilities that go beyond notions of a fixed identity or geography.**5**

The NSK Passport Project proved to be a truly intense and ambivalent experience – certainly for the three of us, but also, in different way, for the CCA Lagos team (Bisi Silva, Hansi Momodu, and Jude Anogwih). Two of the NSK State's founders, who had always thought of the state as an abstract concept and an intellectual tool, were suddenly confronted with a position that no longer maintained a "safe" ironic distance from the promise made by the NSK passport. They found themselves in a situation where it was necessary to speak very clearly and directly about what their state was and was not, and what its passport could and could not do. Ambivalence and irony did not prove helpful when the genuine fear was that the promise made by a document – acquired directly from the artists or bought on the black market – would soon prove to be empty.

During the two-hour discussion at the CCA it became clear that what once had been conceived as an "escape vehicle" had, in the minds of the Nigerian applicants and passport holders, transformed into an "entry vehicle," or at least the promise of such. Originally, the NSK State was founded as an alternative to the exclusively national (Slovene) identity that the artists were confronted with when Slovenia seceded from Yugoslavia. It was conceived as almost the opposite of the new Republic of Slovenia, which had declared its independence in 1991. As an artistic concept of a state, it defined itself neither through a concrete geographical territory nor through an ethnically fixed *Staatsnation* (nation state). Instead, the NSK emphasized the notion of time, understood as a new productive category for the definition of space. Within this terminology, time was equated with the individual accumulation of experiences. Eda Čufer and IRWIN defined this new "geography of time" as follows: "The real ... 'fatherland' of the individual is limited É to the circle of his own individual experience, to that which exists and *not that he was born into*." Therefore, the "territorial borders of the NSK state can by no means be equated with the territorial borders of the actual state in which NSK originated."[6] Rather, the NSK State in Time is defined as an abstract body whose borders are in a state of constant flux depending on the activities of its physical and symbolic body, and whose territory is situated in the consciousness of its "members." Eda Čufer and IRWIN define the State in Time as

an abstract organism, a suprematist body, installed in a real social and political space as a sculpture comprising the concrete body warmth, spirit, and work of its members. NSK confers the status of a state not upon territory but upon the mind, whose borders are in a state of flux, in accordance with the movements and changes of its symbolic and physical collective body.[7]

The State issues passports as a "confirmation of temporal space." There are many instances where fiction crosses into reality – like the story about NSK using the same passport printing house as the Republic of Slovenia. But telling this story in Lagos during the panel discussion, where about twenty-five Nigerian applicants or passport holders eagerly awaited any kind of proof of the "real" potential of the passport, would have fed into the very economy of expectations that the NSK state founders came to Nigeria to discourage. Similarly, telling the amazing – and true – stories of Bosnians who managed to cross international borders in the late 1990s with nothing other than the NSK "document" would have been irresponsible.8 That is why these stories were never mentioned during the panel discussion in Lagos. Even if these (few) cases really did happen, it did not feel right to mention them, as they could easily be read as "proof" of the validity of the passport, for which it would then be worth paying large amounts of money on the black market.

Miran Mohar and Borut Vogelnik very explicitly discussed the reasons for creating the NSK State in Time and the intended purpose of the passport. They stressed that the NSK State in Time was not an existing country and that it should by no means be confused with the actual Republic of Slovenia. Towards the end of the event we were convinced that the audience had "understood the initial artistic concept" of the NSK. However, at the very end of the panel discussion, two memorable statements were voiced. One member of the audience said, "A friend of mine has a friend who knows somebody who has already been there. He said that it is a beautiful country." Shame on us who had thought that the roller coaster of emotions had ended! The IRWIN members once more explained patiently that the NSK State in Time is a state of mind rather than an existing state that one can travel to. The second – and positively devastating – statement came from a young man with stylish 1970s sunglasses who had been sitting silently throughout the whole event: "Listen, I think that everybody in this room perfectly understood what you have been telling us over the last two hours [meaning: don't think we Africans are stupid!]. But, still, I think that holding an NSK passport is a good thing. Because the

NSK State in Time could come into being at some point in the future, you know?"

"Lock your doors, I will not stop": The NSK Passport and the Nigerian 419 Scam

Lagos Island, located just opposite Lagos Mainland, is a huge gated community for the very rich – the upper class of Nigerian society as well as expats working for international oil companies. The property prices are beyond comprehension, even higher than in Paris, London, or Tokyo. The three highway bridges connecting the island to the mainland are guarded by heavily armed police forces dressed in splendid uniforms. One night, we stayed out after nightfall. Leaving the bar around 10:30 p.m., Eddy drove us back from Lagos Island to our hotel on the mainland. It was pitch dark again. Suddenly, we saw a group of young men dancing into the street in front of our car, lit only by our headlights. "Lock your doors," Eddy said calmly as he rolled up the automatic windows. "I will not stop." Luckily, we did not hit any of the dancing men. A few days after this incident an artist at the CCA told us that on that very night he had made the mistake of stopping his car at the same spot. He was robbed – the thieves used the exact same "dancing onto the street" trick and took his money and camera.

Imagine if only one out of every five hundred cars stops. Possibly one in five hundred will also hit one of the dancing men – but that's the risk, I guess, of what Giorgio Agamben has called "bare life." That one successful theft in a sea of failed attempts reminded me of the logic of e-mail spam, or more precisely, of something called the "Nigerian Letter," the "419 fraud," or the "Nigerian bank scam."[9] Millions of e-mails are sent out and perhaps one person will answer and fall for the fraud.[10] The 419 scam began in the early 1980s as the oil-based Nigerian economy went into decline. Several unemployed university students first used this scam to manipulate visiting businessmen who were interested in shady oil deals. They later targeted businessmen in the West, and then the wider population. According to Insa Nolte of the University of Birmingham's Centre of West African Studies, advance-fee fraud boomed in Nigeria in the 1990s as government corruption and economic stagnation fuelled poverty and disillusionment in the country. To some, internet scams looked like an easy way to bag some quick cash. Scammers in the early-to-mid 1990s targeted companies, sending scam messages via letter, fax, or Telex. The spread of e-mail and easy access to e-mail harvesting software significantly lowered the cost of sending the scam letters.[11] "The availability of e-mail helped to transform a local form of fraud into one of Nigeria's most important export industries," says Nolte.[12]

Is it possible that the NSK passport is read by Nigerians as some kind of 419 scheme? As the promise of an unexpected fortune waiting out there, which you can obtain by paying a small fee? Or, formulated differently, do they believe in the NSK passport because one in five hundred just might be genuine? Did the Nigerian applicants and passport holders seriously regard the NSK passports – originally conceived as escape vehicles – as entry vehicles which would allow them to cross international borders? Ultimately, we did not find out. But we realized that the power of belief, even if supported only by rumors, even against better judgment, is a force to be reckoned with.

On our last day in Nigeria, a Sunday, Eddy invited us to attend church at Redemption Ministries. Before the service there was a business seminar addressing the question "Where to find money?" – especially poignant in a church made up of half-finished walls and a makeshift corrugated metal roof. During the service, after the preacher warned insistently against "witches in the household," members of the parish got up one after the other, raised their arms, and began speaking in tongues. It occurred to me that I was in a Pentecostal church whose members believed not so much in Jesus or God the Father, but in the Holy Spirit which takes possession of their bodies and tongues during the service. This led me to realize that in Nigeria, the NSK passport functioned not so much as a "confirmation of temporal space" but as a material vessel for something spiritual – a fierce hope in the possibility of a better future. The passport is neither of these – or, rather, it is something in between. It exists simply because people have heard rumours about it and have become convinced that it might come in handy some day if they already have legal travel documents. A utopian-pragmatic position, so to speak, that trusts in the power of believing.

Inke Arns, "The Nigerian Connection: On NSK Passports as Escape and Entry Vehicles" originally appeared in *e-flux journal* no. 32 (April 2012).

1.   On the strategy of overidentification see Inke Arns, "Mobile Staaten / Bewegliche Grenzen / Wandernde Einheiten. Das slowenische Künstlerkollektiv Neue Slowenische Kunst (NSK)" in *Netzkritik: Materialien zur Internet-Debatte,* ed. nettime / Geert Lovink, Pit Schultz (Berlin: Edition ID-Archiv, 1997), 201–211; Inke Arns,*Neue Slowenische Kunst (NSK) – eine Analyse ihrer künstlerischen Strategien im Kontext der 1980er Jahre in Jugoslawien* (Regensburg: Museum Ostdeutsche Galerie, 2002); Inke Arns and Sylvia Sasse, "Subversive Affirmation: On Mimesis as Strategy of Res*istance," in* East Art Map: Contemporary Art and Eastern Europe, ed. IRWIN (Cambridge, MA: MIT Press, 2006), 444–455; "Subversive Affirmation," eds. Inke Arns and Sylvia Sasse, *Maska* 19.3–4 (2006): 98–99.

2.   See, for example, http://saharareport ers.com/column/my-brief-dete ntion-okey-ndibe

3.   Like most residential houses in Lagos, our hotel was surrounded by a high wall topped with barbed wire (or, alternatively, glass splinters). There were two generators in the courtyard beneath our windows that ran all night. Like our neighbors' generators, they were pretty loud.

4.   Speakers included Dr. Inke Arns, IRWIN members Miran Mohar and Borut Vogelnik, and Nigerian NSK passport holders. The panel was moderated by Loren Hansi Momodu and took place on July 31.

5.   The passage omitted from this quote reads: "This project forms part of CCA Lagos' year-long program *On Independence and The Ambivalence of Promise,* celebrating 50 years of independence by seventeen African countries including Nigeria on the 1st October 2010. It provides an avenue to interrogate notions of nationhood at a time when our idea of citizenship is continuously being challenged by state policies such as Nigeria's contentious 'federal character' system or through religious and ethnic disturbances such as the recent unrest in the city of Jos, as well as the perennial civic unrest of the oil-rich Niger Delta."

6.   Eda Čufer and IRWIN, "Concepts and Relations" (1992), in IRWIN, *Zemljopis Vremena / Geography of Time,* exh. cat. (Umag, 1994). The full quote reads: "The role of art and artists in defining time which belongs to them individually is more effective than in defining territory. The real, not imaginary, 'fatherland' of the individual is limited to the circle of the house in which he was born, the classroom or the library in which he acquired knowledge, the landscapes in which he walked, the spaces to which he is oriented, to the circle of his own individual experience, to that which exists andnot that he was born into. The territorial borders of the NSK state can by no means be equated with the territorial borders of the actual state in which NSK originated. The borders of the NSK state are drawn along the coordinates of its symbolic and physical body, which at the time of its activity acquired objective values and objective status."

7.   Eda Čufer and IRWIN, "NSK State in Time" (1993), ibid. NSK makes a distinction between its "citizens" and its "members." In practice, "citizens" are anyone who can scrape together the money for a passport, while only fifteen special people qualify as "members" (paraphrasing Michael Benson).

8.   Bosnians did this because Bosnia was not then internationally recognized and so people had no papers that would allow them to cross international borders.

9.   The number 419 refers to the article of the Nigerian Criminal Code dealing with fraud (part of Chapter 38: "Obtaining Property by false pretences; Cheating").

10.   See http://en.wikipedia.org/wiki/Advance-fee_fraud.

11.   The 419 scam has been imitated by people in other Africa nations and in countries throughout

the world, including the Philippines, Malaysia, Russia, Australia, Canada, the United Kingdom, and the United States.

12. Quoted in Robert Andrews,

"Baiters Teach Scammers a Lesson," *Wired*, August 4, 2006. See http://www.wired.com/tec hbiz/it/news/2006/08/71387.

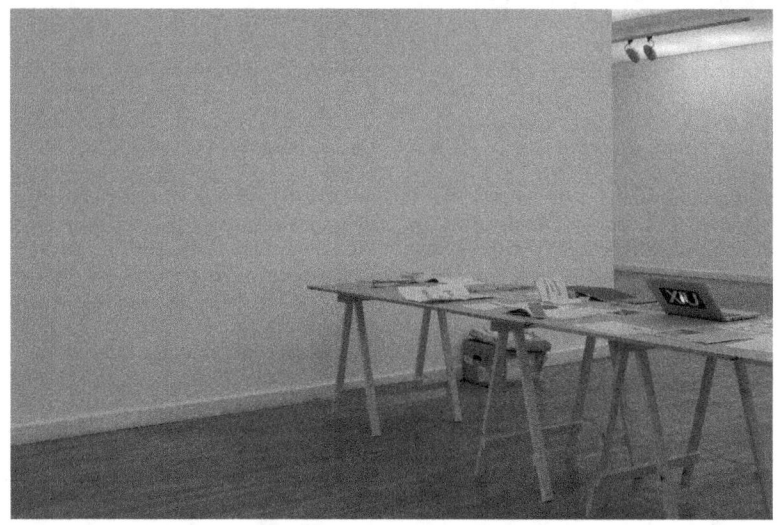

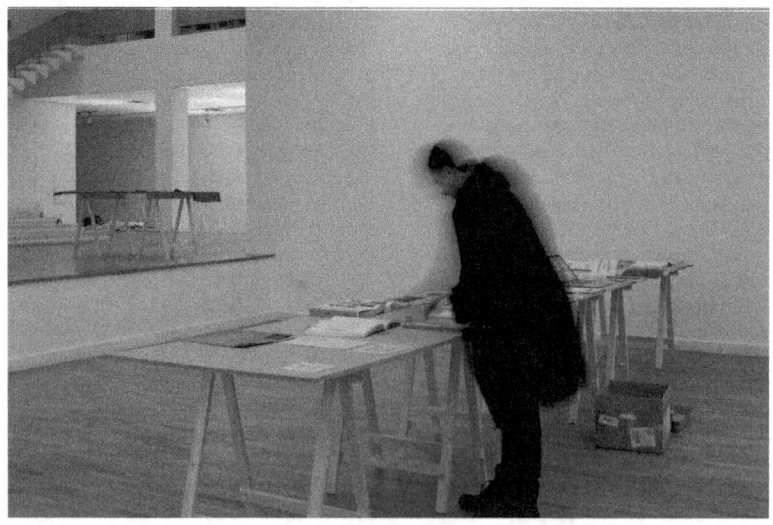

Ciprian Mureşan: Communism Never Happened

The work is an archive of the many lives and after-effects of Mureşan's strange slogan, cut out of propaganda music records printed in Romania before 1989. The initial "message" of that work (did communism not happen because it did not reach its philosophical and social conclusions, did it cease to happen because we forget about it today, or maybe undo and replicate it in the liberal fervor of post-communist transitions?), is interspersed with the many paths that compose the work's destiny in the art world: exhibitions borrowing its title, texts that interpret or misinterpret it, that think about it or adapt it to their own agenda, curatorial or otherwise, bureaucratic emails, letters from the work being stolen: all forms in which Mureşan's initial, resonant ambiguity is echoed, refracted, and maintained.

Ciprian Mureşan: Komunizmi nuk ndodhi kurrë Puna është një arkiv i jetës së shumëllojshme (dhe efekteve të mëpasme) të sloganit të veçantë të Mureşan-it, të prera nga kopertinat e regjistrimeve muzikore propagandistike të shtypura në Rumani para vitit 1989. "Mesazhi" fillestar i kësaj pune (komunizmi nuk ndodhi sepse nuk arriti qëllimet e tij filozofike dhe sociale, pushoi së ndodhuri sepse ne e harrojmë sot, apo sepse ndoshta sepse e zhbëjmë dhe e zëvendësojmë në entuziazmin liberal të tranzicionit post-komunist?), është shpërndarë mes drejtimeve të shumta që përbëjnë fatin e veprës në botën e artit: ekspozita që e marrin hua për titull, tekste që e interpretojnë apo e keqinterpretojnë, që mendojnë për të ose e përshtasin me axhendën e tyre, kuratoriale apo gjithfarësh, emaile burokratike, letra (pjesë nga puna) që vidhen: të gjitha forma nëpërmjet të cilave ambiguiteti fillestar dhe resonant i veprës së Mureşan jehon, përthyhet, vazhdon.

130

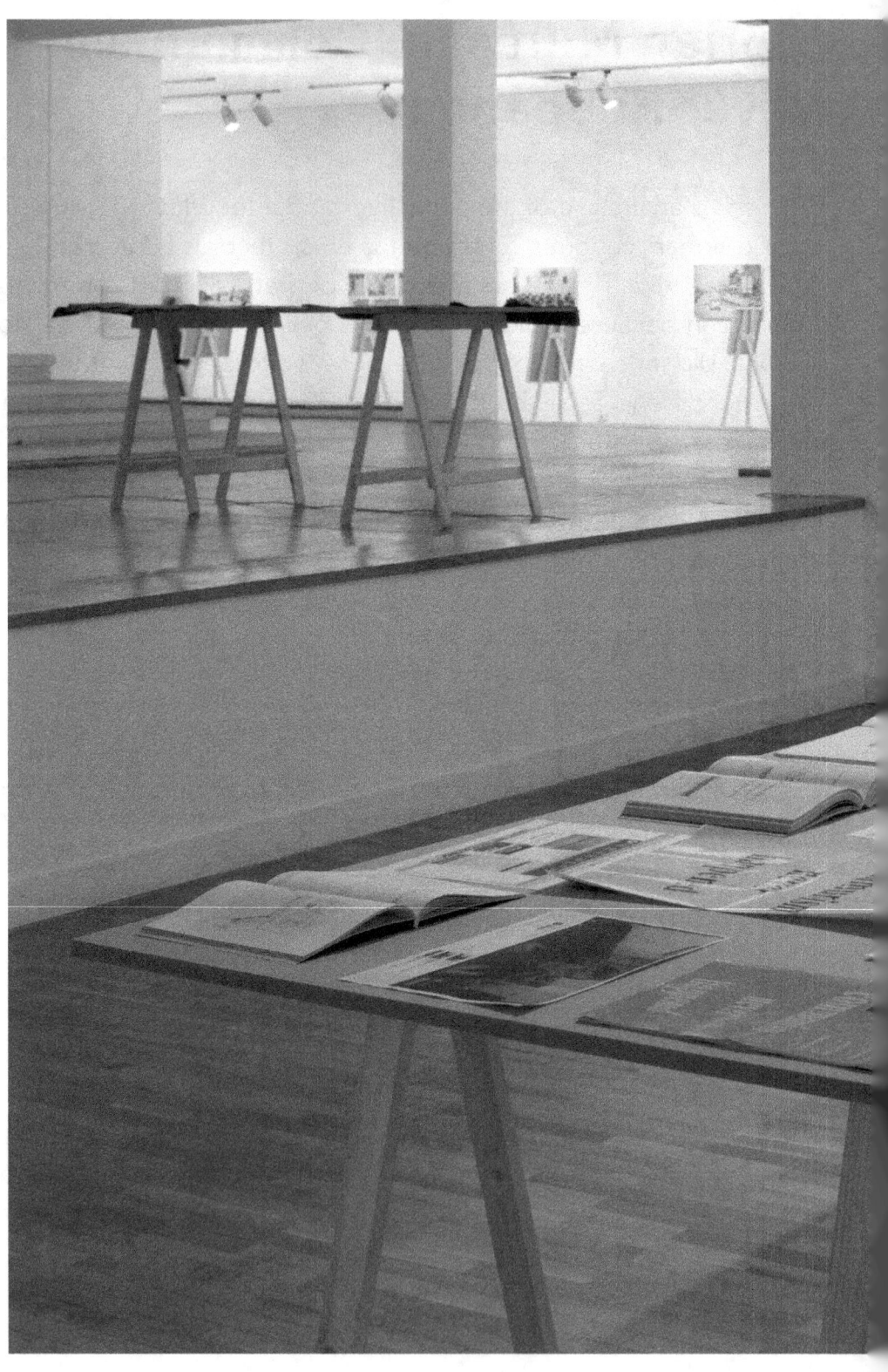

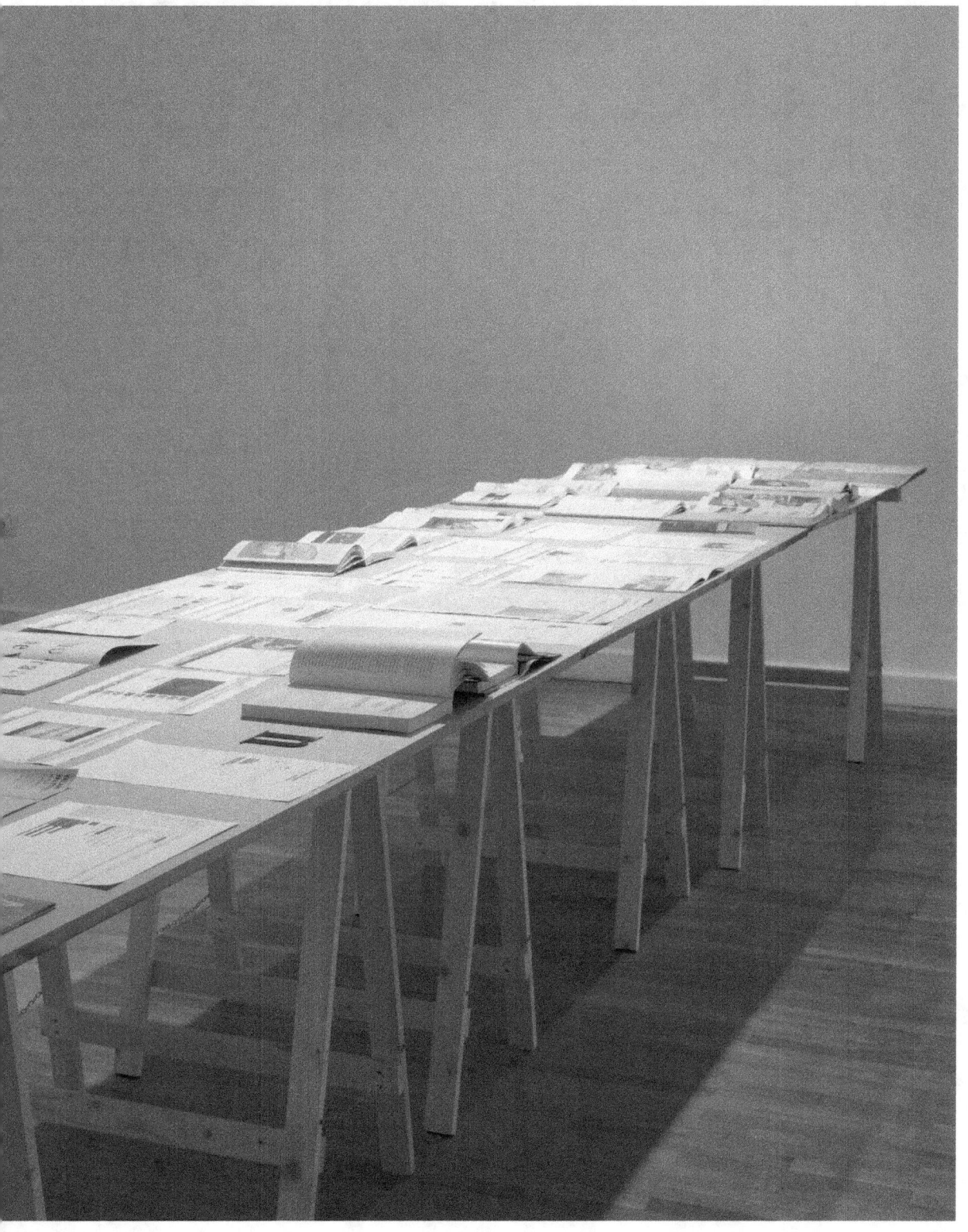

Ciprian Mureşan, *Communism Never Happened*, mixed media, 2006–ongoing.

Ciprian Mureşan, *Komunizmi nuk ka ndodhur kurrë*, media e përzier, 2006–në vazhdim.

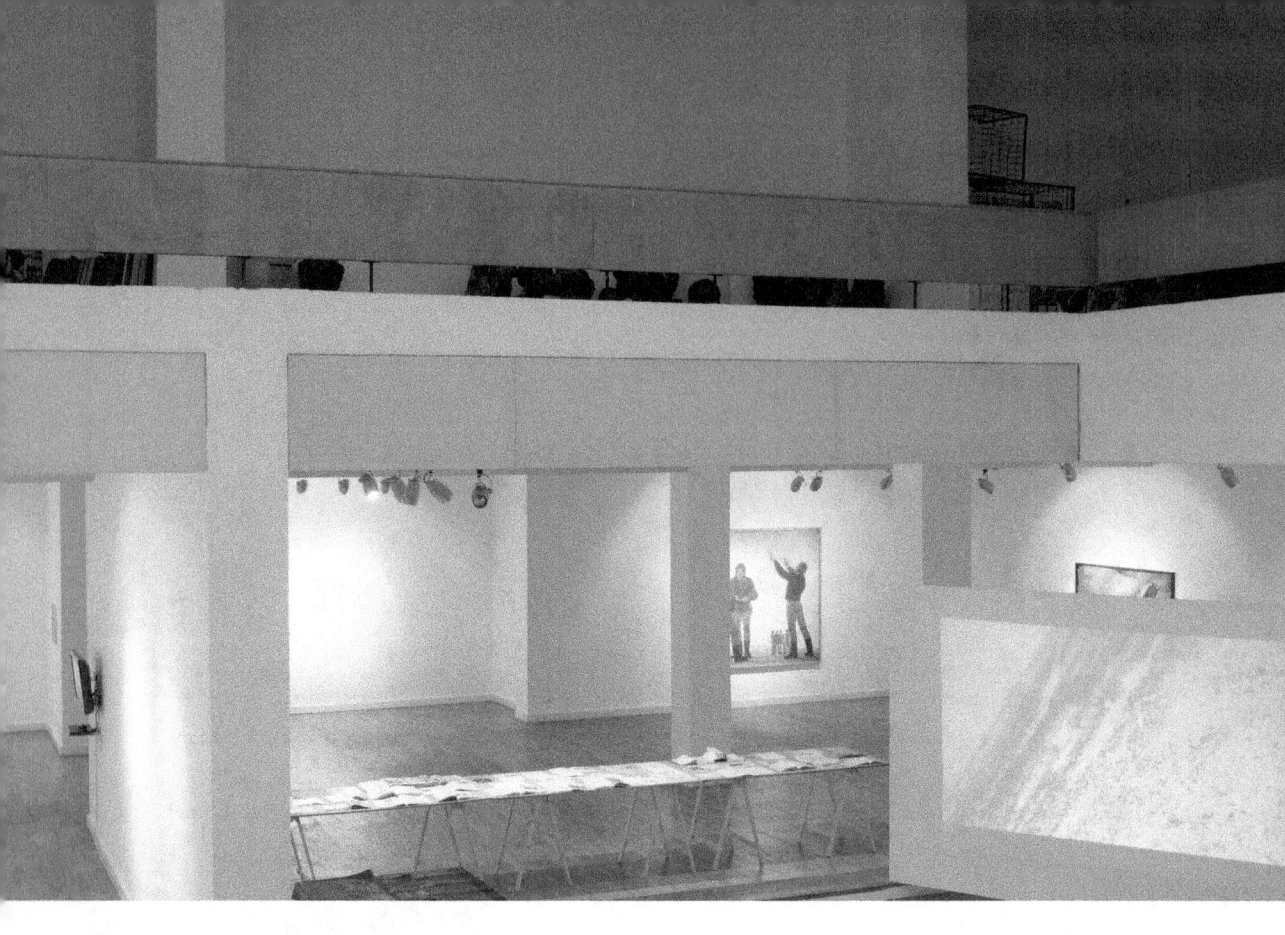

Exhibition view.

Pamje ekspozite.

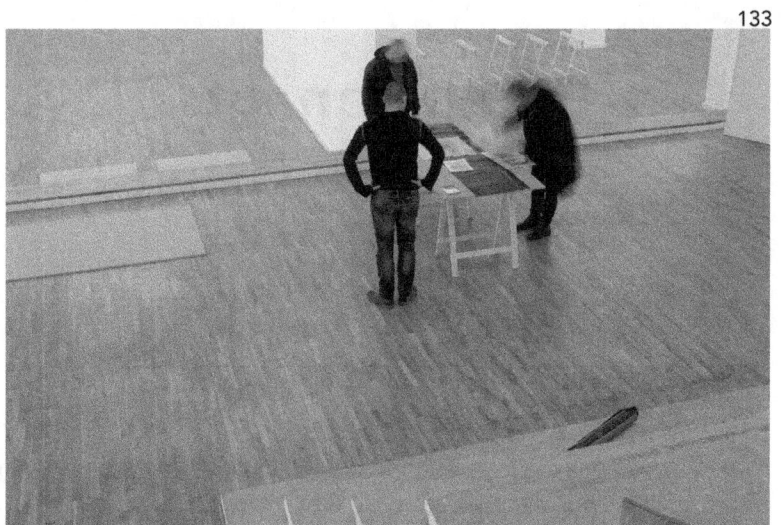

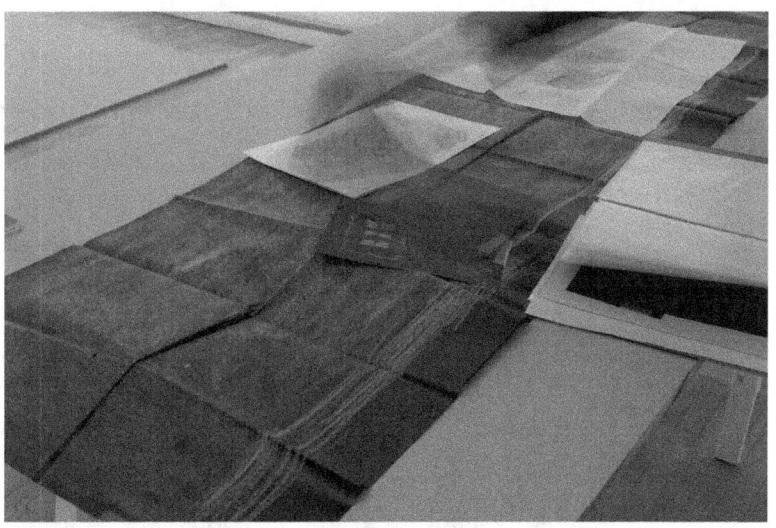

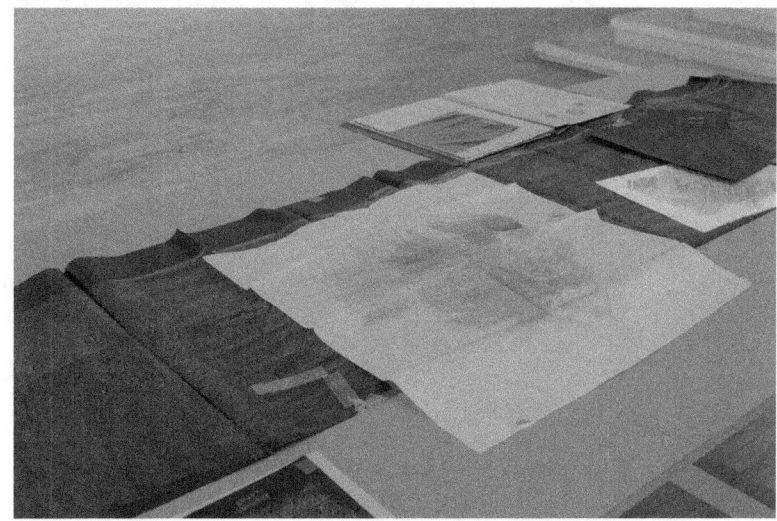

Sarah Vanagt: Élevage de poussière (Dust Breeding)

What is the value of images as objective testimonies of a conflict? In this work, Sarah Vanagt turns her attention to the International Criminal Tribunal for the former Yugoslavia in The Hague. All court hearings were translated simultaneously in four languages, filmed by six cameras, edited in real time, streamed online with a 30-minute delay and then archived, creating an electronically-expanded scenography for the verification of judicial truth. The project draws on the video documentation of the trial of Radovan Karadžić, which ended in 2014: all images of the court proceedings were sent to the artist by the Tribunal's Press Office. In parallel, Vanagt carries out a series of pencil rubbings inside the courtroom, juxtaposing the unfolding of the trial with another, older, modality of (visual) truth: the imprint, an immediate relation between previously imperceptible details and the paper. Her frottaged imprints remind us of the very source of our notion of the image, the event where the energy of the model registers directly on the support, where representation and that which is represented are indistinguishable. Technologically-mediated testimony is doubled by the elaborate creation of a "material witness."

Sarah Vanagt: Élevage de poussière (Rritje pluhuri) Çfarë vlere kanë imazhet si dëshmi objektive të një konflikti? Në këtë punë, Sarah Vanagt kthen vëmendjen e saj nga Gjykata Ndërkombëtare për Krimet në ish-Jugosllavi, në Hagë. Të gjitha seancat gjyqësore përktheheshin njëkohësisht në katër gjuhë, filmoheshin nga gjashtë ekipe kameramanësh, redaktoheshin në kohë reale, transmetoheshin online me një vonesë 30-minutëshe, dhe më pas arkivoheshin, duke krijuar kështu një skenografi të zgjeruar elektronike për verifikimin e së vërtetës gjyqësore. Projekti i Vanagt bazohet në video-dokumentimin e gjyqit të Radovan Karaxhiqit, që përfundoi në 2014: të gjitha imazhet e procedurës gjyqësore ju dërguan artistit nga Zyra e Shtypit e Gjykatës. Paralelisht, Vanagt nisi një seri kopjimesh me laps të gjurmëve të lëna brenda në sallën e gjyqit, duke kundërvënë zhvillimin (në këtë rast zbulimin) e seancave gjyqësore me një zbulesë tjetër, më të vjetër, të së vërtetës (pamore): gjurmën e lënë, raportin e menjëhershëm mes detajeve të padukshme e të pavëna re më parë me letrën. Vizatimet e saj frottage na sjellin ndërmend thelbin e nocionit tonë për imazhin, momentin kur energjia e modelit regjistrohet drejtpërsëdrejti në mbështetësen nën të, e kur paraqitja dhe subjekti që paraqitet nuk dallojnë më nga njëri-tjetri. Dëshmia e transmetuar dhe ruajtur nëpërmjet teknologjisë dyfishohet nga gjurma e marrë me detaje e një "dëshmitari material".

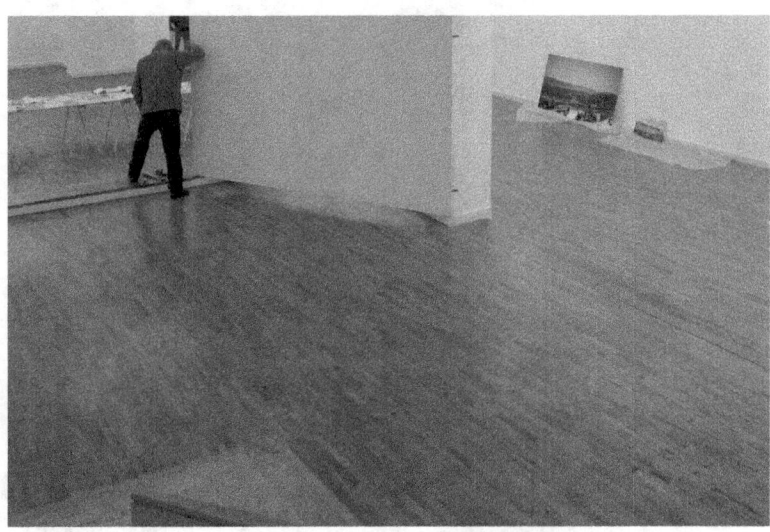

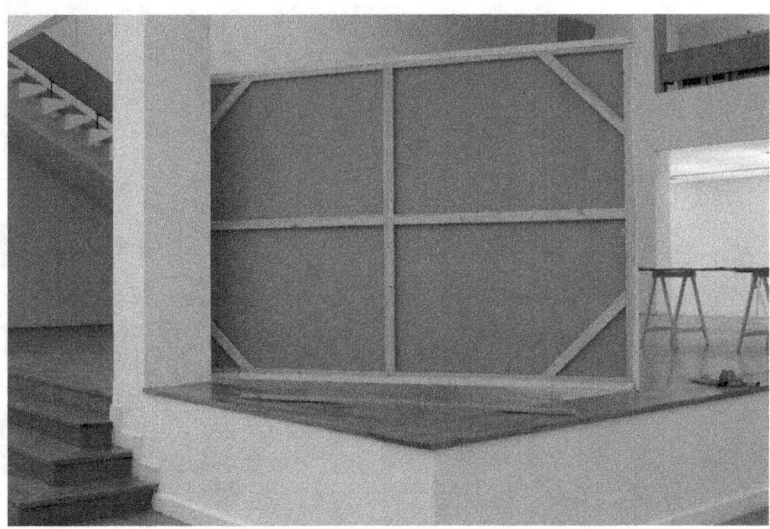

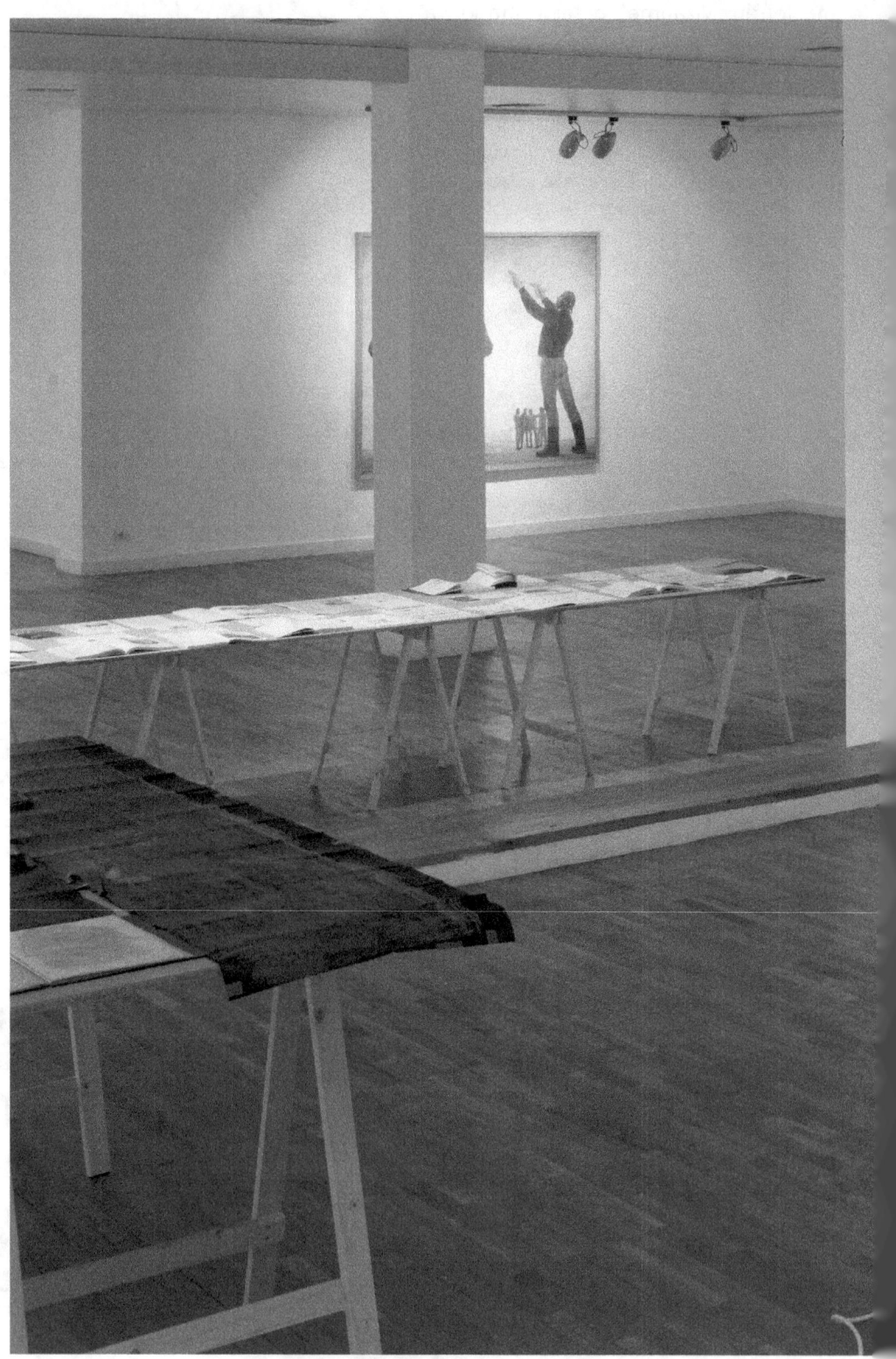

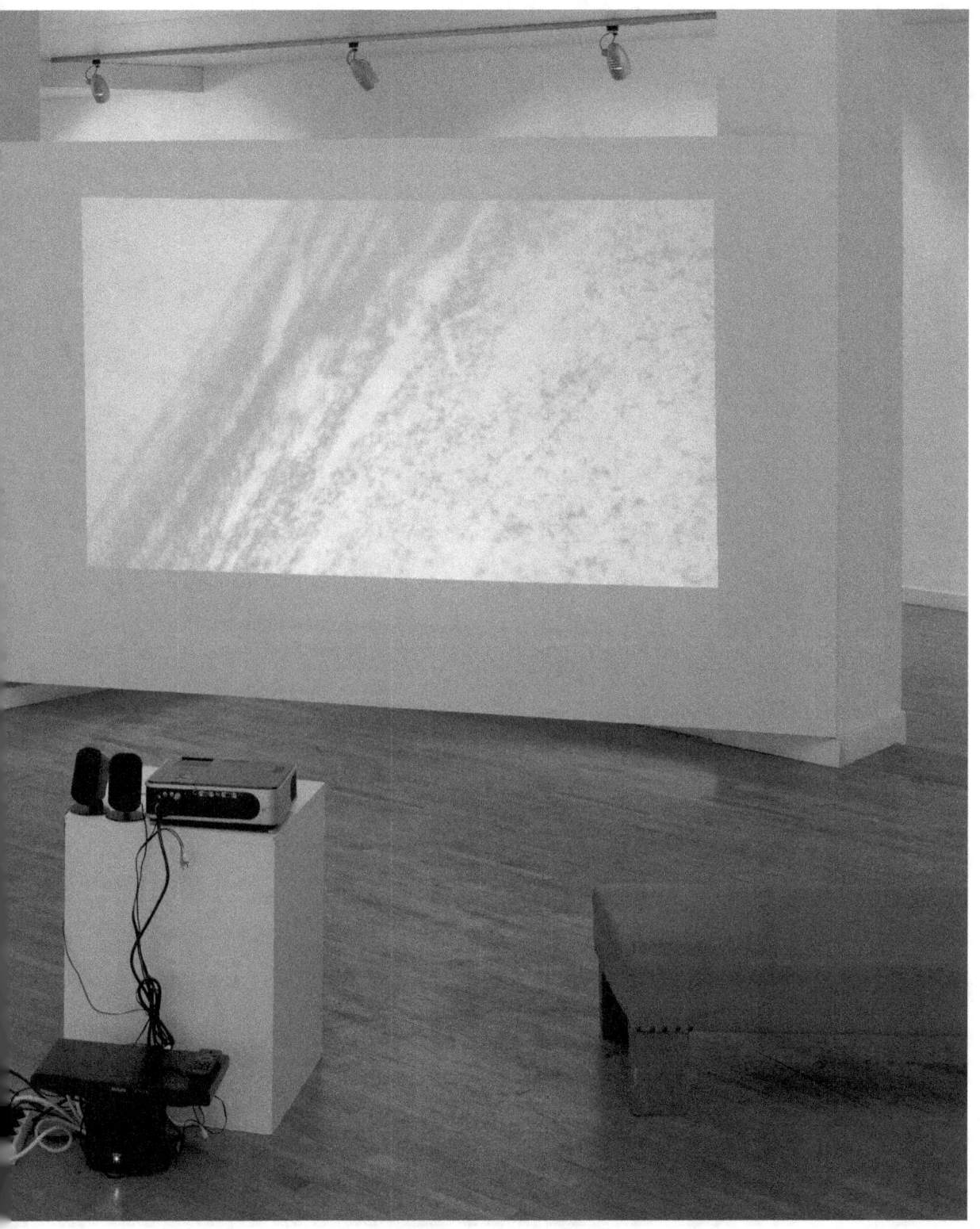

Sarah Vanagt, *Élevage de poussière
(Dust Breeding)*, video, 46', 2013.

Sarah Vanagt, *Élevage de poussière
(Rritje pluhuri)*, video, 46', 2013.

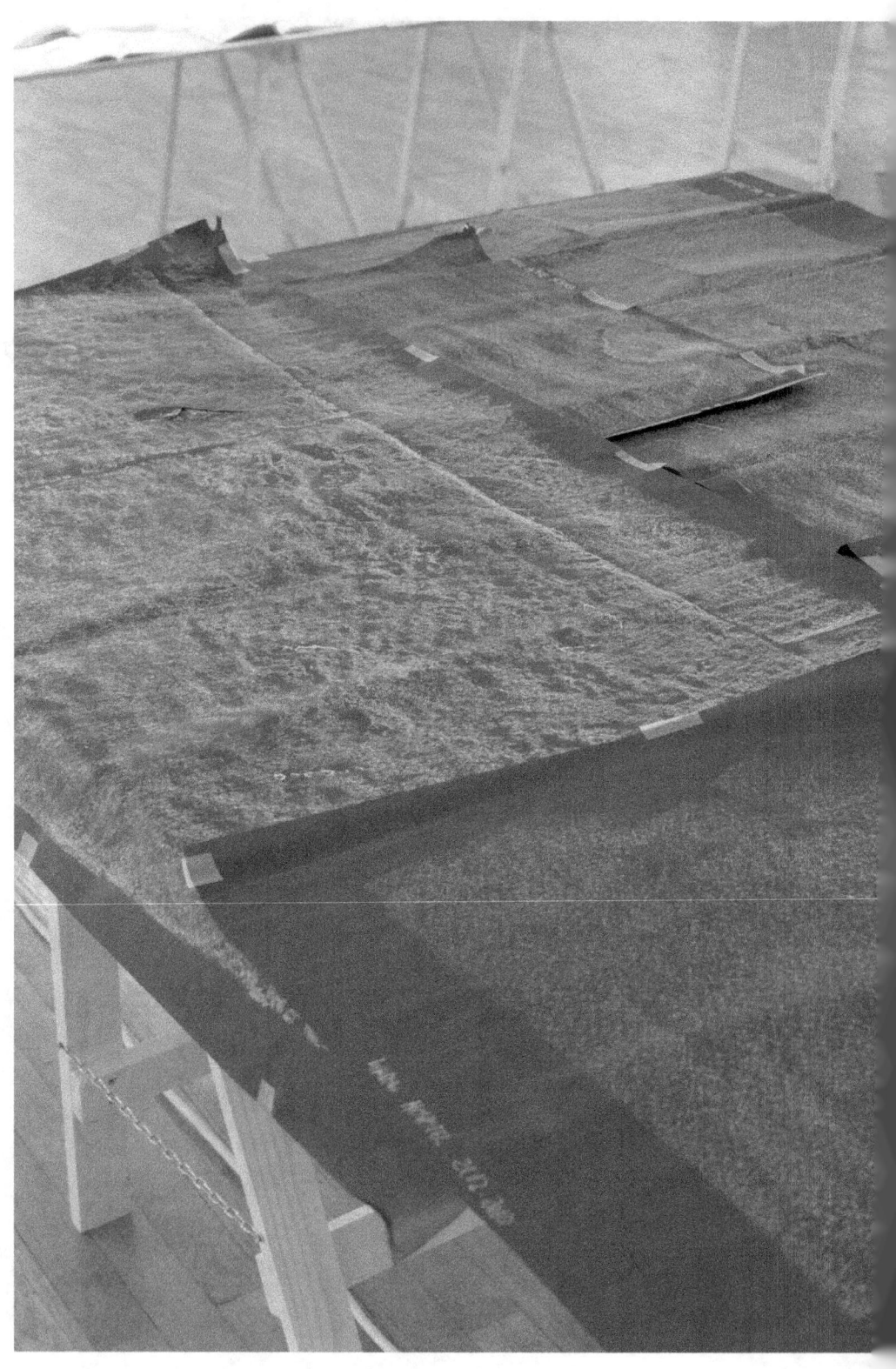

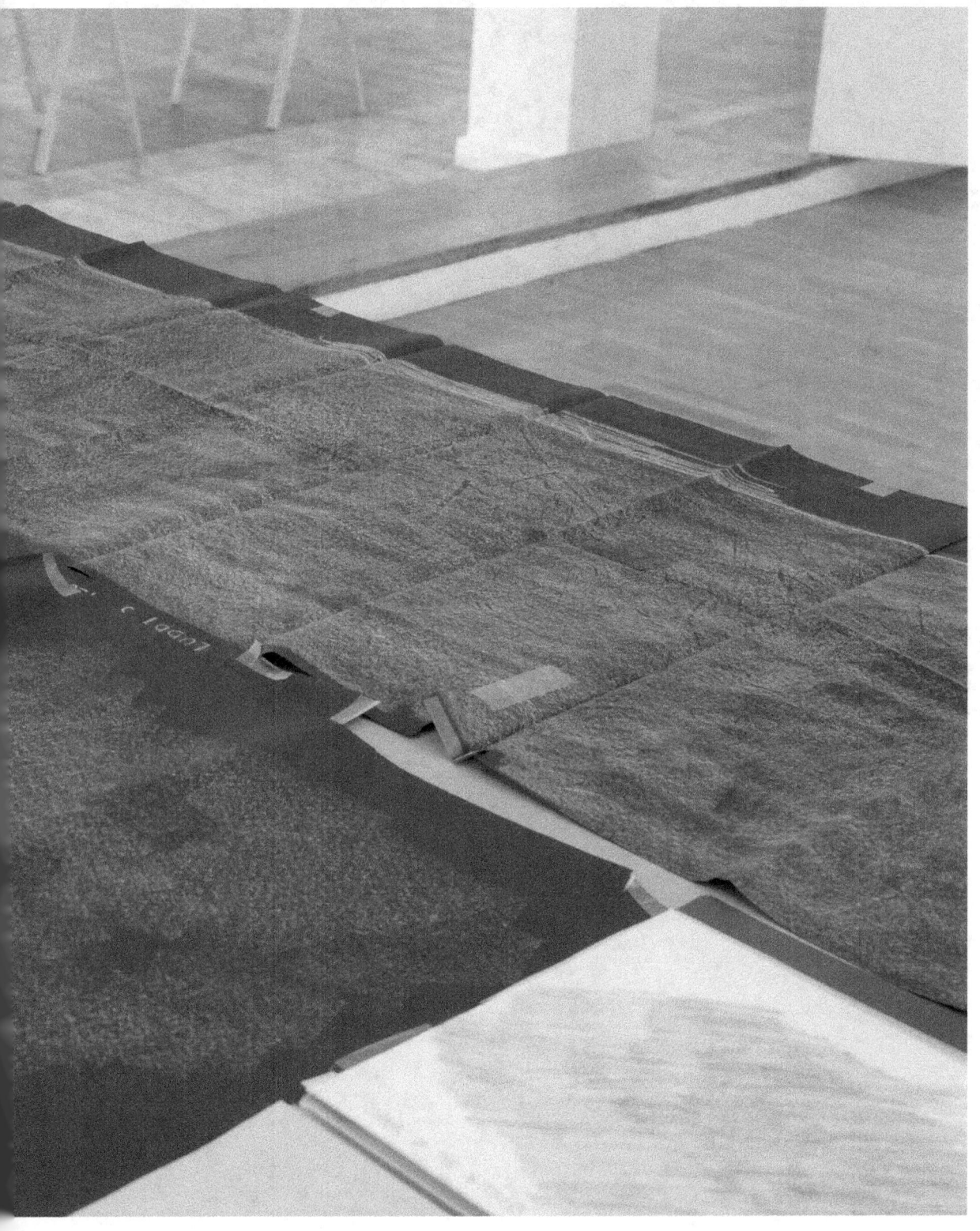

Sarah Vanagt, *Élevage de poussière (Dust Breeding)*, crayon and pencil on paper, 2013.

Sarah Vanagt, *Élevage de poussière (Rritje pluhuri)*, laps në letër, 2013.

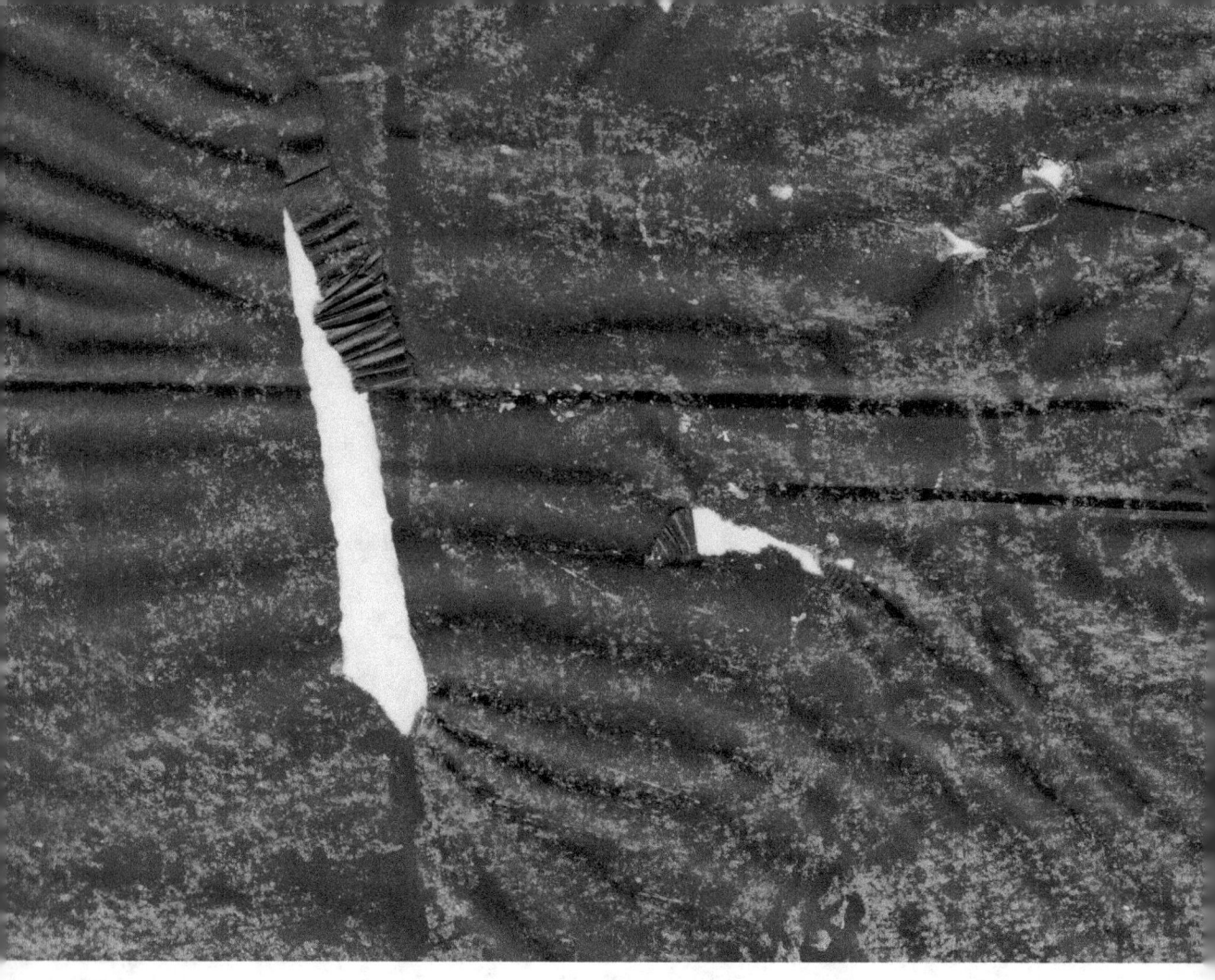

Sarah Vanagt, *Élevage de poussière
(Dust Breeding)*, crayon and pencil on
paper, 2013.

Sarah Vanagt, *Élevage de poussière
(Rritje pluhuri)*, laps në letër, 2013.

Disturbed Earth

Contact images? Images that touch something and then someone. Images thatcut to the quick of a question: Touching to see or, on the contrary, touchingto no longer see; seeing to no longer touch or, on the contrary, seeing to touch.Images that are too close. Adherent images. Image obstacles, but obstacles thatmake things appear. Images coupled to each other, indeed even to the thingsof which they are the image. Contiguous images, images backing each other.Weighty images.

Or very light images that surface and skim, graze us andtouch us again. Caressing images. Groping or already palpable images. Imagessculpted by developer, modeled by shadow, molded by light, carved by exposuretime.Images that catch up with us, that manipulate us, perhaps. Images thatcan ruffle or chafe us. Images that grasp us. Penetrating, devouring images.Images that move our hand.

– Georges Didi-Huberman[1]

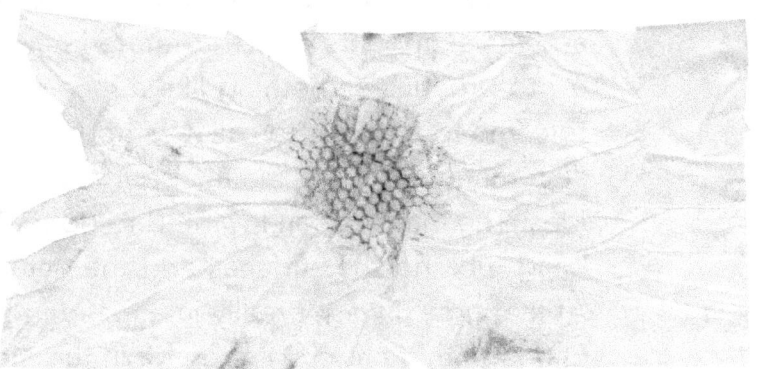

Brussels, April 2012

Sarah Vanagt: My project on the ICTY (International Criminal Tribunal for the former Yugoslavia) began with an encounter with someone. In 2007, I went to present my video installation *Power Cut* in Filmhuis Den Haag in The Hague. The exhibition was part of a festival titled "Cinema and Justice," an annual festival obviously inspired by the presence of the International Courts in the city. At the opening night of the festival, which was attended by lawyers and judges working in the international tribunals, I talked to a researcher from the court who had also been involved in the Rwanda tribunal in Arusha. He said that the entire court system is based on the spoken word, that this was where it originated. Seeking for truth requires the ability to put things in words, to connect facts to a story. And he said: "We are very bad with images." It seemed that there was a growing concern among people involved in court cases that, even though images have become extremely powerful and influential, the legal sphere still hasn't really found a way to incorporate them. This was something I found really interesting: this inability he was talking about and that had become the source of a fear. For a long time, on and off while working on other projects, I thought about this question: What could be the role of images in *justice*? What could be an image of justice, or a *just image*? (In the sense of *mot juste*?) It might have been after reading a text by Georges Didi-Huberman that I suddenly had the idea to go and make imprints of the furniture in the courtroom, of all the surfaces; to produce something like a record of 18 years of this... of trying to come to a – what to call it without being vague? – ... this search for "international justice," in this courtroom. First there was a very intuitive idea. The main reason I wanted to go to the courtroom was to film my hand rubbing the surfaces and the actual appearance of the traces. At that time, I wasn't really interested in the final results on the paper, although that has changed a bit in the meantime. I wanted to film the movement of the hand trying to rub something away, while the same gesture actually makes something appear. This something seems to be abstract, or in any case unreadable, like sign-language perhaps.

To get permission to film in the courtrooms I contacted the ICTY's press office and explained what I wanted to do. The people working there were very open to my suggestion. It took three weeks to get the permission and they suggested that I should come very soon, because it was just before the Christmas break, and that is the only time when the courtrooms are not used. Otherwise I would have had to wait one more year for the next Christmas break. So I went to an art supplies shop and bought all kinds of paper and pencils, preparing for the different surfaces I might encounter. I bought silk paper, and the best tool for most surfaces turned out to be this triangular-shaped children's wax crayon.

Tobias Hering: *So the idea to make rubbings was already there before your first encounter with the actual site, before you went to this court for the first time?*

Yes, absolutely. And I chose the Tribunal for the former Yugoslavia, and not the International Criminal Court, because the ICTY is not only restricted geographically but also restricted in time. It had already entered its "completion phase," which gave me a sense of urgency. When the ICTY was founded in 1993, nobody really expected that it would take so long. Now that they have captured Mladić it will probably take a few more years, but they are not taking any new cases. The wars in Yugoslavia must already be – thanks to these trials – the best documented wars ever. For twenty years now the court archive has been continuously growing, so that we are talking about literally millions of documents, all translated into four languages: English, French, Albanian, and Serbo-Croatian. Whatever is said in the courtroom is transcribed immediately into these four languages and put online. The court sessions themselves are filmed by six cameras and streamed live online, with a thirty minutes delay. Except for some closed sessions, when a particular witness needs to be protected, for example so that they conceal his or her identity.

This means you didn't enter a situation of secrecy, where there would be an initial lack of information and where you would have to do extensive research to find out what's going on behind closed doors. Quite the contrary, it seems: it was a situation where everything, or almost everything, was visible and accessible and given to the public via an internet archive.

Yes – to a point where there is such an overload of information that it effectively becomes *inaccessible*. That might be a general problem of our age and time, but in this case the transparency is so detailed and so meticulous that it reaches a point of absurdity. The material is so dense, so vast, that you don't know how to find a way into it. This means that there is a constant sense of vertigo when working on this film.

In the ICTY database, there is a section "Exhibits," which signposts all documents or photos of objects that were brought to the trial as 'evidence.' Another section is "Transcripts": the transcripts of the court sessions in the four languages. What I often do is search these for keywords, for example "traces." Now in the Karadžić trial you get lots of hits for the search term "traces," because the entire trial is based on traces, of course.

What is the difference between "evidence" and "trace"?

For the court, I think, evidence is merely the more juridical term, but often they use traces as evidence. That's actually a core issue, because the court does not deal with the war as such, but with *traces of* the war. It analyzes traces and often to incredible detail. It happens that they discuss one piece of evidence for several days, for example a photo of a bomb crater, a completely abstract image, which looks even more abstract than my rubbings, but from which experts can presumably tell the type of bomb and where it came from, thus eventually who launched it. Recognizing this level of detail in the discussions, and at the same time the level of abstraction of many of the photographs, made me more and more interested in my drawings and the actual patterns that had come out through the rubbing. At first I had only been interested in the gesture itself and in what it transmits: the anger, the obsession.

Are you thinking of the work you are going to produce as a linear video? Is video the 'container' in which your research is to find its final form?

Yes, but I have started to think about a way to also use the original drawings, that is the rubbings, in an installation. The idea could be that entering a space one first encounters the drawings, and then proceeds to the room where the film is projected. The film should also work on its own, but I like the idea of showing the audience the actual drawings before or after the film. It's a difficult question, however:

Why show the original objects, if they are already part of the film? I am
not sure yet what I will eventually decide.

Karadžić Trial (Case IT-95-5/18-I)
Witness: Richard Wright,
archaeologist
Cross-examination by the accused,
Radovan Karadžić
1 December 2011

JUDGE KWON: So one – was one of your mandates to establish the timing of the death of those bodies?

THE WITNESS: Yes, Mr. President. I – it would have been. Or I was asked to advise whether it was reasonable to think that these people had died after the fall of Srebrenica.

JUDGE KWON: Very well. Yes, Mr. – back to you, Mr. Karadžić.

THE ACCUSED: [Interpretation] Thank you.

MR. KARADŽIĆ: [Interpretation]

Q. Did you establish and did they show you graves – or, rather, was it your obligation to investigate all the accessible mass graves?

A. No, Mr. Karadžić. I was shown aerial images that the – that had fresh patches of soil on them dating from October 1995, and I was shown photographs that, on my analysis, had about 28 of these patches of soil that appeared, you know, over a period of a couple of days in October 1995, and I went to all of these and decided which of them we could excavate in the season that was available, in the season that was available which was about six months. And so my advice was sought as to how many we could reasonably excavate in that time. It was not possible to excavate more than seven of those in that time. But as I said earlier in my testimony, we probed the other sites it showed on the aerial photographs to establish that they were – that they had multiple human remains in them, but we didn't exhume them. So in answer to your question, was it my obligation to investigate all the accessible mass graves, yes, to investigate, but not to excavate. Excavation was restricted to seven.

Q. Thank you. Which method did you apply, and in which way did you establish the time of death?

A. Well, we – we – we established

that the watches that were worn by some of the individuals were consistent with the date of the executions, and that analysis is in my report. They're consistent. The – we also found artefacts of a sort, which, again, are in my report, such as a Dutch newspaper that was cut up into cigarette papers and was in the pockets of the victims. But the main way in which we established the age of those graves was that they – that is, the secondary graves of the 1998 season, is that they do not appear before October 1995. We have images of the ground before October 1995 and then suddenly these graves appear. So that is the best way of determining the age of the graves.

Q. The age of the graves. But the time of death is something different. That's not the age of the graves. How did you establish when a man had died?

A. I was not able to establish when a man had died other than by the context of the artefacts that came out of the grave.

Q. Thank you. Are you trying to say that a watch would show the hour, day, month, and year of execution?

A. The particular watches that I'm talking and which are in my report are Seiko mechanical or automatic watches that stop within 24 to 48 hours of the last movement of the watch. Now, I'm told that the executions took place on Friday, the 14th of July, and eight out of the ten watches that we found in the 1998 season showed a day and a date, that is, Saturday 15th or Sunday 16th, which is consistent with the information I received about the date of executions. But apart from that, apart from that I have evidence of the age of the graves. But if I look at an individual, I can't tell you when that individual died, no.

JUDGE KWON: Yes, Mr. Mitchell.

MR. MITCHELL: Mr. President, just – if there's going to be more questions on the topic of watches, I think the report in question is – it's – it had 65 ter 2496, and it might be helpful to bring it up if there's going to be further questions on this. And it starts

– there's a section on this topic that starts at around page 28.

JUDGE KWON: Thank you. Yes, Mr. Karadžić. Please continue.

THE ACCUSED: [Interpretation] Thank you.

MR. KARADŽIĆ: [Interpretation]

Q. So all of these watches were automatic mechanical ones? There were no battery operated watches? Electronic ones?

A. There were windup watches and there were electronic watches, but they do – the windup watches do not show day and date in the window. I really believe at this stage I should have a picture of the watch – of one of the watches to explain what I'm talking about.

JUDGE KWON: I think it's the penultimate page of the first report. Exhibit P4000. Page 181. E-court page. Did you refer to this?

THE WITNESS: I referred to this type of watch, yes.

MR. KARADŽIĆ: [Interpretation]

Q. And this is not a windup watch, right? This is an electronic or an automatic mechanical watch. Oh, it says automatic, doesn't it?

A. Yes, it's an automatic mechanical watch that is self-winding but stops after no movement within 24 or 48 hours. And this watch is showing in its window the day 'Sab', which is either Italian or Spanish for Saturday, 15th. And this is one of the watches that I'm talking about where eight out of ten were consistent with an execution on Thursday – on Friday the 14th. And I argue in my report that the probabilities of eight out of ten watches showing these day/dates that are consistent with the supposed execution date is trillions to one. Some special event happened that made these watches stop, not at random, but in a pattern.

It's very disquieting to think of the violence and destruction that took place during that war, of the disappearance and all that will probably remain unspeakable, in contrast to the meticulous and orderly court procedures and especially the word-by-word protocol of everything that's being said. The contrast between this total transparency and oblivion. How could we complain about not being informed, not being able to judge or have an opinion, when everything is online and accessible? But, as you already said, the amount of information also has a silencing and paralyzing effect. Even if that were not somebody's actual strategy, only very few would overcome their sense of being overwhelmed and actually make their way through to the details.

The two elements combined, the amount of information and the level of detail, enhance this effect. Whenever you tune in, you will find them talking about such small details. If you don't follow the procedures closely, it is virtually impossible to understand what is being talked about. Here, for instance, this is Jean-René Ruez, an expert-witness and former police officer in France. He was in the courtroom for four or five days to talk about a criminal investigation he pursued on the basis of the events at Srebrenica: a overall report, including witness accounts, survivor accounts, ballistic reports and forensic reports.[2] This is an important term in this case: "the angle of descent." That means: "of the bullets." Depending on the surface and where the bullet hit, they can tell where it came from.

What does this mean: "MR. KARADŽIĆ: [Interpretation]"?

It means that this is the translation of what he said, because he is not speaking in English. Karadžić is interrogating Ruez here.

So you hit on these documents following keyword searches.

Yes, I work a lot with search terms. For example, "crater," "surface," "residue," "exhumation." Everything to do with surface.

Which means you are trying to contextualize your own approach to the courtroom within the vocabulary of the trial.

Exactly. And then I hit on something that actually overlaps with the other film Katrien Vermeire and I are currently making on the exhumation of a mass grave from the Spanish Civil War.[3] It's the notion of "disturbed earth," which is very prevalent in the Karadžić trial. The way they locate mass graves in Bosnia is by comparing satellite images of the same location taken on different dates. Through this before-and-after comparison one can recognize disturbed patches of earth, which are believed to mark the sites of mass graves. These aerial images themselves already look similar to some of the rubbings I made.

Karadžić Trial (Case IT-95-5/18-I)
Witness: Jean-René Ruez, police investigator
Cross-examination by the accused, Radovan Karadžić
2 February 2012

THE ACCUSED: [Interpretation] Thank you. Could we zoom in on this rectangle with the bodies.
MR. KARADŽIĆ: [Interpretation]
Q. In this football pitch, they are sitting. We heard from witness statements that they are sitting, and they were guarded by several men. Do you agree that that is information we got from witness statements?
A. Yes. That is correct.
Q. Thank you. These individuals that we see standing apart in the front, in the foreground, would those be the Serb soldiers, the guards?
A. No. Those who are grouped are prisoners. The guards would be standing around. There is no need to have a huge amount of guards on the left side, no need.
Q. Thank you. Could you try to assist us. I'm now counting the shortest side, one, two, three, four, five, maybe six. And the longest side, one, two, three, four, five, six, seven, eight, nine, ten. Ten, eleven at the outside; correct?
A. One, two, three, four, five, till eleven, what? Centimetres, people, metres? I don't understand.
Q. Individuals, Mr. Ruez, those who are sitting. The shortest side of the rectangle. We can count five to six, and the longest side of the rectangle, we can count 10 to 11 individuals. Can you count more than I did? And when you do the arithmetic you get 60 to 70 people.
A. Your counting skills are far better than mine. I would not even try to do such a counting, but I think any reasonable person who would take a dot as you can see some of them on – on this photograph, would have a much, much larger number than the one you come up with. But this type of counting I never attempted and would not even attempt, because it would at the end be, anyhow, extremely fuzzy.

In the video material you find in the online archive you can sometimes see how, while a document is being discussed, there are lines appearing in it, lines drawn as if by an invisible hand. It's the witnesses drawing on the screens in front of them, and these screens are interactive touchscreens, so they transmit the line onto the other screens in the room and of course onto the recorded video image. So while someone speaks, one can see what he is talking about. This is a typical one …

What is it?

It's a wall where many people were executed. ... This is where they found bodies … This is another example of disturbed earth. ... These are notebooks they found, military notebooks. ... This is also evidence: they show this photo of a tractor to explain what kind of machinery the Bosnian Serb army was using and how the tire tracks of these look like. ... Much of this evidence is so abstract, as an image, that you really need to know, or be told, what you're looking at.

> *When you decided to make the rubbings and to work with the visual aspects of this process of rubbing, was there anything you decided "against"? Was there anything that you were foreclosing by this decision?*

It was clear by then that it wouldn't be a film "about the war," recounting what happened in the war, in Srebrenica or other places. Rather, a film that concerns the fact that this is a war, which, for a while now, has been dealt with in a court case, dealt with in very meticulous ways, where they are examining these traces. So my decision meant that I would not try to document the war, but that I would document the traces of the tribunal. This was a conscious decision. On the other hand, it is of course impossible to claim that one *isn't* dealing with the war. The evidence that the court is dealing with is evidence of the war and it's bringing this war back into the image.

> *It seems to me that you're taking a step back, that you're seeking a distance out of which things can be seen in their proper relation (a desire which might be related to seeking justice). After deciding that you won't be making a film about the war, you realized that you also don't need to reconstruct a public image of something going on "behind closed doors," like for example Eyal Sivan did in his film on the Eichmann trial, Un Spécialiste. Once you had permission to film, you didn't enter the courtroom the way one would most likely expect from a documentary filmmaker. With the rubbings you are taking what seems to be a detour, challenging not only the juridical concept of evidence, but also the modes of*

producing documentary images.

I soon started to have trouble with the level of abstraction both in what I was doing and in the court procedures. It becomes quite surreal if you're not looking at the evidence as an expert (but then, even for them it might sometimes seem surreal). The court procedures seem so far removed from the reality of war and also from the reality of living with the consequences of war afterwards. Related to the human loss and trauma and guilt we're dealing with, what's happening on the image level seems sometimes painfully abstract and distant. Some of the evidence images look like microscopic images of a plant structure. It's as if the entire war – by means of *images* of its traces – is put under a microscope. The legal judgment will ultimately be based on these images, but it won't be abstract at all, because it may mean that someone is going to prison for life. On this problematic level of abstraction I think that the work I did with the rubbings matches the work they are doing in the court. It provokes similar questions. In fact, "abstraction" is not even the right word to describe this shared element. What we might call the "abstract" quality of the evidence material does not result from a *denial* of reality or a *turning away* from it. On the contrary, there is a radical return *toward* reality, a desire to zoom in on the smallest particle of reality. And in the same way one could argue that the rubbings are not abstract images either, but that they are radically realistic images.

Since this understanding of the visual similarities came later, I wonder, however, if in the beginning the rubbing gesture with its sense of futility was intended as a critique of the truth practices applied in the court, a critical reflection of you as an artist, and also as an historian, on the use of evidence or images?

What is certainly related is a reflection on the *desire* to have images, to find images or produce images as evidence of something. What is an image of justice, how does justice become visible, or rather: what is a visual documentation of it? Can you represent an abstract notion like justice, and what are the images that are circulating in this respect? So with this distance that I felt existed between the court and everyday life I went there and performed this tactile gesture, this touching and rubbing, which is of course meant to include the meaning that you cannot grasp "justice." It was an attempt to perform a critique by reflecting on the impossibility of what the gesture is performing. Does it minimize the distance or does it make it even bigger? A paradox, which is related to the "anachronism of imprints" that Didi-Huberman writes about: imprints are traces of a physical contact that have a physical presence themselves and at the same time they are evidence of the absence of that which left the trace and which the trace is "of."

> *To conclude, such is the paradox of objects produced by imprint: the contact involved, of which they remain the legitimate agents; an often poignant, undeniable contact, which nevertheless does not allow a categorical identification of its real-life referent. There was adhesion, but adhesion to whom, to what, at which moment, at which body origin? [...] No matter how much the imprint might affect us by the adhesion from which it was derived, this contact almost inevitably ends up by conceiving itself in the element of separation, of loss, of absence. For a footprint to appear as a process, the foot needs to sink in the sand, the walker needs to be present, in the very same place where the mark is to be made. But for the footprint to appear as a result, the foot needs to be lifted, separated from the sand and moved away to produce more footprints in other places. And from this moment on, of course, the walker is not there anymore. On this double condition doubtlessly rest the power and fragility that mingle in the imprint. They form together what I would like to call the critical function of the imprint or its symptom function. The imprint at once touches and escapes us in that it creates a kind of malaise in the representation: a "symptom-likeness." In each unique imprint, in fact, the game of contact and gap reaches, overwhelms, transforms the expected relationships of the likeness, so that the optical and tactile, the image and its process, the "sameness" and its alteration are suddenly intertwined*

again, at the risk of disturbing a thought that, for the purposes of its own clarity or distinction, spontaneously tended to disentangle any contradictory elements.[4]

I went to The Hague the day when Mladić, who had recently been arrested, was made to appear in court for the first time. I took a hotel room right opposite the court, from where I could film the media commotion in front of the building. Since the events were broadcast live, I could also watch them on the TV screen in my room. I used this hotel room as a place where I could establish some distance from what was going on in the court case. I had with me some documentaries that had already been made about the tribunal and about the Bosnian Wars, and I watched those on my laptop in the hotel room, occasionally panning with the camera from computer screen to TV screen and to what I could see from the window. At one point I taped a piece of silk paper to the laptop screen, strapped a mini-camera to my forehead and filmed my hands rubbing over the images that appeared on the laptop screen, trying to capture the outlines, the silhouettes of figures in the images which was of course futile, impossible, because the images were moving.

For me, the term "surface" is becoming crucial now, because here you are introducing a third surface: the screen, the computer screen and the TV screen. The courtroom rubbings negotiate the materiality of the surfaces in the courtroom against the surfaces of the Bosnian topography interpreted through aerial photography and ballistic analysis. And now the screen: a totally smooth and unstructured surface. On this surface, the gesture of rubbing becomes really desperate, because it reveals no traces whatsoever, or it only reveals the traces of its own movement.

This time, I gave myself time to really get lost in the project, not only in the material. I knew that things connected, but I got almost lost in trying to find a way to create the connection and how to make it work in a video. In the scene that we're discussing, I was watching one of my favorite films – I mean not just favorite films about the former Yugoslavia, but one of my favorite films in general: *Serbian Epics* by Pawel Pawlikowski. I was in this hotel room, it was late at night, a few days before Christmas. I had already seen the film some years before, and that film may well have been another starting point for making this film I'm working on now. I don't know. Anyway, The Hague was covered in snow, and I watched the film while doing camera tests in the hotel room, preparing myself for the series of rubbings I would go and make in the courtroom the next morning. When, in *Serbian Epics*, Karadžić started to recite his poem "Nocturno – A poem about fear and about snow," I decided to film this while making a rubbing of the screen. Again, it was an intuitive idea, not something I constructed in my head or in a script beforehand. This might become the opening scene of the film.

> *I think the image of your hand rubbing the computer screen touches the limits of what is at stake. The gesture is becoming absurd, and from this point of absurdity we are forced to reflect back on the relation between the surface and what's underneath, between the image and the reality for which it is taken as evidence. It makes you realize that the surface must be structured, that it must already have contrasts – that means traces – in order for something to appear. The rubbing gesture can only reproduce traces that have already been there before.*
>
> *The technique you're applying in this project – creating imprints of surfaces – is a common technique both in art and archeology. But the way you're applying it here is at odds with the demands of the disciplines. The site you are dealing with, the courtroom, is not an archeological site, and its temporality is not historical but the present.*

I would say it's a place where history is in the making. If the trial were closed, it would already make a difference to my project. But even a pre-historian or an archeologist, when he creates imprints of the trace of a hand in a cave, is not only dealing with something a thousand years ago, but also with something present, something in the present. He is taking an imprint of all the layers of time between the moment when the hand touched this surface and the moment when he, the archeologist, is taking this imprint.

One of the main difficulties for me in this project is caused by the fact that the trial is not over yet. How do I decide when to start editing, when new material is continuously being produced in the court? Usually I start editing when I have the rushes. Of course, many filmmakers keep filming even while they are already editing, but in this case I don't even know what's coming, with the Mladić case yet to start. On the other hand I have so many hours of footage and material already that it doesn't make sense to not start editing. The fact that new material keeps coming in is challenging my mind as someone who was trained as a historian in the first place. Yes, as if I were longing for an even greater distance. Because the sense of drowning in the material is never far away.

Is your identity as an artist then something you take refuge to? Is the artist's mindset what enables you to start editing?

I wouldn't even make this a strong opposition, because it's not easy to make a clear distinction within myself. I am less and less inclined to decide whether my work contributes to one discourse or the other, whether I am acting as an artist or an historian or something else. I guess that on the artistic level what I am doing in this project is finding a new way of dealing with such a topic. So I'd say I have no refuge for the moment. I am just doing it, trying things out. For a while, I was inspired by the Arab Spring artists who went out during the day with their cameras and put on the internet in the evening what they had filmed. That is such a different way of dealing with historical events. In the tribunal you are confronted with a strange layering of historical times. You are not watching the war while it is unfolding, but you're looking at something that is going on now, the trial, and you're reflecting on it without having a distance. That's very difficult for me.

*Let's talk about the objects that you're creating, what we some-
times call rubbings, and sometimes drawings. The different accent
of these two terms made me think that it is here, in these objects,
that something comes together that we usually keep separate.
What could be the role of these objects? Isn't their very status what
is at stake in this negotiation between the artist and the historian?*

As I said before, when I started out I was expecting to throw them out
once I had filmed the process of their production, because I was only
interested in the rubbing gesture itself. In the first few days I didn't
treat them as valuable objects at all, just folding them up any odd
way, dropping them on the ground. On some of them the traces of
this rough handling remain visible. Only on the last day I noticed that
there was something strong in these objects themselves; that I was
producing new traces and that for the moment I should keep them. I
wasn't sure what I would do with them and I still am not.

*Reconsidering some of your earlier works, it seems that at the core
of the very different topics and landscapes that you've been dealing with so far we often find elements of "objectified history." I am
thinking, for example, of the statues of King Albert and Queen Eliz-
abeth, between whom you animate a dialogue in* Little Figures[5]*; or
the children's games depicted in* First Elections[6] *– disturbing enact-
ments of a past which these children probably didn't experience
themselves, but which their bodies, their toys and the games they
play express nevertheless.*

Looking back it seems there has always been an interest in the ways
the past is, so to speak, seeping through the stones. I realize that I am
more and more interested in material traces than in narrated traces.
With the children in Goma [in *First Elections*] it comes together: an
oral narrative and a play with objects and gestures. But for the film
about the exhumation of the grave in Spain [*The Wave*] there has
been a clear decision to only show images of the exhumation and to
not include any of the witness accounts and memories. When I started

the project in The Hague, the initial idea was, again, not to give any words, but all I had in mind was this gesture of rubbing.

How can you avoid narration?

It's not that I want to avoid it. I like to think of this work in terms of Brecht's *Kriegsfibel* [War Primer], the *abécédaire de la guerre*. The idea of a simple structure like this: the desk of the judge, the seat of the defendant, the microphone of the witness.

An inventory?

Sort of an inventory, yes, but with this child-like connotation of learning an alphabet. The alphabet of the tribunal. In children's books you read "chicken" and you see the image of a chicken. So here you read "desk," but you don't see the desk; you see the rubbing of the surface of the desk. I wish I could keep it very simple like that, plainly visual, but I think it doesn't work.

—

Kassel, November 2012

There is something very emotional about this frenetic, repetitive rubbing movement of a hand in close-up, especially when you see it on three screens simultaneously. An emotional acuteness that I hadn't fully anticipated, since the initial idea had been more on an intellectual level, more concerned with the symbolic meaning of the gesture. Of course the context of seeing it in Sarajevo with this audience helped to bring unforeseen elements to the foreground.

At first I hesitated to accept the Sarajevo invitation, since I don't like the idea of showing work-in-progress to an audience. But this time the situation was quite different. I had spent two years following the trials online and doing research in the online archive, all on my own, from my workspace in Brussels. Somehow the distance we talked about earlier on had become too big. I felt I had become detached from the reality, both the reality of the courtroom now, and the reality of the war twenty years ago. And with this sense of detachment came all sorts of other doubts: Who am I to deal with this war? Will people who have lived through the horrors not be offended by my "performance' in the courtroom? And so on. I felt it was time to be confronted with the people for whom the tribunal in The Hague is closely connected to their very person. I don't think I exaggerate when I say that my stay in Sarajevo has been crucial for continuing the work on this film. It has given me the courage to stop the somehow addictive research in the archive, to lock myself up in the editing room with Effi Weiss, the editor, and to make a film. To stop being an observer – a collector even.

The general reception of the installation in Sarajevo was very positive. However there were also people who told me that they were sick and tired of seeing images of witnesses or of evidence, which they feel they have seen more than enough of, especially if they had been engaging with this subject or were witnesses of the war themselves. It obviously mattered what age people were, but it also made a big difference at what moment someone would enter the room: Since the video segments on the three screens had different lengths and were set to loop, the combination of simultaneous images was random and the combined impact of the installation therefore quite unpredictable. Entering the room with all three screens showing a hand rubbing made it more likely that people would stay and move closer than a combination of witnesses testifying to the court. The most likely 'worst case scenario' for some visitors to the exhibition would have been a combination of three screens showing Karadžić defending himself. It made some people just back straight out again. Someone explained to me afterwards that he just didn't want to see this face ever again. "Show it anywhere in the world," he said, "but don't show it to me." This person also said that he appreciated the rubbings and that he wished he could have just seen a room full of these. For this exhibition I finally decided I wouldn't show the originals, but digital prints of the originals in B1 size. As there were three screens, I also chose three rubbings: the table of the judge, the table of the accused, and the marble steps in the hallway. For the latter I chose a photo of the actual rubbing that I had taken after it had already been handled and transported several times, and traces of this handling were visible on it. I gave the prints to people who had invited me, and I was surprised how important they seemed to be for them, how happy they were to receive them. I don't know if they valued the object, or what the image shows, or the meaning they gave to it. I am not sure what the rubbings mean to people; for someone who has been through this war and who might appreciate the vague, aesthetic quality of the rubbings; or to someone from the outside – you for example, for whom they are first and foremost abstract and might remain inaccessible.

The level of abstraction in the rubbings, or let's say their aesthetic presence, might originate a separation between those who were physically affected by the war at the time and those who are post-witnesses, so to speak, who have only witnessed the aftermath, the politics and the tribunal for example. It seems inevitable that for those who have seen and suffered the concreteness of that war, the rubbings will signify something different than for those whose relation to this war is mainly through images. For someone who has experienced more than could be successfully shown or proven with images the enigmatic quality of the rubbings might come as a relief, because they might signify what's beyond the dominance of the "visible"; while those of us for whom the war in Yugoslavia spells a breakdown of the belief in the civilizing (or at least peace-keeping) power of media presence and the visibility of events might feel a need to compensate retrospectively for a lack of me-dia responsibility (or rather: ur own responsibility); to exercise a "right to look" which, at the time, was either censored, ridiculed or instrumentalized in propaganda. There is something to say about these not easily reconcilable perspectives around image evidence, and from what I have seen so far of your work I think that you are trying to bring these perspectives together: not in the sense of merging them into one, but in the sense of having them in the same space, negotiating the conflict between them as something that plays out alongside the court scenario, yet by definition out-side of it. There is a moment in one of the Sarajevo videos where you do this by overlapping sound: when we see the sequence of the hand rubbing the desk, we already hear the beginning of the following court scene in which they are interpreting evidence. So here, through this overlapping of image and sound, we are enticed to look at the rubbings in similar terms in which the court is looking at aerial photographs. The two aesthetics – artistic practice and forensic image – are forced to negotiate what's between them.

I ask myself all the time how to deal with these levels. At some point, I even thought of the possibility of overlapping an image of the hand rubbing with an image from the courtroom, so as to create the visual impression that the rubbing movement makes another image become gradually visible. It might be absolutely too much, but I would only know after I had tried it.

I was imagining that the voice-over from the courtroom could be-gin over a moment of black screen, so that we already hear the ex-pert explaining what can be seen in a certain photograph, but we don't see anything yet and have to imagine the image instead. This relates to what we said earlier, when we talked about elements for this text: invisible images, images that are being talked about and described, but that the reader is not always given to see.

Yes, these are all possible connections and disconnections that we are currently trying out in the editing room. But from what I tried so far, I see that without a visual reference – that is, as soundtrack only – the courtroom sessions become even more difficult to follow. It helps to see the judges, the accused, to see the strange protocol, the details. Otherwise you are even more distanced from it all, and it's already so far away. The eye needs to be grounded in the courtroom, it seems. Even if it's through the glass of the public gallery, through the com-puter screen, through the window of the hotel room opposite the tri-bunal. And then there is this "urge" – where does it come from? – to put one's hand on the window, to touch what lies beyond. I remember an incident from a day when I was visiting the court and sitting in the space that's reserved for the public. It was the opening session of Karadžić's defense on 16th October 2012, which was attended by many international journalists, and also by a group of survivors of the war. The public gallery is separated from the courtroom by a thick glass pane, through which you can see what's going on, and the sound is transmitted through loudspeakers. Additionally, there is a TV screen under the ceiling through which is transmitted the almost-live documentation of the court sessions as it is simultaneously broadcast on the internet. Sitting in front of me was an elderly woman, maybe in her seventies, who was talking non-stop to Karadžić throughout the entire session. A constant monologue. She would not face him through the window, though, but only look at his image on the TV screen. Every once in a while a guard asked her to lower her voice, but everyone in the room was tolerating it. The tension in the room was enormous; I sat next to a survivor of the Srebrenica massacres, who asked the guards to leave the woman alone. Of course I didn't understand a word of what the woman was saying.

In Sarajevo, I was introduced to Jovan Divjak, a retired general who had served in the army of the Republic of Bosnia and Herzegovina from 1992 to 1995, during the Bosnian War. After he had been to my exhibition, he suggested that he would take me to various strategic wartime places in and around Sarajevo the next morning. While walking through the city with him – a tour he obviously had done many times before with foreign visitors – I saw glimpses of a man who walks endlessly through the city's deep traces of the war. It was a very moving, but also estranging experience for me: being at the places of which I have seen so many photos and videos, images that have been dismantled into the smallest fragments during the court hearings in The Hague.

After working with all this material for two years, I really thought I knew what the city would look like, but I was completely disoriented. It was an interesting experience because I realized the distance from which I am working, which is also a reflection on the distance of the court. And then you end up with this ultimate question, which is of course a crucial question for the documentary filmmaker: Can we, or how can we, *film* reality? We can't, we all know that. And yet we try it. With six remotely controlled cameras in a courtroom. Or, in my case, with a wax crayon and a small camera on a helmet, a camera designed to film miniature sets for animation films.

This text was based on several conversations between Sarah Vanagt and Tobias Hering that took place in Brussels and Kassel in April andNovember 2012. During that time, Sarah was engaged in an extensive researchand art project dealing with the International Criminal Tribunal for theformer Yugoslavia (ICTY) in The Hague and in particular with the ongoing trial against Radovan Karadžić. What was then still a work-in-progress would subsequently become the 47-minute video *Dust Breeding*, which was released in May 2013. From the beginning, the conversations were meant to result in a collaborative text to be published before or after the release of the finished film. They were accompanied by a regular exchange of thoughts and images through email and further informed by Sarah's parallel collaboration with Katrien Vermeire on *The Wave* (2012), a 20-minute video about the exhumation of a mass grave from the Spanish Civil War. Both works – *The Wave* and *Dust Breeding* – are concerned with juridical evidence and historical justice,and more obviously with the treatment of soil and surface, under which are buried the remains of the murdered. In November 2012, Sarah was invited to present for the first time a work based on her research around the ICTY at duplex, an art gallery in Sarajevo, as part of the "Pravo Ljudski Film Festival." Her experience of this exhibitionbecame subject matter during our following session in Kassel.The text that follows includes parts of the transcripts of the recorded conversations as well as text and image material which had been viewed or read together.

1. Georges Didi-Huberman, *Contact Images* (1997), translated by Alisa Hartz, no page ref. (quoted from online source: www.usc.edu/dept/comp-lit/tympanum/3/contactimages.html [last accessed November 2013].
2. See www.antablog.com/jean-rene-ruez-thelonesome- investigator-srebrenica-hero [last accessed November 2013].
3. *The Wave* (Katrien Vermeire, Sarah Vanagt, 2012).
4. Georges Didi-Huberman, *La ressemblance par contact: archéologie, anachronisme et modernité de l'empreinte* (Paris: Les Éditions de Minuit, 2008), p. 309f. The quoted excerpt was translated by Alexandra Bordes.
5. *Little Figures* (Sarah Vanagt, 2003) is a short lyrical experiment creating a dialogue between three statues on Brussels's Mont des Arts brought to life by the voices of three children.
6. *First Elections* (Sarah Vanagt, 2006) is one of several video works that resulted from repeated visits to the war-torn border region between Rwanda and the Republic of Congo. The video was shot in the Congolese city of Goma which in January 2002 had suffered heavily from the eruption of the Nyiragongo volcano. *First Elections* depicts children "playing politics" on the lava covered lots in front of their houses. All images indicated to be taken from the ICTY Court Records Database are courtesy of the United Nations International Criminal Tribunal for the former Yugoslavia.

Ilustrimi i instruksioneve ose Gjigandi dhe Shkurtabiqi

Nga një shënim i vogël me laps, që duket në cepin e poshtëm të saj, mësojmë se në vitin 1968, piktori Spiro Kristo pikturoi tablonë *Ditë Fluturimi*. Ky vit, pra gjashtëdhjeteteta, për arsye që unë nuk i di me saktësi ka qenë një vit që i përket një periudhe të begatë (duke përdorur termat e asaj kohe) për pikturën shqiptare, pasi disa piktura të rëndësishme janë prodhuar ato vite, ndër to edhe *Vojo Kushi* e Sali Shijakut (1969). Në versionin tim jozyrtar të historisë së artit shqiptar, mendoj se janë këto, vitet kur fillon Realizmi Socialist në Shqipëri, pavarësisht se për shumë njerëz, mes tyre edhe akademikë, ai fillon në vitin 1944, ndërsa ushtria gjermane largohej në mëdyshje nëse duhej ta linte në 28 apo në 29 nëntor, territorin e këtij vendi. Gjithësesi Spiro Kristo nuk pati asnjë mëdyshje kur pikturoi tablotë e tij, në fund të viteve gjashtëdhjetë, se ai po pikturonte Realizmin Socialist. Këtë unë nuk e di nga ndonjë e dhënë që mund të më ketë lënë piktori, sepse nuk kam patur fatin ta takoj, por prej tablove të tij, të cilat janë ndër të preferuarat e mia mes koleksionit të Realizmit Socialist shqiptar. Megjithëse ky koleksion është i madh, (ai përbën pjesën më të madhe të gjithë fondit të Galerisë Kombëtare) mendimi im (gjithmonë jozyrtar), është se në të vërtetë ai është i vogël. Sado e çuditshme të tingëllojë kjo që po them, jam i bindur se nuk ka qenë e lehtë ta bëje Realizmin Socialist, e aq më tepër në Shqipëri. Koleksioni ynë nga vitet e "epokës socialiste" mund të jetë vërtet i madh, por jo shumë vepra, mendoj unë (si jo akademik i devotshëm) ia kanë dalë të jenë Realizëm Socialist. Pyetjes se çfarë janë ato vepra, nëse s'janë Realizëm Socialist, ndoshta mund t'i përgjigjem herë tjetër sepse sot dua të merrem me atë që është e tillë, pra tablonë *Ditë Fluturimi*. Në fakt nuk është se kam parë shumë punë nga Kristo, por ato pak që kam parë në fondin e Galerisë Kombëtare janë të gjitha Realizëm Socialist

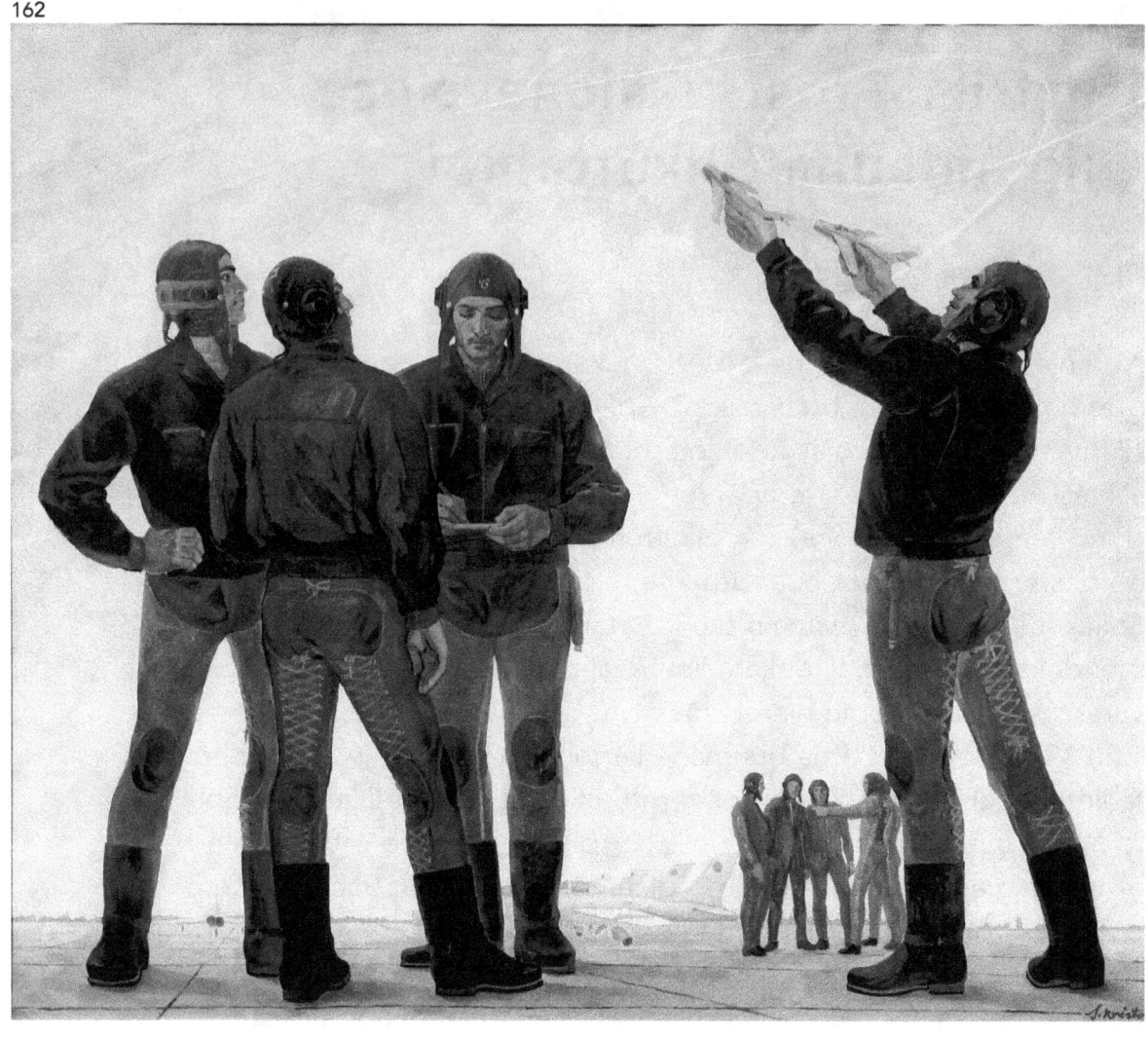

Spiro Kristo, *Flying Day (The Pilots of Division 7594, Rinas)*, oil on canvas, 183 x 209 cm, 1968.

Spiro Kristo, *Ditë Fluturimi (Aviatorët e repartit 7594, Rinas)*, vaj në pëlhurë, 183 x 209 cm, 1968.

i pastër. Termi *i pastër* në këtë rast është termi më i papërshtatshëm sepse Realizmi Socialist ishte një tendencë e kundërt me *artin e pastër*, nëse do ta përkthenim kështu në shqip termin *pure* dhe *purist*. Por nga ana e tij, ai përpiqej të ishte një metodë sa me rigoroze dhe e mirëpërcaktuar, pavarësisht se historia, për ironi të fatit, ia dha këtë emërtim edhe shumë veprave që fillimisht u privuan nga mbajtja e tij. Kjo ndodhi kur babai i Realizmit Socialist, ose siç quhej në atë kohë, në vendin tone, baba Stalini, e kishte lënë këtë botë dhe të tjerë pas tij bënë ç'deshën me pjellën e tij artistike duke e përçudnuar dhe kthyer atë në diçka banale, ose gjithëpërfshirëse (siç kishin qejf ta quanin). Por edhe një herë për ironi të historisë, rreth pesëmbëdhjetë vjet pasi Stalini ishte tretur dhe harruar, disa piktorë shqiptarë e ringjallën doktrinën e tij të preferuar artistike. Edhe ky është një fakt që akademikët tanë s'e kanë zënë ndonjëherë në gojë, pra faktin që Realizmi ynë Socialist (unë me këtë term jam i prirur të etiketoj ngushtësisht atë art që u zhvillua nën regjimin e Stalinit) filloi kur në vendin e vet të origjinës, kishte kohë që kishte mbaruar. Si erdhi dhe si u fut Realizmi Socialist prej Moskës e Leningradit në Tiranë, Durrës, Shkodër e Vlorë, këtë duhet ta thonë njerëzit që e sollën me vete, pra artistët që studiuan në akademitë e Bashkimit Sovjetik dhe vendeve të tjera të Lindjes dhe u kthyen në vend me këtë doktrinë në valixhet e tyre. Natyrisht, unë nuk mund të flas për këtë, sidomos nëse kjo është një zanat akademikësh, të cilin s'e njoh, siç e thashë që në fillim. Ajo që mua më mjafton është vëzhgimi i punës së atyre artistëve që ia dolën të prodhojnë me sukses Realizmin tonë Socialist. Këta jo aq për faktin që ishin ish-studentë të Bashkimit Sovjetik apo Rumanisë (si në rastin e Kristos), sepse kishte po aq bashkëstudentë të tyre që s'kanë dhënë prova se mund të realizonin një vepër të Realizmit Socialist sipas normave që ajo duhej të përmbushte në kohën e Stalinit, ndonëse kishin arritje të admirueshme akademike, apo njëherësh kishte ish-studentë të Institutit të Lartë të Arteve, Tiranë, që s'kishin qenë kurrë në Bashkimin Sovjetik apo vendet e tjera lindore, që për mendimin tim ia arritën të futen në lëkurën e Realizmit Socialist. Arsyeja është se veprat e tyre kanë atë gjënë e veçantë që i bën Realizëm Socialist, atë pjesën e imët që nuk dallohet dhe aq lehtë dhe që kërkon një thellim në

doktrinë që ta kuptosh. Nuk e përjashtoj që një pjesë e Realizmit Socialist vjen në pikturën shqiptare që etiketohet si e tillë, si klishe dhe
imitim i drejtpërdrejtë prej ilustrimeve të librave që kishin ardhur në
vitet 1950–1960 nga Moska drejt Tiranës njësoj dhe bashkë me doku-
menta, mallra konsumi apo armë, por mendoj se disa autorë (gjithësesi të pakët) kanë prodhuar diçka që reflekton ndërgjegje dhe njohje të
atyre problemeve që shqetësonin Realizmin Socialist në periudhën e
regjimit të Stalinit. Një nga këta autorë mendoj se është Spiro Kristo
dhe një nga këto vepra është tabloja e tij *Ditë Fluturimi*.

Ajo është një tablo e përbërë nga dy grupe figurash njerëzore
(aviatorësh) të vendosura në një rrafsh horizontal, hapësirën e gjerë
të pistës së aerodromit të Rinasit (sipas një shënimi të lënë nga autori në pjesën e pasme të tablosë). Në sfond duken edhe avionët,
gjithësesi larg prej grupeve të figurave e sidomos prej grupit të parë
që zë pjesën më të madhe të tablosë duke krijuar një lloj plani të parë
njerëzor. Përveç këtyre dy grupeve aviatorësh, të ndarë në dy plane
dhe një grupi avionësh ushtarakë të rreshtuar në pistë, tabloja duket e
pashqetësuar nga gjë tjetër. Vija e horizontit ndodhet fare ulët, pranë
brinjës së poshtme të kuadrit, duke bërë që qendra e tablosë dhe pjesa më e madhe e sfondit të saj të jetë qiell. Një qiell i hapur ku duken
fashat e bardha të gazrave që çlirojnë motorët a avionëve, por jo aq
avionët që i kanë lëshuar ato. Kjo është diçka thelbësore mendoj, për
një vepër adekuate të Realizmit Socialist. Sublimimi tipik me të cilin
ngarkohej vepra nuk na vjen prej avionëve metalikë e të pashpirt që
çajnë qiellin por prej aviatorëve, figurave njerëzore që zënë pjesën më
të madhe të tablosë dhe përbëjnë planin e parë të saj. Në këtë rast,
siç e përshkruam, figurat njerëzore mbushin qiellin, meqë ai përbën
gjithçka shohim pas tyre. Ka një arsye pse shohim fare pak tokë në
tablo dhe figurat e aviatorëve kanë si sfond apo janë të vendosura
në qiellin e hapur. Janë ata që "fluturojnë" dhe jo avionët e tyre. Pra,
të fluturosh, sipas Kristos (për mendimin tim), bëhet të fluturosh mes
thonjëzash. Krijimi i këtyre thonjëzave (të cilat do ti përdor me shumicë
gjatë këtij shkrimi) është një tipar i veprës së Kristos ku dua të ndalem.
Përshkrimi i një situate të zakonshme ishte diçka që Realizmi Socialist
sipas Stalinit e përçmonte edhe më shumë se vetë modernizmin. Ky

do të ishte pak a shumë realizmi, le të themi, arti përshkrues i cili e linte realitetin siç e shihte dhe linte shikuesin të gjykonte për të. Jo. Kjo ishte diçka që ishte tejkaluar me kohë, që me Endacakët e fundit të shekullit të nëntëmbëdhjetë, dhe sovjetikët nuk kishin më kohë për të humbur me *një art që i kishte paraprirë revolucionit dhe kishte shërbyer thjesht për të ndërgjegjësuar masat popullore për gjendjen e mjeruar ku ndodheshin.* Tani ata kishin plane të tjera. *Ata duhej të ndërhynin në realitet dhe jo ta përshkruanin atë.* Stalini kërkonte transformimin e realitetit dhe këtë duhej të merrte përsipër edhe arti i kohës së tij. Këtë ose asgjë! Vetëm se kishte një problem të vogël. Ky transformim nuk duhej të vinte prej makinave dhe zhvillimit marramendës që kishin marrë ato në shekullin e njëzetë. Një nga detyrat që dilte përpara Realizmit Socialist ishte mesazhi i fitores së njeriut mbi teknologjinë. Për këtë arsye tek Kristo shohim një plan të parë ku "fluturojnë aviatorët" por pa avionët e tyre. *Qielli iu përket njerëzve dhe jo makinave.* Pra, nëse Kristo do t'i pikturonte aviatorët në kabinat e avionëve duke drejtuar mjetet e tyre, ai do të prodhonte një situatë përshkruese, tregimtare e të pavlerë për Realizmin Socialist. Nga ana tjetër, kjo është ajo që bëjnë aviatorët gjithandej – fluturojnë me avionët e tyre. *Këtë bëjnë dhe ata të perëndimit që i shërbejnë sistemit kapitalist.* Kështu që fluturimi në thonjëza bëhet fluturimi i vërtetë për Realizmin Socialist dhe jo fluturimi i njëmendët. Ishte e nevojshme që ky fluturim të kryhej pa u ngritur aspak në qiell, (ai i duhet lënë së ardhmes) sepse ashtu ai fluturim mishëronte më së miri natyrën dialektike të realitetit dhe të vetë aviatorëve. Ata janë qënie në transformim e sipër. Janë produkt i drejtpërdrejtë i revolucionit. Sinteza marksiste (apo hegeliane) e paraqitjes së tyre duhej përbërë nga fluturimi i tyre (teza) ndërkohë që janë ende në tokë (antiteza). Natyrisht ishte e nevojshme që e gjithë kjo të kryhej me mjetet tradicionale të pikturimit dhe t'i përmbahej metodës realiste të paraqitjes së formës (deviza ishte e qartë: *socialiste në përmbajtje, realiste në formë*). Këmbët e aviatorëve janë të mbështetura në tokë por vija e horizontit ndodhet mu aty ku mbarojnë kyçet, duke ia lënë kështu komplet trupin e tyre marrëdhënies me qiellin. Asgjë e pazakontë këtu për shikuesin e mësuar me formën realiste të paraqitjes. Madje figurat janë në pozicione bashkëbisedimi krejtësi-

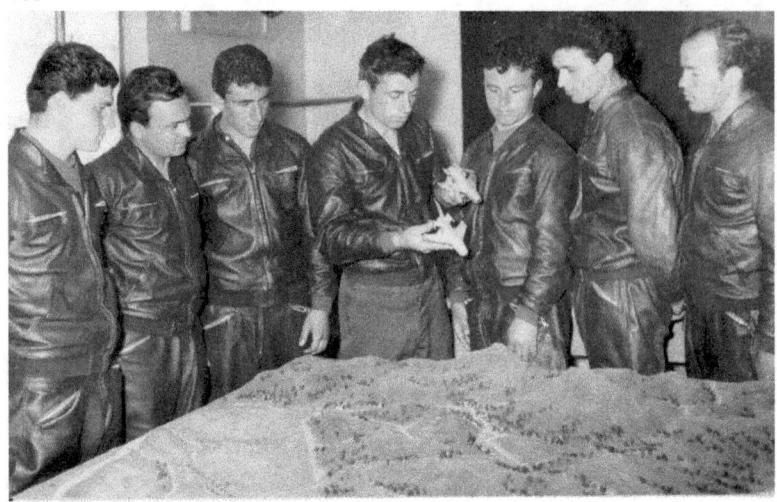

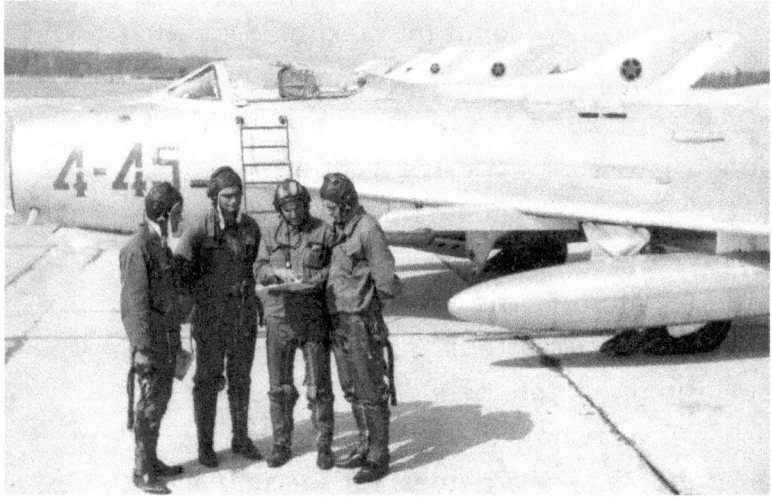

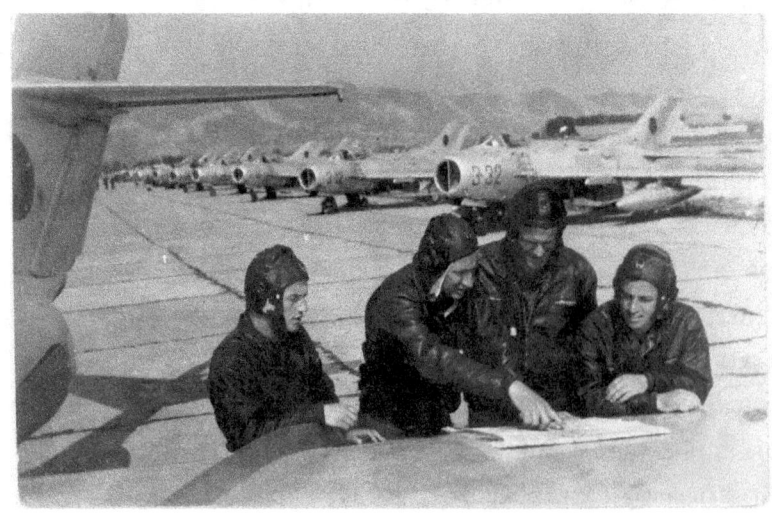

Armando Lulaj, *Pilots Playing with Airplanes* (1970), b/w print, 10 x 15 cm, 2015.

Armando Lulaj, *Aviatorë që luajnë me avione* (1970), stampim bardhezi, 10 x 15 cm, 2015.

Armando Lulaj, *Flying Day / 2* (1968), b/w print, 37 x 50 cm, 2014.

Armando Lulaj, *Ditë fluturimi / 2* (1968), stampim bardhezi, 37 x 50 cm, 2014.

Armando Lulaj, *Flying Day / 1*, b/w print, 37 x 50 cm, 2014.

Armando Lulaj, *Ditë fluturimi / 1* (1968), stampim bardhezi, 37 x 50 cm, 2014.

sht të natyrshme, mes tyre duke e bërë gjithë interpretimin artistik një operacion shumë delikat e pothuajse të padukshëm që nuk bërtet por përpiqet të depërtojë butësisht tek spektatori. Ky i fundit duhej përfshirë në vepër pasi ajo i drejtohej atij, jo si një shikuesi që gjen kënaqësinë tek soditja e artit, as si një blerësi potencial të saj (tregu i artit nuk ekziston) por si një qenie që duhej edukuar përmes artit dhe për këtë arsye duhen respektuar shqisat e tij të perceptimit mimetik. Ajo që modernistët kërkonin të arrinin me shpërbërjen e paraqitjes së formës dhe shkatërrimit të mimesisit, tek Realizmi Socialist arrihet me riformësimin e tij nëpërmjet përmbajtjes. Synimi i të dy palëve ishte në fakt krijmi i një njeriu që shihte dhe perceptonte ndryshe botën: Njeriut të Ri. Ky synim gjithësesi, për stalinistët të cilët e kishin hedhur tutje artin e avantgardave të periudhës së revolucionit, i duhej lënë së ardhmes sepse vetëm ajo ishte ende e pakapur dhe e paperceptuar. Prandaj ky art, Realizmi Socialist, duhej të manifestonte atë që nuk kishte ndodhur akoma, dhe jo atë çka ishte realitet. Kjo është dhënë më së miri nga Kristo. Por ai shkon edhe më tej duke ndërtuar në planin e parë të tablosë një marrëdhënie të çuditshme mes një aviatori dhe dy modeleve të vegjël avionësh nga ata që përdoren për ushtrimet e instruktimit taktik të aviatorëve, qe ai mban në duar dhe ngre lart. Në pamje të parë kjo duket groteske, gati-gati infantile dhe qesharake! Si ka mundësi që një aviator që ngrihet në fluturim me avionin e tij modern të marrë pozat e një fëmije që ngre në duar avionë të vegjël lodra e i projekton ata në qiell? Si mundet që ajo që tashmë, për aviatorin është një rutinë të jetë njëkohësisht një ëndërr? Me sa duket, është pikërisht kjo pamundësi ajo që Kristo kërkon të sugjerojë me veprën e tij. *Aviatori nuk është bërë ende aviator. Ai e projekton veten si të tillë çdo ditë nga fillimi.* Ky proces është i pafundmë dhe Kristo do të na tregojë këtë pafundësi.

Ndërkohë që avionët e vegjël të instruktimit dhe ilustrimit të fluturimit janë vendosur në planin e parë të tablosë, (në fund të fundit Realizmi Socialist është çështje ilustrimi instruksionesh) avionët e vërtetë janë tej në pistë, në një plan të tretë si objektet e fundit për nga rëndësia në tablo dhe kjo siç e thamë nuk është një rastësi. Ata nuk duhet të marrin prioritetin e objekteve instruktuese, madje përbëjnë një rrezik për instruktimin e duhur njerëzor. Kjo nënshtresë filozofike me prejardhje romantike ishte një kusht i domosdoshëm për Realizmin Socialist stalinist, i cili përpiqej me të gjitha mënyrat për të shmangur produktin e një Frankensteini socialist, qënien fatale gjysmë njeri e gjysmë makinë, që propagandonte Perëndimi dhe fashizmi si ideologji në vitet mes dy luftrave botërore. Ajo që formësoi Realizmin Socialist në fillim të viteve 1930 më shumë se çdo gjë tjetër ishte në fakt nevoja e një arti të ndryshëm prej atij perëndimor. Gjetja e këtyre ndryshimeve u bë pista e kërkimit të artistëve dhe ideologëve sovjetikë, ose e përzjerjes së këtyre dy specieve në një, më mirë të themi, kur vjen fjala për artistët e Realizmit Socialist. Gjithësesi gjërat më thelbësore na vijnë prej vetë Stalinit, apo të paktën kështu janë servirur. Një nga këto ka qenë edhe shprehja e famshme, apo jehona e saj, që (ndonëse tridhjetë vjet me vonesë) mbërriti deri në Shqipëri "Të mësojmë nga klasikët", e cila në të vërtetë nuk donte të thoshte se Realizmi Socialist ishte vazhdimësi e artit klasik por se ky art duhej parë si një trashëgimi e cila dikur kontrollohej nga klasat sunduese por që tashmë duke ndërruar "pronar" e duke rënë në duar të tjera, nëpërmjet interpretimit marksist duhej vënë në shërbim të klasës punëtore njësoj siç u vunë në shërbim të saj mjetet e prodhimit, fabrikat, armët, avionët...

E gjithë trashëgimia kulturore e botës ishte në shërbim të Realizmit Socialist, përfshirë edhe modernizmin, i cili thjesht duhej fshehur brenda paraqitjes "realiste". (Në fakt Realizmi Socialist është një lloj derivati i tij.) Pikërisht këtë arrin Kristo me anë të avionëve të vegjel në duart e aviatorit "infantil". Ata janë një lloj mekanizmi modernist i fshehur që shërben për të krijuar shpërbërjen mimetike me anë të mjeteve realiste. Ky lloj figuracioni i cili më kujton letërsinë e Edgar Allan Poe-së (e cila i parapriu letërsisë moderniste apo le të themi ishte njëherësh romantike dhe moderniste), është mënyra më e mirë për ta ripropozuar figuracionin pa e shpërbërë mimesin siç bënin artistët modernistë. Tek "Sfinksi" (1846), Poe flet për një personazh i cili pas një tronditjeje të fortë, fillon të shquajë në horizontin që shihte prej dritares së tij, një përbindësh gjigand i cili në fund të tregimit del se ishte thjesht një insekt i vogël që dukej i tillë për shkak se personazhi kishte humbur aftësinë për të shquar distancat dhe perceptonte si diçka që ishte larg atë që kalonte fare pranë syrit të tij. Pikërisht nocionin e distancës vë në lojë edhe Kristo në tablonë e tij nëpërmjet aviatorit që ngre "në fluturim" dy modele avionësh në duart e tij. Ajo që ai synon është "humbja" e kësaj aftësie apo një lloj modifikimi "i vogël" perceptues pa hequr dorë nga piktura figurative. Piktura e tij mbetet "realiste" por ajo është një ripropozim mimetik i realitetit pas shpërbërjes së tij konceptuale. Ky modifikim i aparatit perceptues të përmasave, distancave dhe hapësires dhe rindërtimi i tij pas kolapsit të nevojshëm (ajo që tek "Sfinksi" për Poe-në është fundi i botës, sëmundja e kolerës, për sovjetikët është revolucioni) do të thoshte ndërhyrje tek shikuesi dhe jo tek tabloja. Kështu që Kristo e përdor figuracionin në kah të kundërt me "Sfinksin" e Poe-së. Ai nëpërmjet tij synon të tregojë rritjen e përmasave të njeriut që projekton avionët në qiell, dhe jo atë të modeleve të vogla të avionëve siç mund të duken prej perspektivës së aviatorit. Ai e transferon modifikimin e perceptimit nga personazhi, aviatori i tablosë, tek shikuesi i saj, duke i kërkuar këtij (ky është edukimi i masave) të dallojë në tablo njeriun gjigand që mban në duar dy avionë "të vërtetë". Madhësia e modeleve të vogla të avionëve është e tillë në tablo që ata mund të perceptohen fare mirë si avionë në fluturim, nga perspektiva e shikuesit. Kjo është arsyeja pse Kristo e mbush qiellin me shiritat e bardhë të gazrave të cilët lidhen mirë me avionët e vegjël në duart e njeriut dhe "e gënjejnë" shikuesin sikur kanë dale prej këtyre avionëve dhe jo prej avionëve në fluturim, të cilët siç e thashë që në krye të shkrimit, nuk i shohim ose janë pothuajse të padukshëm për t'i prishur punë këtij inskenimi. Kjo i "vë" avionet në qiell dhe në "fluturim", kurse gjigandin e kthen në një lloj dirigjenti të realitetit dhe në arsyen e vërtetë pse këta avionë janë në fluturim. Këtu kemi një problem, ose të pakten ky ka qenë i tillë për stalinistët. Gjigandi është një përbindësh! Sado të fshihet pas figuracionit dhe interpretimeve të perspektivës ai rriskon të mbetet i tillë për atë që do të mund ta lexojë tablonë. Sigurisht që baba Stalini nuk e fshihte ambicjen për të qenë një Frankenstein, një ringjallës, modifikues dhe prodhues i një përbindëshi që u pagëzua me emrin Njeriu i Ri, por mbështetja e tij tek parimi i dialektikës kërkonte që procesi i ringjalljes (kjo kushtëzohej nga vdekja e njeriut të vjetër) nëpërmjet modifikimit të aparatit perceptues të realitetit të ishte i përditshëm dhe i pafundëm. Ndërkohë nga ana tjetër besoj se një nga zgjidhjet e Realizmit Socialist ishte përbindëshi i mirë. Gjigandi naiv apo infantil të cilin Kristo e ka realizuar me shumë sukses. Ndërhyrja e tij "kirurgjikale" tek "hipofiza" e aviatorit është krejtësisht e padukshme por njëkohësisht e mjaftueshme për të na zbërthyer tërë tablonë si një sërë instruksionesh të ilustruara. Siç sapo e përmenda, krijimi i gjigandit kompesohet me faktin që ai është naiv, fëminor, ka aftësinë për të luajtur apo për të ëndërruar dhe rrjedhimisht është edhe i parrezikshëm për botën. Një nga pretendimet e Realizmit Socialist përballë kundërshtarëve të tij ishte humanizmi që ai manifestonte dhe lidhja e tij me humanizmin e gjetur tek trashëgimia kulturore e para revolucionit. Prandaj aviatori merr përsipër rriskun të duket pak i leshtë në sytë tanë. Në fund të fundit vetë uniforma që ai mban veshur është një aspekt shumë i rrezikshëm për humanizmin që ky art merr përsipër të manifestojë. Ku ndryshon ajo nga uniforma e një aviatori të perëndimit që i shërben sistemit kapitalist? Madje ndër gjithë uniformat e mundshme të armëve të ndryshme ushtarake, ajo duket më aliene, më e huaj dhe më futuriste (fashiste) se të gjitha. Ky aspekt naivizmi i këtij aviatori përpiqet të kompensojë hostilitetin e uniformës që ai mban veshur dhe të profesionit të tij, atë të individit të pregatitur të mbartë në ajër kilogramë të tëra arsenali vrasës dhe të shkaktojë viktima të panumërta njerëzore në kohë rekord. Me shumë takt Kristo ka krijuar, aspak rastësisht, një marrëdhënie kompozicionale mes katër figurave të aviatorëve që përbëjnë planin e parë të tablosë. Ndërkohë që i pari (naivi), paksa i veçuar prej të tjerëve, ngre lart avionët e vegjël të ilustrimit taktik në klasa, ai tërheq vëmendjen e dy shokëve të tij, të katërtit dhe të tretit, të cilët ndërkohë janë pranë të dytit, i cili nga ana e tij, nuk tërhiqet nga gjestet e të parit. I dyti vazhdon ta mbajë shikimin mbërthyer mbi bllokun e tij të shënimeve ku diçka shkruan dhe iu shpjegon të tjerëve. Ky, me gjasa komandanti i skuadriljes është i përqëndruar tek blloku i tij, ndoshta tek itinerari i fluturimit, kuotat e lartësisë etj., dhe duket sikur po ua shpjegon ato të tjerëve, të tretit dhe të katërtit, por këta e kanë shpërngulur shikimin e tyre prej bllokut

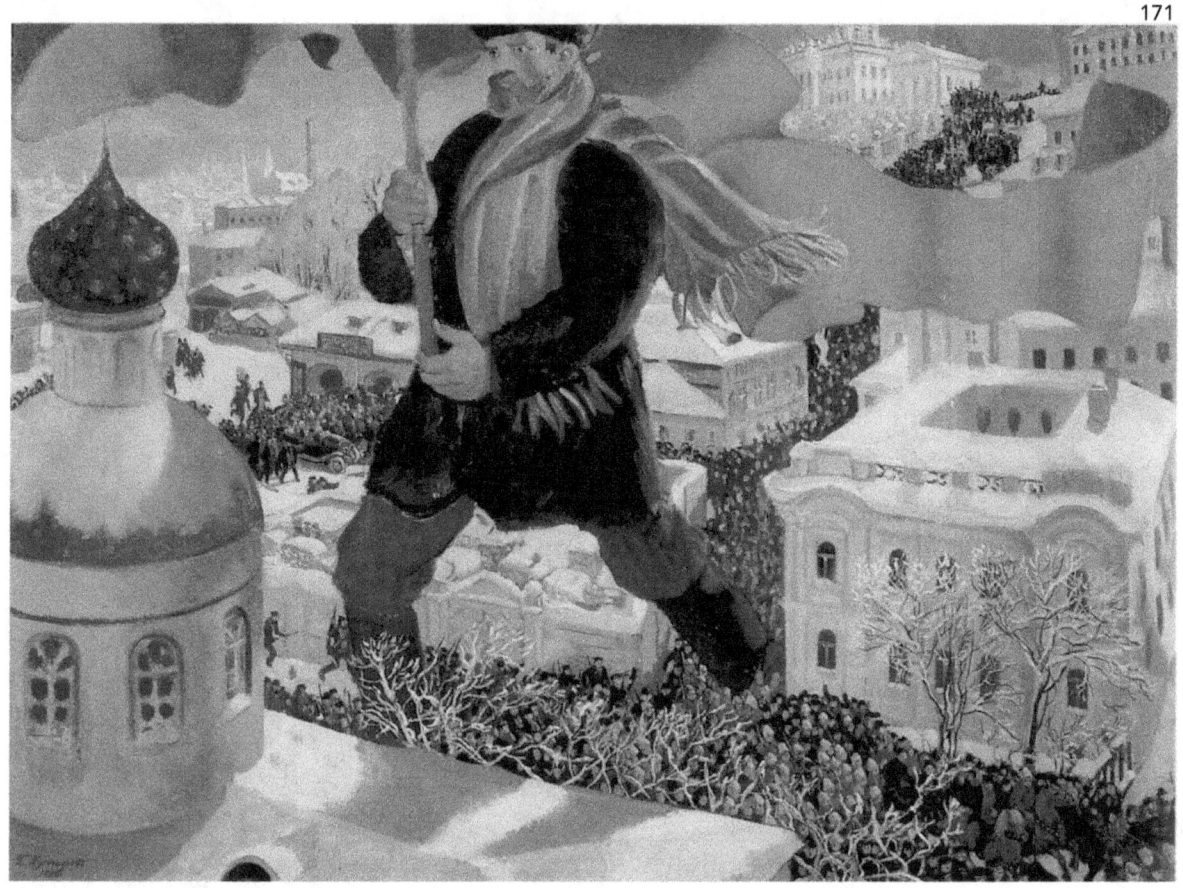

dhe duket se janë "marrosur" edhe ata prej avionëve lodër që ka ngritur lart naivi. Pra është i dukshëm superioriteti numerik i naivëve në
forcën e aviacionit dhe kjo bën që rreziku i këtyre qënieve, që mbartin
dhe zotërojnë një arsenal kaq shfarrosës, të jetë i vogël për të dekon-
spiruar humanizmin e Realizmit Socialist. Ata ndryshe nga sivëllezërit
e tyre të flotave ajrore të kapitalizmit nuk janë thjesht makina lufte. Ata
janë humanë që ëndërrojnë. *Të qënit aviatorë është thjesht një rastësi,
siç është çdo profesion tjetër i kanalizuar prej procesit historik të kapitalizmit.* Madje Kristo e ka kthyer në avantazhin e vet uniformën e tyre
aliene duke krijuar me të një lloj standarti për t'u përdorur. Aviatorët
naivë janë në konflikt me uniformat e tyre. Kjo ndërton dialektikën e
domosdoshme të aviatorit. Uniforma është antitezë e natyrës njerëzore të atij që e mban atë veshur dhe kjo natyrë duhet theksuar nëpërmjet
gjesteve që ai bën dhe që janë kontradiktore me paraqitjen e tij.
Ndërkohë ka edhe një marrëdhënie tjetër po aq interesante. Ajo e

Boris Kustodiev, *The Bolshevik,* oil on
canvas, 140 x 180 cm, 1920.

Boris Kustodijev, *Bolsheviku,* vaj në
pëlhurë, 140 x 180 cm, 1920.

grupit të aviatorëve të planit të parë me ata të planit të dytë. Këta si-gurisht në perspektivën e qëllimtë të ndërtuar nga autori, ku ndodhen pak a shumë në të njëjtin rrafsh me figurat e planit të parë duken të vegjël dhe të kujtojnë artin mesjetar ku madhësia e figurave nuk i nënshtrohet normave të perspektivës shkencore që prodhoi Rilindja Evropiane dhe ky është po ashtu një element përbërës i mekanizmit të fshehur modernist brenda tablosë. Marrëdhënia mes dy grupeve të aviatorëve bëhet ajo e "gjigandëve" me "shkurtabiqët". Kjo më kujton një lojë që bënim kur ishim fëmijë dhe që konsistonte në një grup që i përgjigjej komandave të një individi të zgjedhur prej tyre (ose të vetëzgjedhur) që thërriste "gjigandi" dhe fëmijët duhej të qëndronin drejt, pastaj thërriste "shkurtabiqi" dhe fëmijët duhej të uleshin galiç. Thirrjet e këtyre komandave gradualisht bëheshin të shpejta dhe ritmi që krijohej mes lëvizjeve të fëmijëve, të cilët për shkak të kondicione-ve të ndryshme fizike nuk i përgjigjeshin dot njësoj komandave, krijon-te një disharmoni në lëvizjen e tyre kolektive pas harmonisë dhe sin-kronizmit të fillimit kur komandat ishin më të kapshme prej tyre. "Komandanti" i lojës përpiqej me çdo mënyrë t'i ngatërronte lojtarët dhe përsëritja e të njëjtës komandë disa herë ishte mënyra më e mirë për ta arritur këtë dhe për të krijuar entuziazmin e lojës dhe garën e vërtetë mes lojtarëve. Loja "gjigandi dhe shkurtabiqi" duket se mi-shëron më së miri frymën e dialektikës dhe për mua është një kuriozi-tet të kuptoj se si kishte lindur kjo lojë apo pse, fjala vjen, ajo i përket vetëm periudhës së fëmijërisë sime, që përkon me kohën kur stali-nizmi dhe fryma automatizuese e shoqërisë ka jetuar kulmin e vet në Shqipëri, dhe pse që atëherë nuk e kam parë të luhet më!

Sigurisht që Kristo nuk ka aspak ndërmend të na ritregojë artin bizantin dhe mesjetar me gjigandët dhe shkurtabiqët e tablosë së tij. Figura e gjigandit shfaqet edhe në një tablo tjetër të tij (*Zotër të ven-dit*, 1969) dhe mendoj se është një rimarrje që e ka origjinën e vet tek një pikturë e avant-gardës ruse. *Bolsheviku* (1920), i Boris Kustodijev-it tregon një gjigand që shfaqet mes një turrme manifestuesish (liliputë) dhe mban në dorë flamurin e kuq. Tregimi i gjigandit te Kustodijevi bëhet hapur dhe tabloja e tij nuk ndryshon aspak nga modernizmi perëndimor kështu që ajo nuk iu përshtat aspak artit që kërkonin sovjetikët në fillim të viteve 1930, ndonëse i përket së njëjtës ideologji. Tek Kristo gjigandi është i fshehur, ose mes thonjëzash dhe ai mund të dallohet vetëm nëse kemi përvetësuar instruksionet. Kristo kërkon të na tregojë jo thjesht një gjigand përballë një shkurtabiqi në raportin përmasor mes tyre por procesin e zhvillimit të këtij raporti, një proces metaforik, konstant e të pafundëm transformimi të individit nga "shkurtabiq" në "gjigand" apo edhe anasjelltas sepse piktura e tij rreket të transmetojë pikërisht një dinamikë që shkon drejt pafundësisë dhe jo realitete statike e të fundme.

Siç e thashë edhe më lart e gjithë tabloja *Ditë Fluturimi* është një kërkim trajtimesh artistike të sugjeruara nga problematikat dhe njohja e mirë e tezave të Realizmit Socialist. Ajo është një inskenim i botës sipas paradigmave të dhëna nga këto teza dhe jo një përshkrim i saj. Kjo të bën të mendosh se çdo referencë me vende apo njerëz realë është e pavlerë. Kristo ka zgjedhur pikërisht aerodromin dhe aviatorët, si simbolet e duhura për të ndërtuar tensionet specifike që ai do të ndërtojë në tablo dhe jo sepse kishte për qëllim të tregonte punën dhe jetën e aviatorëve të "x" aerodromi. Sigurisht ai mund të ketë përdorur ambjentet e aerodromit të Rinasit por ka ditur se si dhe çfarë do të bënte në Rinas që para se të shkonte aty. Shfaqje të tilla të një përmbushjeje të kërkesave të Realizmit Socialist dhe të një kompleksi marrëdhëniesh të trajtuara me efikasitet brenda një tabloje të vetme, e bëjnë këtë pikturë një shembull të asimilimit të Realizmit Socialist stalinist në artin tonë. Megjithatë siç e thashë në fillim të shkrimit, vepra si *Ditë Fluturimi* nuk gjenden me shumicë në koleksionin e Galerisë sonë Kombëtare. Druaj, madje, se vepra si kjo as nuk janë kuptuar apo zbërthyer nga ana e kritikës së kohës dhe më së shumti për to është shkruar e folur, ndoshta, në ndonjë mbledhje nga ato ku analizoheshin planet dhe realizimi apo mosrealizimi i tyre dhe ku ajo mund të jetë përmendur si një statistikë për realizimin e planit apo si një vepër e realizuar me sukses, me rastin e ndonjë përvjetori të forcave ushtarake, pa i hyrë kurrë analizimit të problemeve artistike që kjo vepër trajtonte dhe zgjidhte brenda vetes.

Kanë kaluar plot dyzeteshtatë vjet që kur kjo pikturë është realizuar dhe gjashtë vjet që ajo është riekspozuar (shpluhurosur) duke zënë

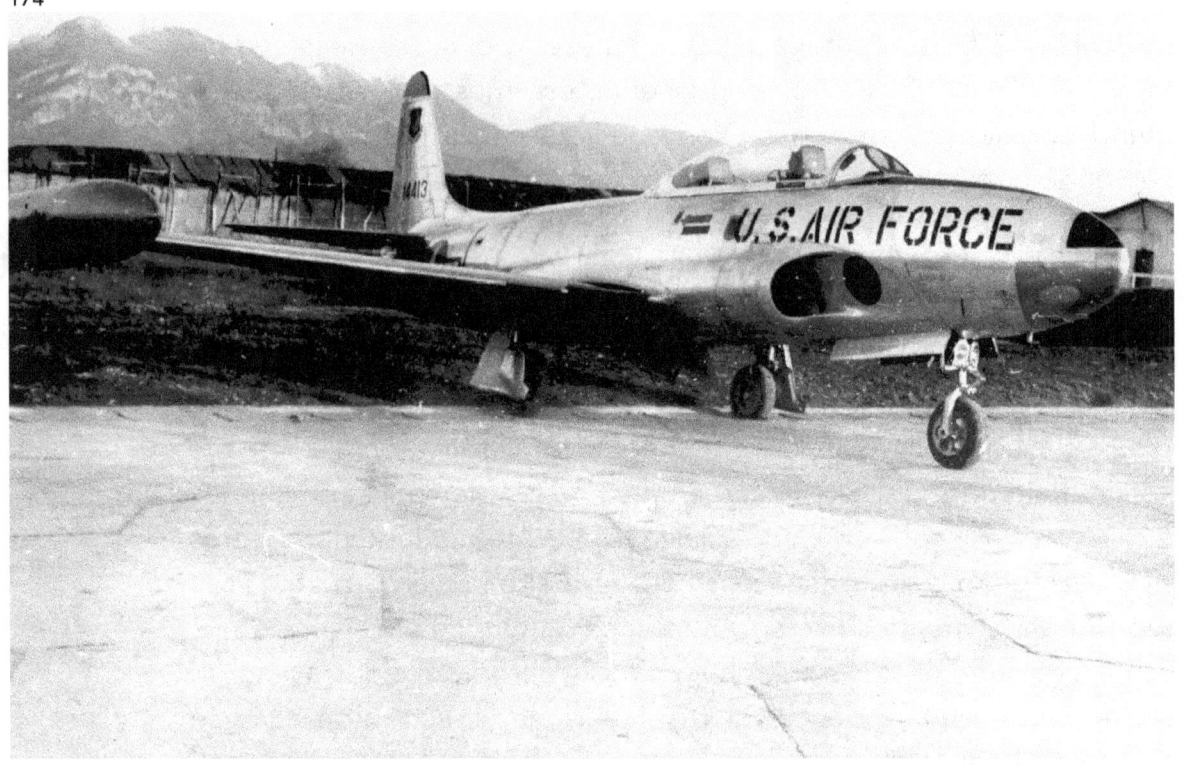

një vend në ekspozitën që tregon koleksionin kombëtar të artit, për të cilën unë kam punar, dhe këtë tekst e shoh si një shërbim të vonuar që i bëj shikuesit të kësaj ekspozite. Edhe vetë vonesa e këtij shkrimi tregon se marrëdhënia jonë me Realizmin Socialist nuk është stabilizuar ende. Ajo mbahet ende peng i paragjykimeve, komplekseve, keqkuptimeve dhe i moskuptimit në masë të gjerë i këtij arti prej audiencave (por jo vetëm prej tyre). Siç e përmenda gjatë shkrimit, dhe siç thotë edhe Boris Groys, shkrimet e të cilit kanë ndikuar mjaft në konkluzionet e mia mbi Realizmin Socialist, ky art i drejtohej në mënyrë impenjative shikuesit të vet. Ai kërkonte përfshirjen dhe përpjekjen e audiencës së vet (dikur klasa punëtore) që ajo të vinte në nivelin e artistit që e realizonte. Pra shikuesi i *Ditës së Fluturimit* nuk mund ta dallojë gjigandin në tablo nëse ai vetë nuk ngrihet në lartësinë e gjigandit (që do të thotë të bëhet i aftë të lexojë instruksionet). Kjo është kërkesa para së cilës e vë Kristo klasën punëtore. Por në realitet kjo nuk ndodhi. Është e qartë se audiencat shqiptare të Realizmit Socialist mbetën shkurtabiqe gjatë periudhës së socializmit, dhe po ashtu edhe ato

Armando Lulaj, *US Spy Plane* (1957), b/w print, 30 x 45 cm, 2015.

Armando Lulaj, *Avion amerikan spiunazhi* (1957), stampim bardhezi, 30 x 45 cm, 2015.

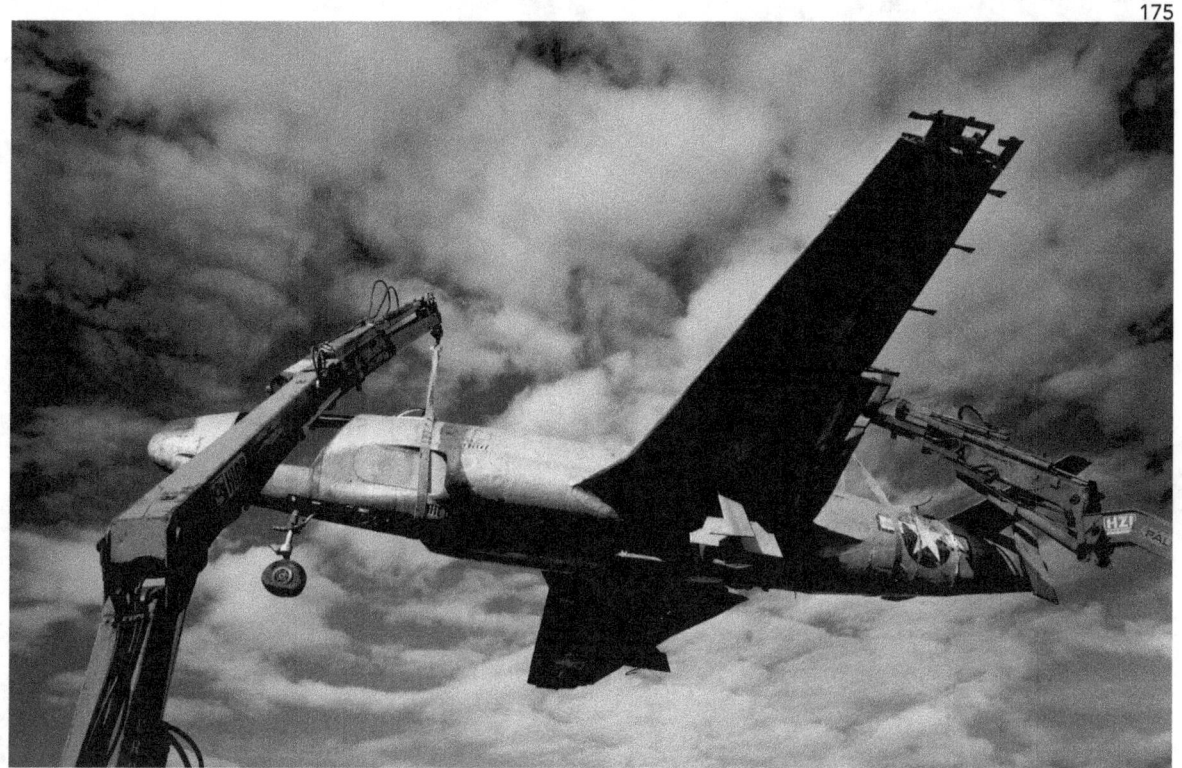

të pas viteve nëntëdhjetë, por duke qenë se projekti (i braktisur) i Njeriut të Ri është një projekt që gjithmonë i përket së ardhmes, misioni i Realizmit Socialist është i destinuar të mbetet i vlefshëm. Këtë, në Shqipërinë e ndarë ende kulturalisht nga Perëndimi e ndihmon edhe mungesa e tregut të artit dhe institucioneve që kontrollojnë dhe sanksionojnë vlerat e tij. Ky art në Shqipëri vazhdon të mbetet ende i lirë prej shtrëngesave të tregut dhe vazhdon të jetojë antagonizmin e tij me sistemin dhe tregun e artit njësoj si në fillimet e veta, por krahas kësaj ai vazhdon të jetojë mungesën e komunikimit me audiencën apo akoma më keq ka filluar të shihet thjesht si një lloj trofeu dekorues për të mbushur sfondin ku shfaqet herë pas here pushteti dhe elitat shkurtabiqe postkomuniste.

Armando Lulaj, *Recapitulation (American Spy Plane)*, b/w print, 115 x 180 cm, 2015.

Armando Lulaj, *Recapitulation (avion amerikan spiunazhi)*, stampim bardhezi, 115 x 180 cm, 2015.

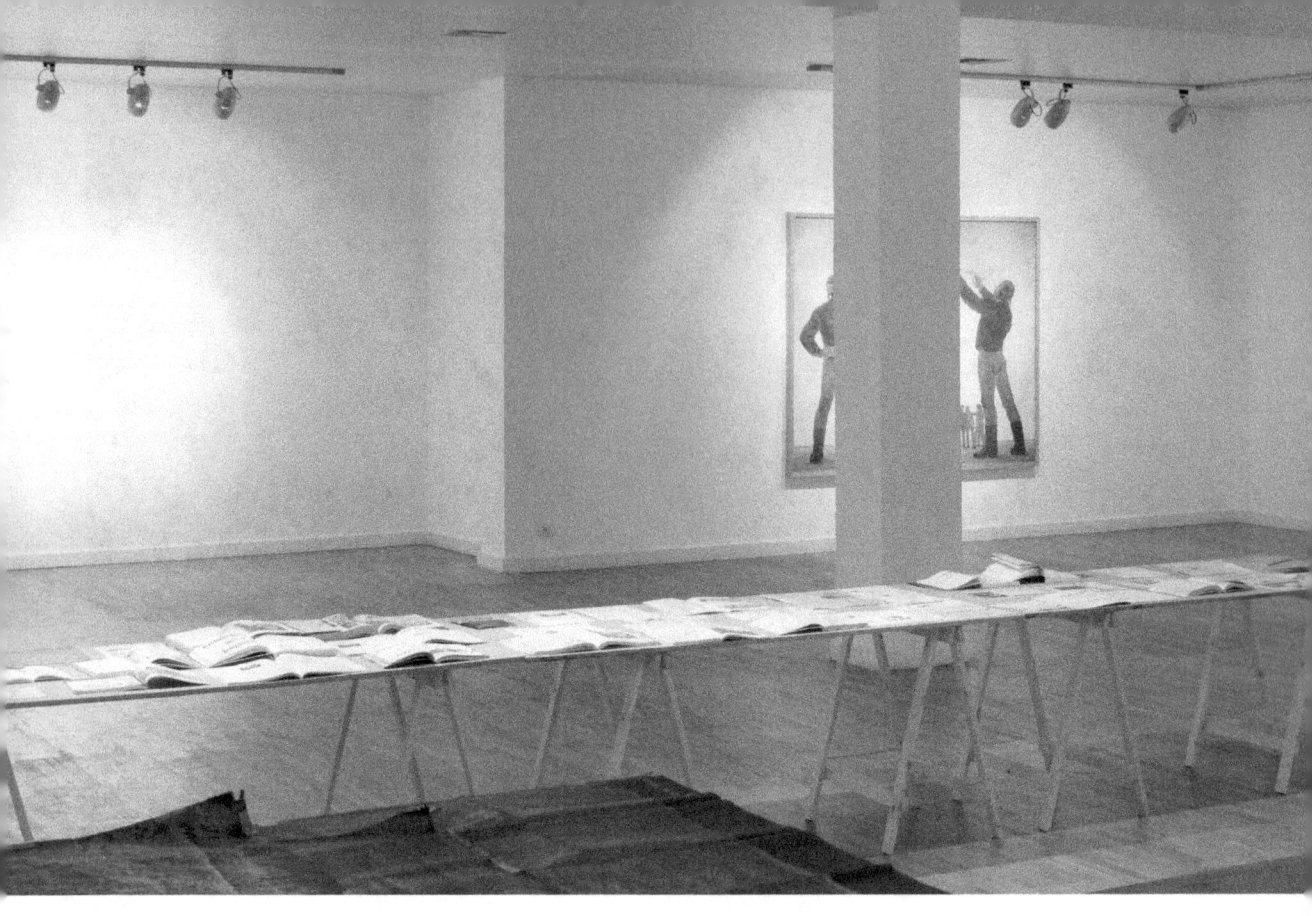

Exhibition view.

Pamje ekspozite.

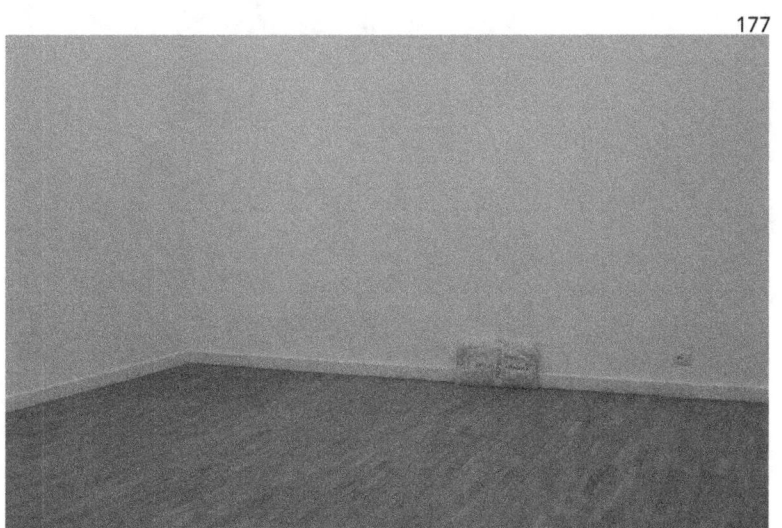

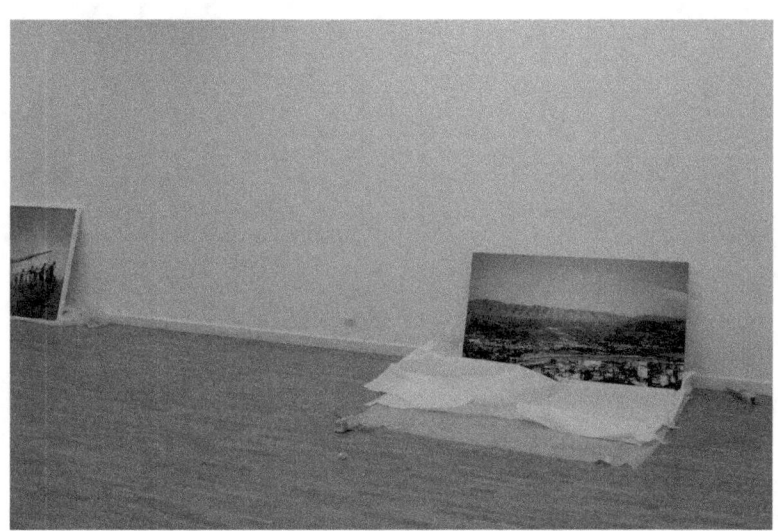

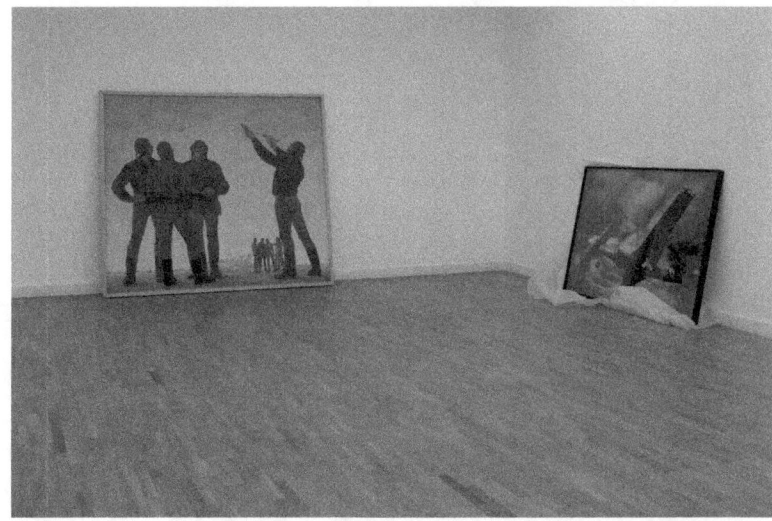

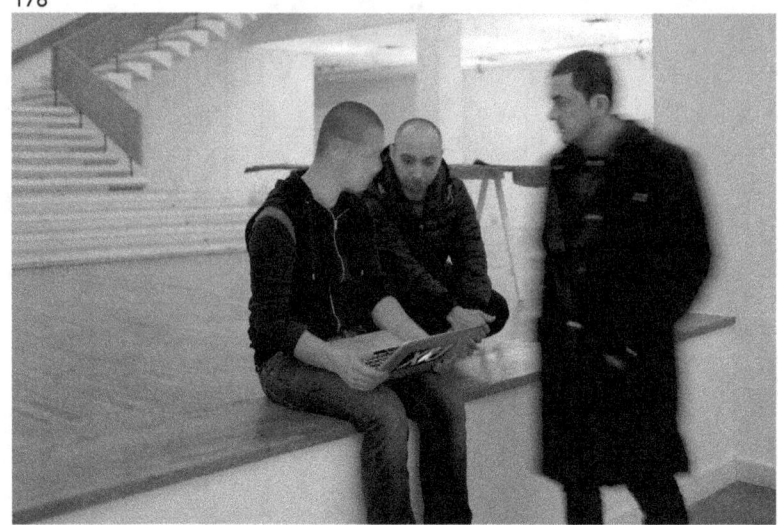

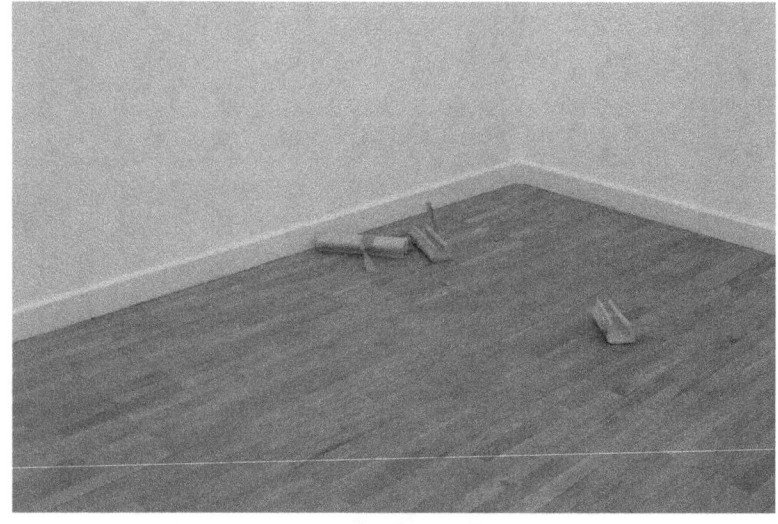

Armando Lulaj

It Wears as It Grows.

On May 25, 1959, at the height of the Cold War, Nikita Khrushchev visited Albania to implement the Soviet Union's plans to arm Enver Hoxha's state with submarines and warships, positioning long and medium-range missiles along the Albanian coast, in order to counter the U.S. missile bases installed in Italy for the sake of controlling the Mediterranean. In 1963, after the break in relations with the USSR, the Albanian navy, in a paranoid fear of enemy attacks, sighted an object that repeatedly appeared and disappeared at the surface of the sea off the coast at Patok. Believing it to be a submarine, they shot it. The object turned out to be a Cachalot, a Mediterranean sperm whale. The whale's remains were displayed in the Museum of Natural History in Tirana. In 2011, the skeleton of the whale reappears in the streets of Tirana, raised onto the shoulders of a group of people, like a ghost wandering around the streets of the city until it found its final resting place inside Enver Hoxha's mausoleum in Tirana, also known as "Piramida," completed in 1987, to glorify his figure and create an eternal monument to him.

NEVER

In 1968, at the height of the Cultural Revolution when relations between China and Albania reached their zenith, the Albanian Labor Party undertook an overtly ambitious initiative to celebrate the magnificence of their leader, Enver Hoxha. Hundreds of young people were forced to join the Albanian People's Army in this endeavor, where by means of enormous stones and white paint they spelled out the first name of the dictator on the side of the Shpirag mountain towering above the ancient town of Berat, across a surface area of approximately 36.000 square meters. In 1993, after the fall of communism, the Democratic Party took power. At their orders, the army attempted to destroy the letters using napalm and heavy military equipment. As a result of the explosions, the letters were almost destroyed, while two soldiers were burned alive in process. The plan was aborted, and, with the passing of the time, what could still be seen of the letters was covered in vegetation. In 2012, the inhabitants of the village return to unearth the letters and rewrite the name. After repeated acts of cleaning, uncovering, and painting, what materializes is however no longer the emblem enver, but something altered and erroneous. At the moment when the indeterminate becomes the determinate, the Albanian name enver returns as the English adverb never.

Recapitulation

On December 23, 1957, a Lockheed T-33 Shooting Star airplane of the us Air Force entered Albanian airspace. Allegedly, it was swiftly identified by two Albanian MiG-15 fighter jets and subsequently escorted and forced to land at Rinas Airport, which at the time was still under construction. The pilot, Major Howard J. Curran, a wwii hero, was held and interrogated by Albanian officials for over two weeks. Due to us diplomatic pressure Major Curran was released on January 11, 1958. The airplane, however, never left Albania. Around 1970, this relic of the Cold War found a home on the outskirts of the castle that hosts the Weapons Museum in Gjirokastër, the birth place of Enver Hoxha, with the label "American Spy Plane." In 2009, the Albanian government wanted to remove the remains of the plane because it was deemed an affront to the now friendly diplomatic relations with the us government. However, that same year, former us Ambassador to Albania, John L. Withers ii, stated that "history should not be revised." Immediately afterwards, a question mark appeared at the end of its label, so that what had been an affirmation turned into a question: "American Spy Plane?" In January 2015, the plane, deteriorated by neglect and the passage of time, has been set free from its confines at the Weapons Museum, entering yet another phase of martial history.

It Wears as It Grows. Më 25 maj 1959, në kulmin e Luftës së Ftohtë, Nikita Khrushchev bëri një vizitë në Shqipëri me synim vënien në jetë të planeve të Bashkimit Sovjetik për të armatosur shtetin e Enver Hoxhës me nëndetëse dhe anije luftarake, duke vendosur raketa me rreze të mesme e të gjata në pika të caktura të bregdetit shqiptar. Kjo ishte një kundërpërgjigje ndaj bazave amerikane të raketave të vendosura në Itali, me qëllim kontrollin e Mesdheut. Në vitin 1963, pas prishjes me brss-në, flota shqiptare, e trembur deri në paranojë nga një sulm i mundshëm armik, dalloi në brigjet e Patokut një objekt që vazhdimisht shfaqej mbi sipërfaqen e detit e pastaj zhdukej nën të. Duke menduar se kishin të benin me një nëndetëse, flota qëlloi. Në fakt, objekti ishte një Cachalot, balena mesdhetare, skeleti i së ciles me pas u ekspozua në Muzeun e Shkencave të Natyrës. Në vitin 2011, skeleti rishfaqet në Tirane, teksa endet porsi fantazmë nëpër rrugët e kryeqytetit, derisa më në fund gjen prehje brenda mauzoleut të Enver Hoxhës, e ashtuquajtura "Piramida", ndërtuar në vitin 1987 për të përlëvduar diktatorin si një monument i pavdekshëm kushtuar figurës së tij.

NEVER. Në vitin 1968, kur Revolucioni Kulturor ishte në kulmin e tij dhe marrdhëniet midis Shqipërisë dhe Kinës më të afërta se kurrë, Partia e Punës së Shqipërisë mori një nismë ambicioze për të kremtuar madhështine e udhëheqësit të saj, Enver Hoxhës. Qindra të rinj e të reja u detyruan t'i bashkohen ushtrisë në këtë sipërmarrje: shkrimin e emrit të diktatorit me gurë e gëlqere me një sipërfaqe rreth 36.000 metra katrorë mbi faqen e malit Shpirag, që ngrihet mbi qytetin antik të Beratit. Në vitin 1993, pas rënies së komunizmit, pushtetin e mori Partia Demokratike. Në zbatim të urdhrit të qeverisë së re, ushtria u përpoq t'i shkatërrojë shkronjat duke përdorur napalm dhe mjete të rënda ushtarake. Për pasojë, ndonëse shkronjat thuajse u shkatërruan, dy ushtarë u dogjën për vdekje. Kjo ngjarje e rënde bëri që plani të anulohet. Me kalimin e kohës, shkronjat u mbuluan nga barishtet. Në vitin 2012, banorët e zonës rikthehen për t'i zbuluar shkronjat e për të rishkruar emrin. Pas proceseve të pastrimit, zbulimit dhe lyerjes, ajo që shohim nuk është më emblema enver por ndajfolja angleze never.

Recapitulation. Më 23 dhjetor 1957, një avion i tipit Lockheed T-33 Shooting Star i Forcave Ajrore Amerikane hyri në hapësirën ajrore të Shqipërisë. Thuhet se avioni amerikan u identifikua menjëherë nga dy MiG-15 shqiptarë që e detyruan të ulet në Aeroportin e Rinasit, që asokohe ishte ende në ndërtim e siper. Piloti, Majori Howard J. Curran, një hero i Luftës së Dytë Botërore, u arrestua dhe u mor në pyetje nga zyrtaret shqiptare për mbi dy jave. Për shkak të presonit diplomatik të Shteteve të Bashkuara, Majori u la i lire në 11 janar 1958, ndërsa avioni mbeti në Shqipëri. Rreth vitit 1970, kjo relike e Luftës së Ftohtë u vendos në skaj të Muzeut të Armëve në Gjirokastër, vendlindja e Enver Hoxhës, dhe u etiketua "Avioni Spiun Amerikan". Në vitin 2009, qeveria shqiptare donte të shkatërronte çfarë kishte mbetur nga avioni duke qënë se marrëdheniet me Shtetet e Bashkuara tashmë ishin mjaft të mira dhe ekzistenca e avionit mund t'i dëmtonte ato. Megjithatë, po atë vit, Ambasadori i atëhershëm i Shteteve të Bashkuara në Tiranë, John L. Withers ii, u shpreh se "historia nuk duhet rishkruar". Në janar të vitit 2015, avioni i rrenuar nga mospërfillja dhe kalimi i kohes, le pas hapesirën e tij në Muzeum e Armeve për të hyre në një tjeter fazë të historisë së tij luftarake.

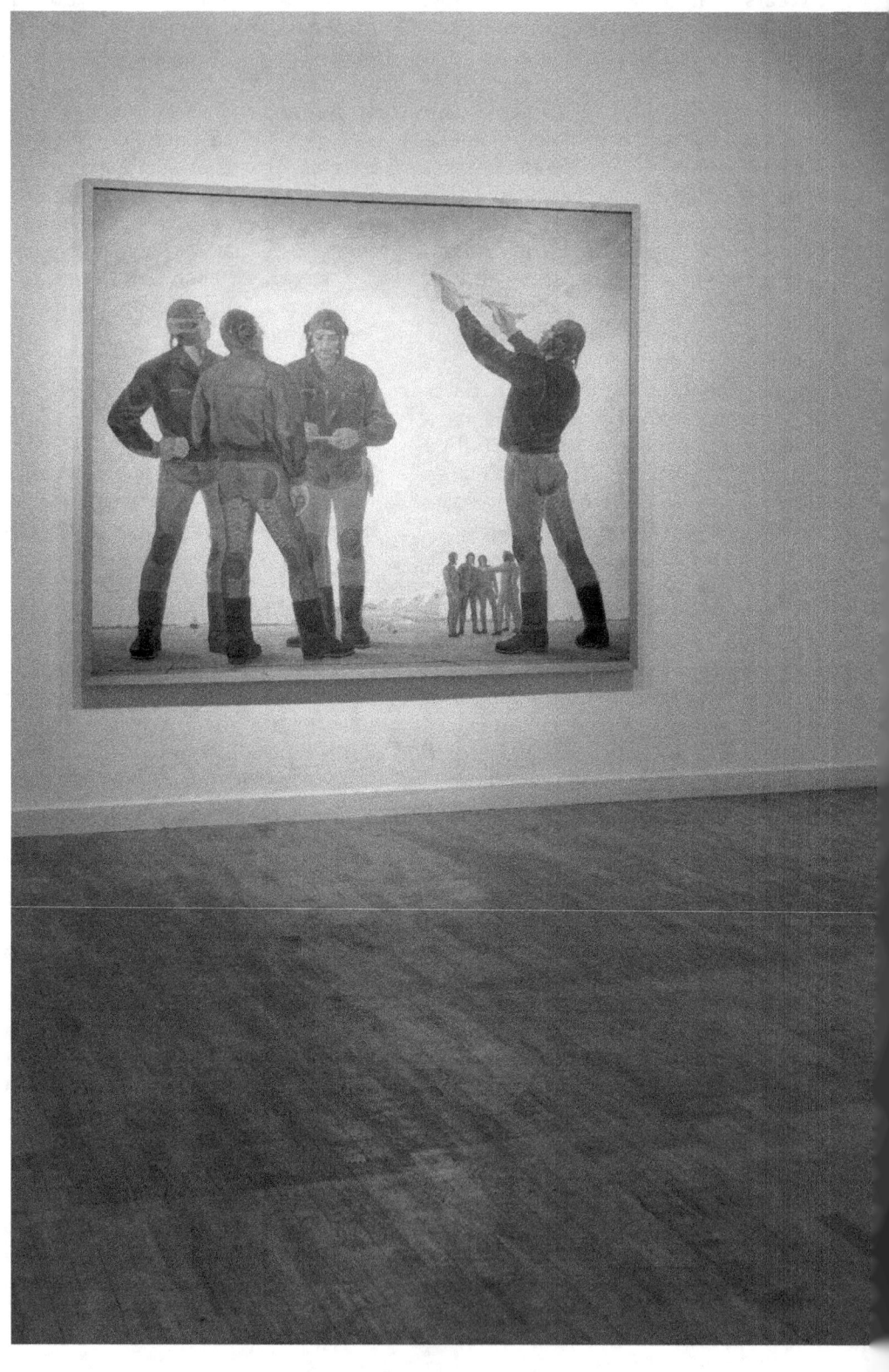

Spiro Kristo, *Flying Day (The Pilots of Division 7594, Rinas),* oil on canvas, 183 x 209 cm, 1968.

Spiro Kristo, *Ditë Fluturimi (Aviatorët e repartit 7594, Rinas),* vaj në pëlhurë, 183 x 209 cm, 1968.

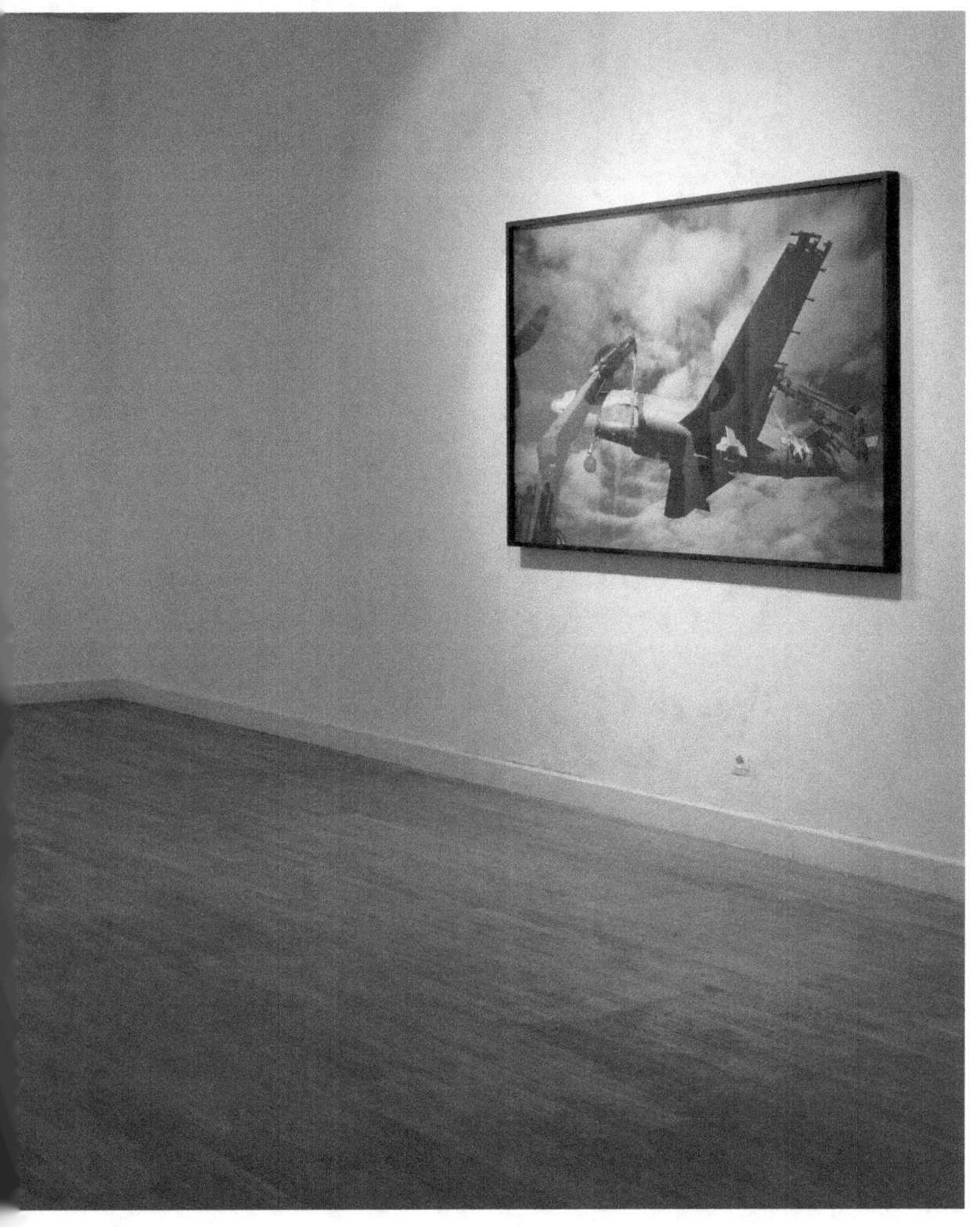

Armando Lulaj, *Recapitulation*, b/w print, 140 x 180 cm, 2015.

Armando Lulaj, *Recapitulation*, stampim bardhezi, 140 x 180 cm, 2015.

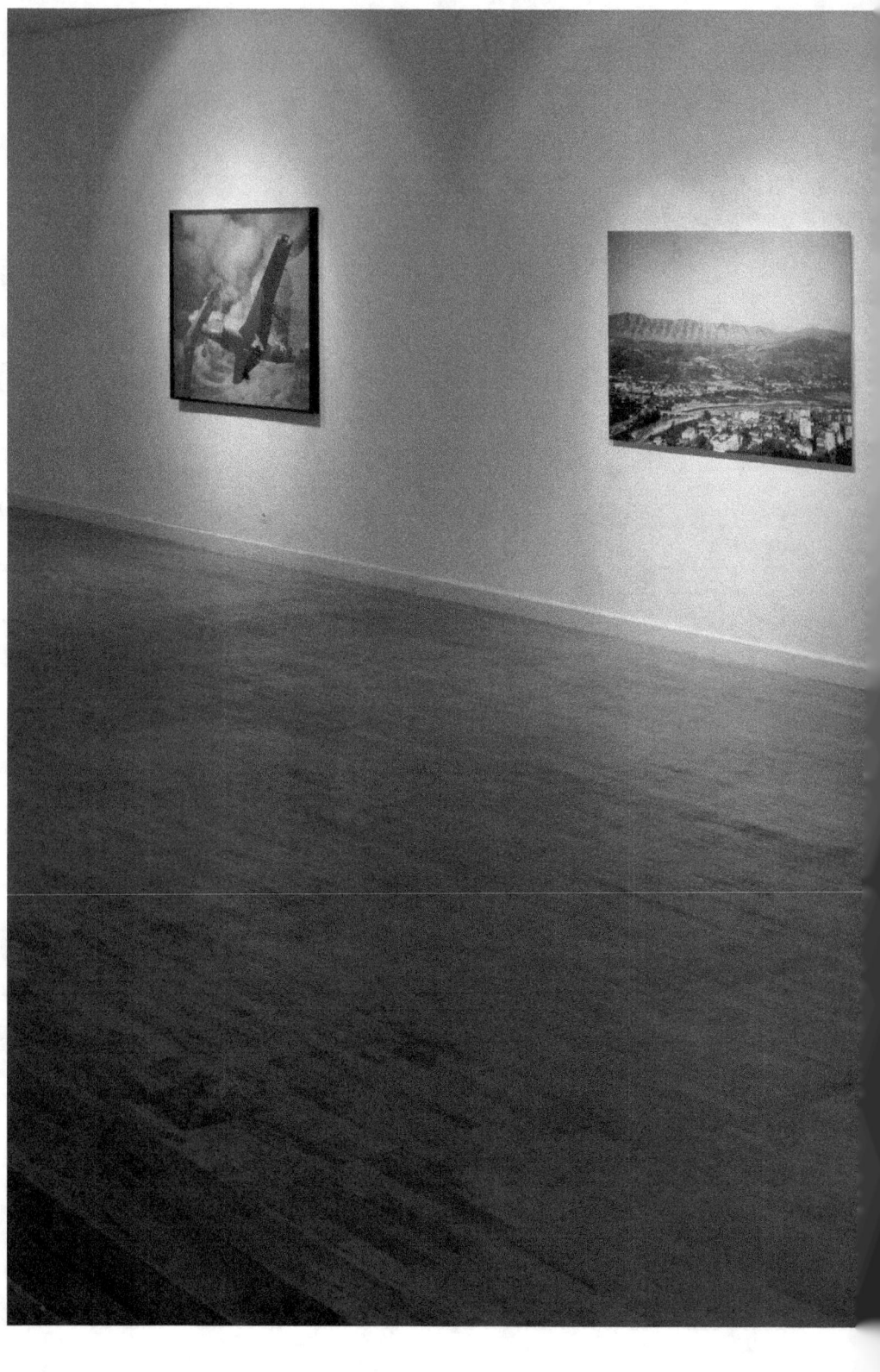

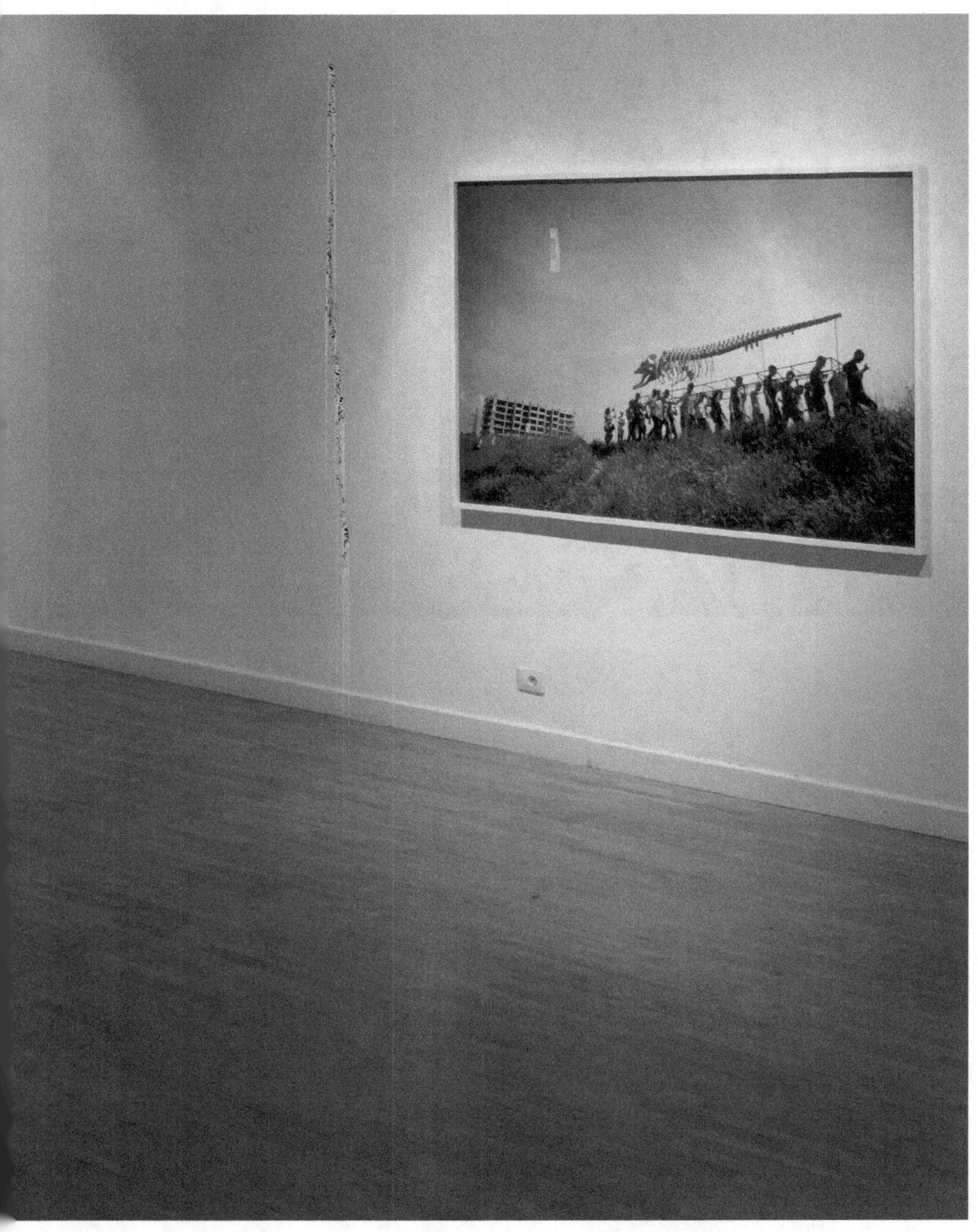

Armando Lulaj, *Recapitulation*, b/w print, 140 x 180 cm, 2015.

Armando Lulaj, *NEVER,* b/w print, 100 x 180 cm, 2012.

Armando Lulaj, *It Wears as It Grows,* c-print, 140 x 180 cm, 2011.

Armando Lulaj, *Recapitulation,* stampim bardhezi, 140 x 180 cm, 2015.

Armando Lulaj, *NEVER,* stampim bardhezi, 100 x 180 cm, 2012.

Armando Lulaj, *It Wears as It Grows,* c-print, 140 x 180 cm, 2011.

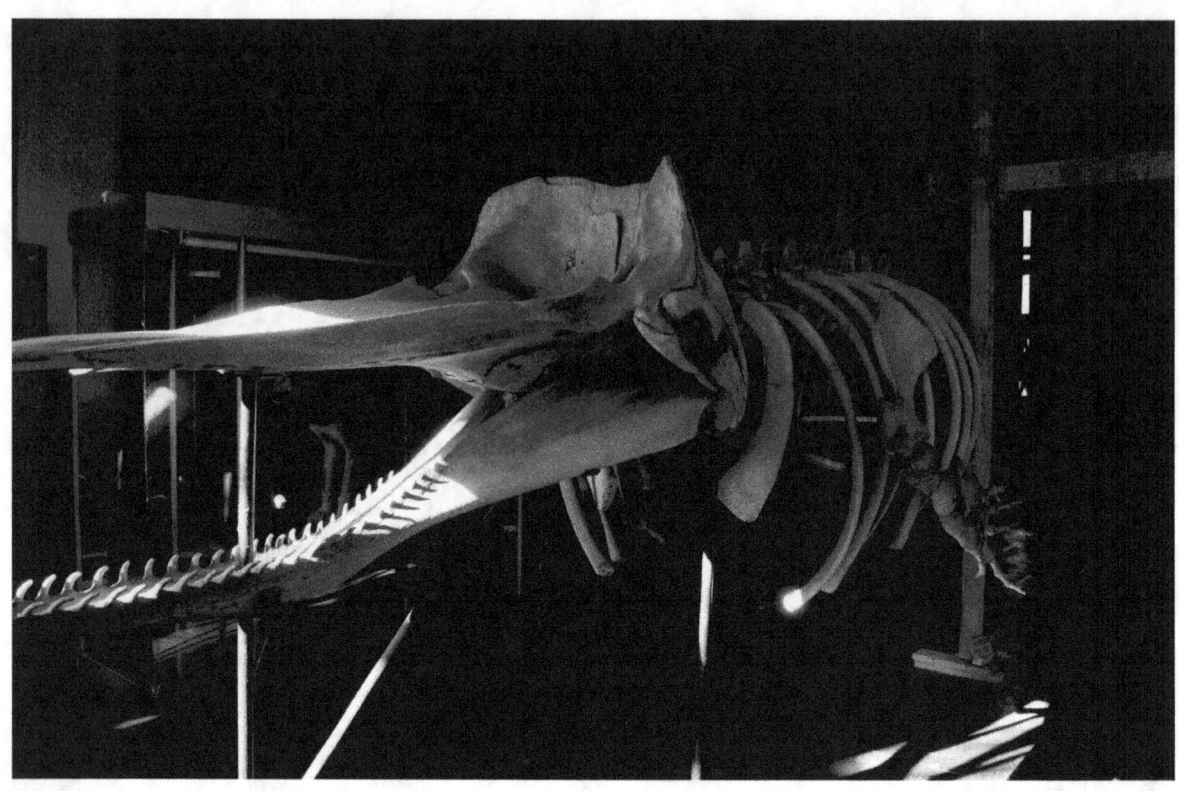

Armando Lulaj, *It Wears as It Grows*,
2011. Original cachalot skeleton
as displayed at the former Natural
History Museum in Tirana.

Armando Lulaj, *It Wears as It Grows*,
2011. Skeleti origjinal i kashalotit siç u
ekspozua në ish-Muzeun e Shkencave
Natyrore në Tiranë.

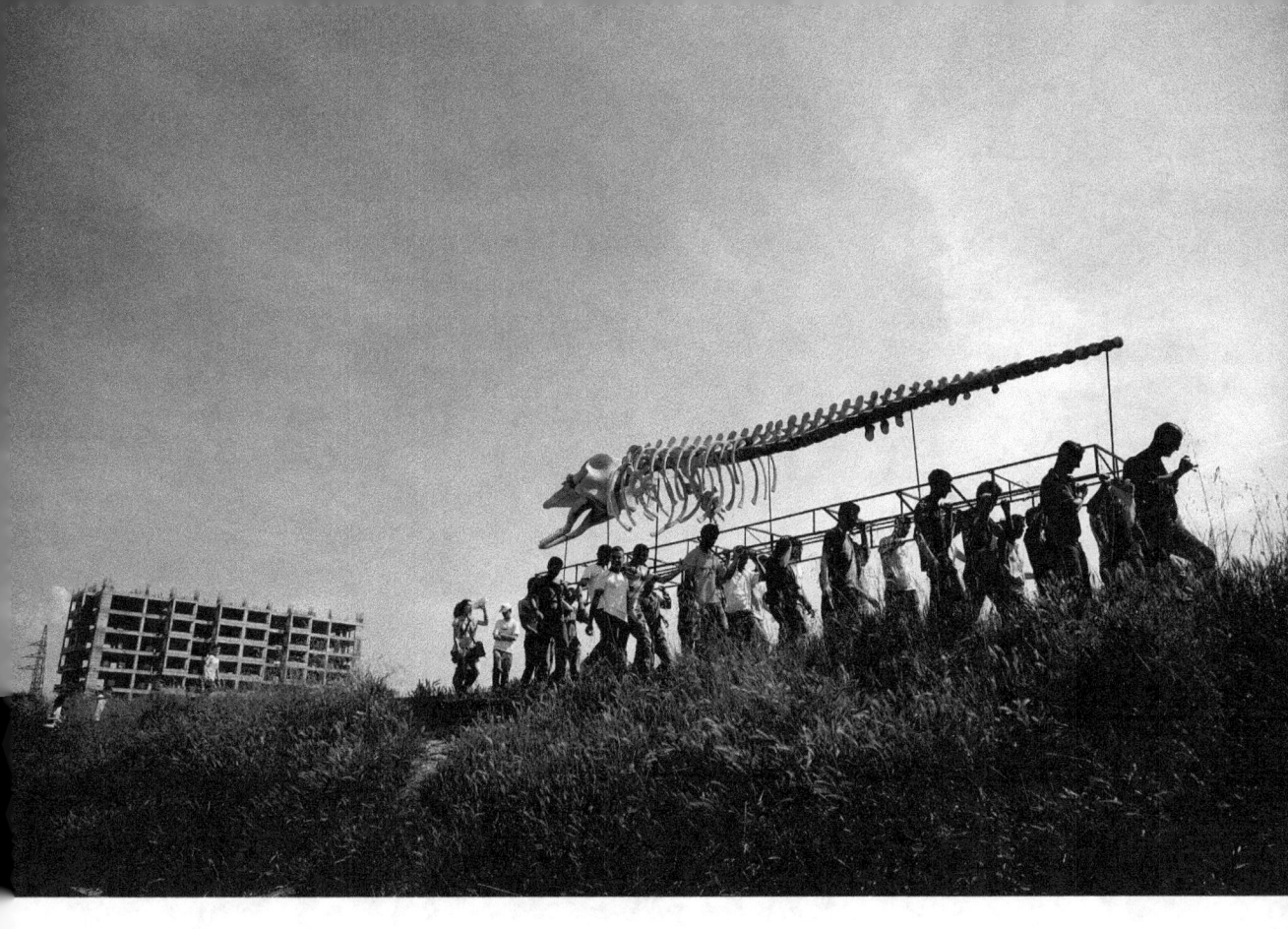

Armando Lulaj, *It Wears as It Grows*,
c-print, 140 x 180 cm, 2011.

Armando Lulaj, *It Wears as It Grows*,
c-print, 140 x 180 cm, 2011.

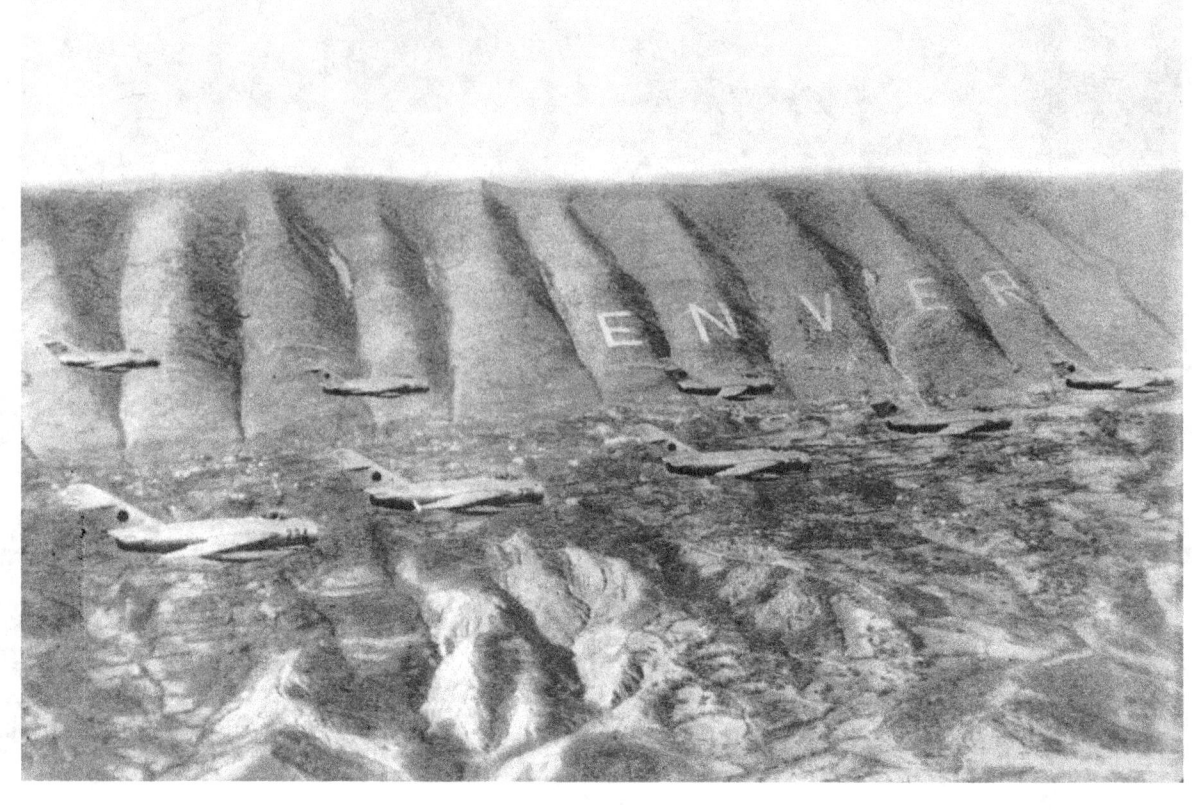

Armando Lulaj, *ENVER* (1974), b/w
print, 50 x 90 cm, 2011.

Armando Lulaj, *ENVER* (1974),
stampim bardhezi, 50 x 90 cm, 2011.

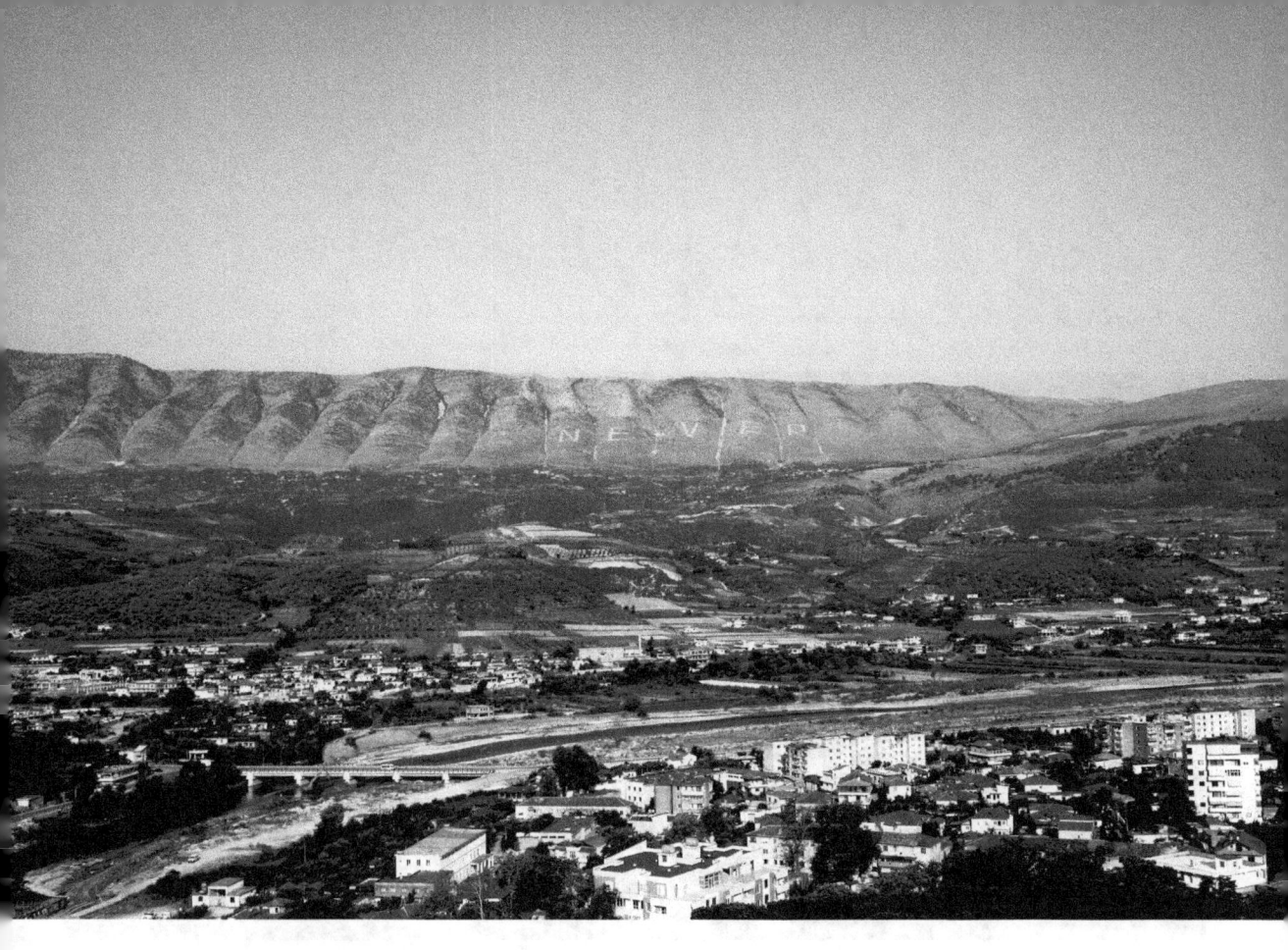

Armando Lulaj, *NEVER,* b/w print,
100 x 180 cm, 2012.

Armando Lulaj, *NEVER,* stampim
bardhezi, 100 x 180 cm, 2012.

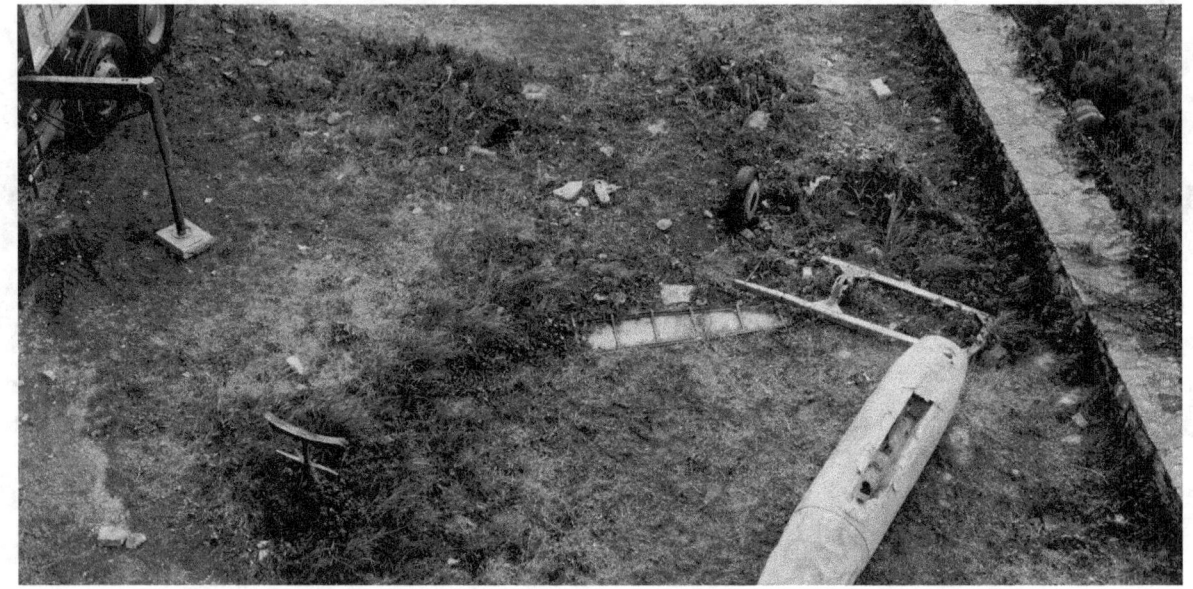

Still image from Armando Lulaj,
Recapitulation, 2015, video, RED
transferred to full HD, b/w and color,
sound 13'.

Imazh nga Armando Lulaj,
Recapitulation, 2015, video, RED
transferuar në full HD, bardhezi dhe
ngjyrë, me zë, 13'.

The Production of Hrönir: Albanian Socialist Realism and After

Write the truth – that will be socialist realism.
– Joseph Stalin[1]

Hlör u fang axaxaxas mlö.
– Jorge Luis Borges[2]

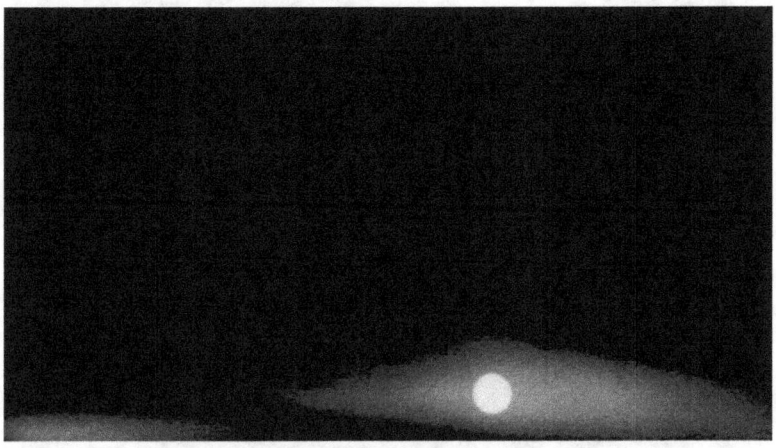

In 1941, Jorge Luis Borges published the short story "Tlön, Uqbar, Orbis Tertius" in the Argentinian literary magazine *Sur*. It outlines a world of unknown origin, "whose language and those things derived from their language [...] presuppose idealism."[3] This world "is not an amalgam of objects in space; it is a heterogenous series of independent acts – the world is successive, temporal, but not spatial."[4] In a world in which *esse est percipi,* to be is to be perceived, objects acquire a questionable status. In fact, they cannot be expressed owing to a total absence of any nouns. Perceiving, thinking, or even hoping for or dreaming of an object is what constitutes its precarious "existence" – a word that becomes dubious itself – as "reality" constituted of objectively observable fact breaks down. "Things duplicate themselves on Tlön; they also tend to grow vague or 'sketchy,' and to lose detail when they begin to be forgotten. [...] Sometimes a few birds, a horse, have saved the ruins of an amphitheater."[5] The name of this world is

Still image from Armando Lulaj, *NEVER*, 2012, full HD video, b/w and color, sound 22'.

Imazh nga Armando Lulaj, *NEVER*, 2012, full HD video, bardhezi dhe ngjyrë, me zë, 22'.

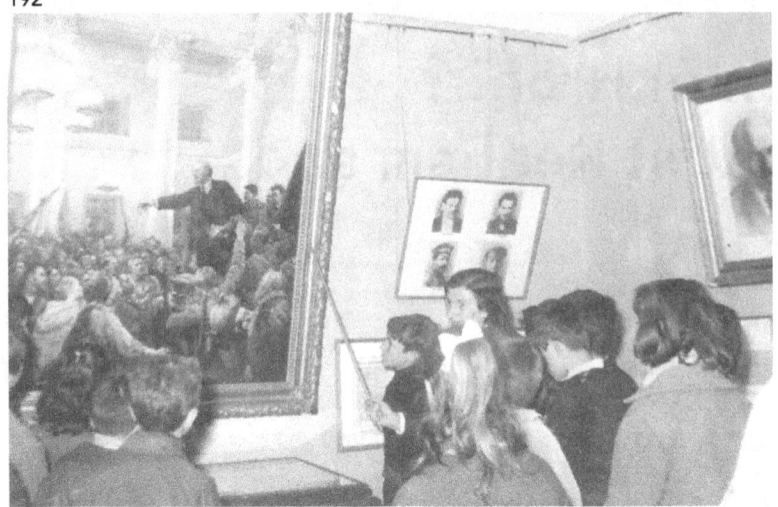

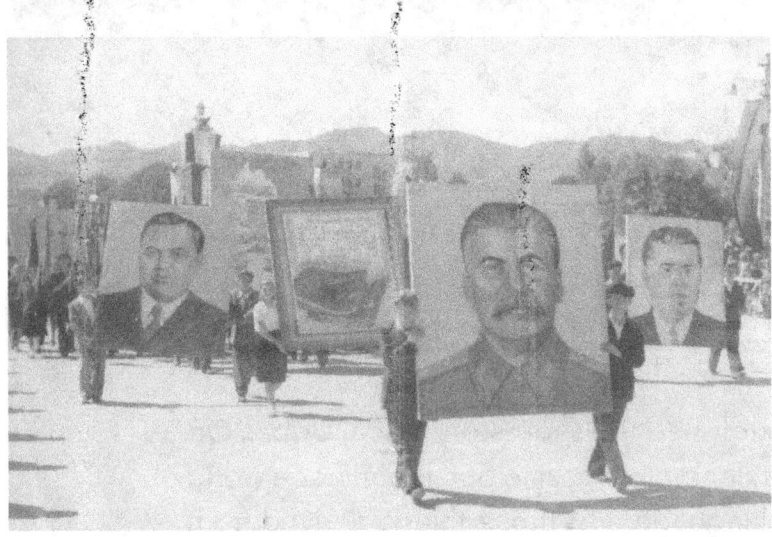

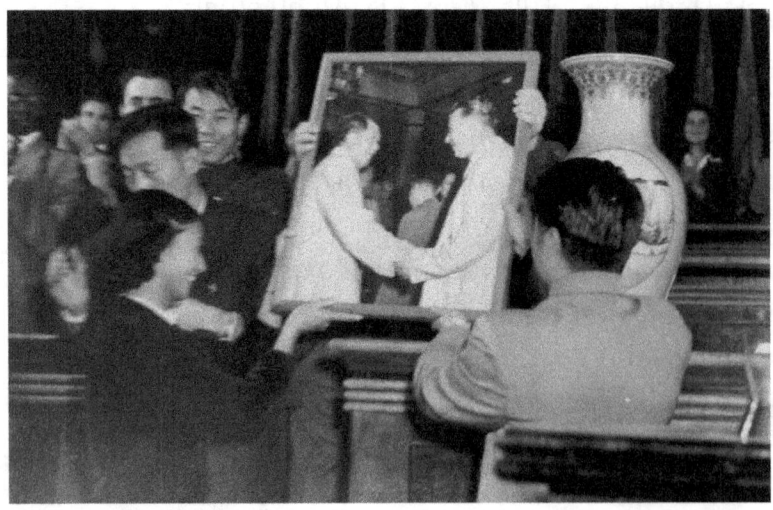

Albanian students in front of Vladimir
A. Serov's *V.I. Lenin Proclaims Soviet
Power* (1954), 1970.

Studentë shqiptarë para Vladimir
A. Serov, *V.I. Lenin shpall pushtetin
sovjetik* (1954), 1970.

Armando Lulaj, *Parade of Workers*
(1950), b/w print, 15 x 25 cm, 2015.

Armando Lulaj, *Parada e punëtorëve*
(1950), stampim bardhezi, 15 x 25 cm,
2015.

Armando Lulaj, *Chinese Friendship*,
b/w print, 10 x 15 cm, 1992.

Armando Lulaj, *Miqësia kineze*,
stampim bardhezi, 10 x 15 cm, 1992.

Tlön, and Borges slowly reconstructs it through a narrative maze littered with plagiarized encyclopedias and secret societies.

Even though the metaphysics or linguistics of this world may be far beyond what we would deem acceptable, there is an important aspect of Tlönian civil life that fails to be mentioned by Borges. Perhaps as a writer of texts that often tend to erase and obscure, to "forget" the borders between fiction and non-fiction, truth and speculation, he was more aware than anyone that, if anything, the visual arts produced on Tlön might not show such a stark contrast with those of Earth. His short overview of Tlönian literature confirms this. The denial of authorship, the absence of a concept of plagiarism, books that contain their own contradiction, poems consisting of a single word – all of these should be no surprise to the average reader of late-twentieth-century literature and philosophy. In fact, we may perversely appropriate Derrida's dictum-turned-cliché "there is no outside-text" as a perfectly acceptable Tlönian point of view, that is, if they were able to understand spatio-temporally determined words such as "there," "is," and "outside."

If we were to imagine Tlönian visual art, its difference with contemporary visual art, in which both authors and grand narratives have died multiple deaths, would be practically indiscernible. Perhaps this is precisely why Borges does not engage in any speculation on this subject. Yet he does make several observations on archeology, which place it in remarkable proximity to certain visual and monumental practices and may therefore perhaps serve as our provisional point of departure. In of those passages on Tlönian archeology he describes the seemingly outlandish idea of the *hrön* (pl. *hrönir*).

> Century upon century of idealism could hardly have failed to influence reality. In the most ancient regions of Tlön one may, not infrequently, observe the duplication of lost objects: Two persons are looking for a pencil; the first person finds it, but says nothing; the second finds a second pencil, no less real, but more in keeping with his expectations. These secondary objects are called *hrönir*. [...] Sometime stranger and purer than any *hrön* is the *ur* – the things produced by suggestion, the object brought forth by hope.[6]

—

Even though socialist realist art from the twentieth century is often discussed under a single heading, there are considerable differences in style and content between national variants, indeed, at least as many differences as there were between the "communist" regimes in Eastern Europe. These differences are not only dependent on the national art-historical context, such as the prior existence of avant-garde movements or local modernisms, but also on political, social, and historical factors. Moreover, we should be aware of the fact that the narrative of "socialist realism" itself assumes a coherency that is much more the result of the Western gaze than of a presumed communication or artistic cross-fertilization between the different nations of the Eastern Bloc that would make it a true "style."[7] Nonetheless, there has been a steady growth of art-historical literature theorizing socialist realism,[8] although the focus remains mainly on its development in the Soviet Union. Also the "other" sides of cultural production in the Eastern Bloc have been increasingly receiving attention, starting initially with the discovery of the historical Russian avant-garde in the wake of Western European left-wing uprisings in the 1960s,[9] and more recently broadening up to include the local underground movements that developed independently in different Eastern European countries,[10] as well as the steady incorporation of "emerging" artists from the region into the global art market, as long as they largely conform to Western artistic narratives.[11]

Deprived of any historical avant-garde that would anchor underground artistic activity or any post-communist "return" to a "lost" modernist tradition, Albania, locked off on all sides by mountains, lakes, and sea, only fits uncomfortably in the dual narrative of Stalinist socialist realism and avant-garde subcultures in the rest of the Eastern Bloc.[12] After cutting ties with Tito's Yugoslavia in 1948 and deteriorating relations with the Soviet Union after Stalin's death in 1953, culminating in Enver Hoxha's denunciation of Khrushchev in 1961, Albania became fully isolated from the Eastern Bloc and the rest of world, first relying on Maoist China, and later only on itself. So if there had been any initial influence from the Soviet Union on the development of socialist realist art in Albania, it was swiftly left to its own devices.[13]

Faced with this art-historical conundrum in which existing narratives seem to collapse, I propose two related approaches, one maybe more orthodox than the other. The first one is to inspect certain fragments of Albanian art-theoretical discourse that are pertinent to the form and content of socialist realism in Albania. This inspection can only be cursory and incomplete, but at least allows us to listen to voices underrepresented in the current art-historical discourse of Eastern Europe. The second one is to consider the work of an artist whose oeuvre, I would argue, hinges on a thorough reinterpretation of the Albanian socialist realist heritage, offering neither a Groysian paradigm of the (failed) continuation of the avant-garde, nor a Greenbergian dismissal of kitsch.[14]

Let us attempt a first approach, an inspection of Albanian art-theoretical discourse from the period of the Cultural and Ideological Revolution in the second half of the 1960s, which for the first time saw a theoretical elaboration of Albanian socialist realism,[15] while at the same time "establishing continuity between Hoxha's regime and the heroes of Albanian history."[16] The fact that Hoxha added "Ideological" to the concept of the Cultural Revolution borrowed from Mao Zedong should here attune us to an all-pervasive aspect of Albanian socialist realism: that ideology, being ever "further revolutionized," prevents any naive, authentic, pre-ideological reality from being distinguished or perceived.[17]

Through several fragments from the writings related to art of party leader Enver Hoxha collected in *Mbi letërsinë dhe artin* (*On Literature and Art*),[18] we may be able to reconstruct this Stalinist conceptualization of Albanian socialist realism. In his speech to the 5th Congress of the Albanian Labor Party on November 1, 1966, Hoxha announces the Cultural and Ideological Revolution with the statement that "the further revolutionization of the life of the country cannot be understood without the development and deepening of the ideological and cultural revolution,"[19] he formulates the role of socialist realist art as follows, characteristically in two breathtaking sentences[20]:

The Party puts forward the duty that literature and the arts become a powerful weapon in the hands of the Party for the education of the workers in the front lines of the struggle to educate an ideologically and morally pure youth, that all artistic creativity have a high ideological level, be driven by the martial, revolutionary spirit of the Party as well as by a healthy national spirit. The Party demands that literature and the arts more broadly reflect the struggle, work, and life of the worker-people, its ideals and aspirations, its noble feelings, its heroic character, its simplicity and majesty, its revolutionary force, that they truthfully and in its own revolutionary development reflect our reality and current situation, that at the center of creativity be placed the heroes of our time: workers, villagers, soldiers, people's intellectuals and revolutionary cadres, young people, educated by the Party, those who with dedication and heroism work and struggle for the building of socialism, for the defense and for the flourishing of the socialist fatherland, that the artistic and cultural institutions are at any time guided by the ideo-political demands of the Party, that they fight and unmask bourgeois ideology, with the aim of exerting a revolutionary educational influence on the masses, and that they be of the people and for the people.[21]

There is much here to unpack – a laborious task that is beyond purview of this text –, but what springs into view first of all is that art is conceived as a tool of ideological education: it should "educate an ideologically and morally pure youth" and exert "a revolutionary educational influence on the masses." This is also what curator Edi Muka points out when he speaks of Albanian socialist realism as "an art of profound educational character that was required to translate the ethics of communism into artistic form."[22] Second, we may note that art itself is, on the one hand, supposed to have "a high ideological level," but, on the other, ought to "truthfully [...] reflect our reality and current situation," in all of this "guided by the ideo-political demands of the Party." Although art historian Raino Isto rightly suggests that socialist realism ought to be considered a "strategy adopted by a particular group (in this case the Albanian Communist Party) to achieve specific ideological goals,"[23] something happens in the consolidation between the seemingly contradictory demands of being highly ideologically charged and the demand to truthfully reflect reality. A few paragraphs further, Hoxha elaborates on this point.

> Socialist realism is the faithful reflection of the socialist life that we are building in all its aspects, of the enormous material transformations at revolutionary tempo happening to our country, our society, our people based on Marxist–Leninist theory and on the masses of decisions elaborated by our Party. But this socialist realism is no way presented in static, solid forms; it boils, is in permanent and constant development through the struggle of opposites, through class struggle, through the struggle of the new against the old: This socialist realism, presented and understood in this way, is related to the present and with the perspective. The present prepares the future and it doesn't prepare this future through dreams and unreal imaginations, but through scientific, materialist predictions, directed by laws that are uncovered, which scientifically help to uncover the new.[24]

So it seems that the "faithful reflection of socialist life" can only be accomplished successfully by a socialist realism that "boils" from the "struggle between opposites," between the reality of the current situation and the ideological demands of the Party. Thus it is in a "constant development," which, while relating to the present and preparing the future does so not "through dreams and unreal imaginations," but through a process akin to the logic of scientific discovery. In other words, socialist realism forecasts the future in a manner akin to scientific methodology, offering a "realistic" perspective on the future in the present. Socialist realist art is summoned to bring out the ideological truth of the present (in both a subjective and objective sense), preparing for the future of its actual realization. Thus, the reality depicted in socialist realism is "more real" than any naturalism could achieve, because it "scientifically" filters out the new from the old. Nevertheless, this artistic process can sometimes fail; not each work will turn out as "successful" as the other. In fact, in a remarkable passage, Hoxha suggests that this is because any art "reflects reality flame by flame, will be created from the void," therefore always risking failure:

> If our socialist realist literary-artistic creativity does not duly correspond to the current situation, has not been fully placed in the frontline of the struggle of the Party and worker-masses for the uninterrupted deepening of the revolution, that doesn't mean that it has left the ranks of that struggle and needs to be put aside, because each new work that will represent reality flame by flame, will be created from the void.[25]

Reality here is precisely the ever "further revolutionization of the life of the country," the intense fire of the building of socialism, consuming the old and making way for the new, or, as slavicist Petre Petrov put it inversely, "socialism is the kind of reality that has realization as its constitutive principle."[26] The effects of Hoxha's discourse on socialist realist art theory and criticism are perplexing, as we gather from the following important passage by Andon Kuqali, one of the leading Albanian art critics of the time, following on a discussion of the concept of the "truth" of the work of art during the "Plenum of Criticism" in 1972:

> The creation of the artistic figure as a meaningful and generalizing figure [...] is a duty with a great ideological responsibility, with is linked to the passage into metaphor, with figurative comparisons, with symbols. These constitute the highest level of artistic realism.[27]

Here we find the synthesis of reality and ideology: metaphoricity, figuration, symbolism are the highest form of realism, or, as Isto has succinctly formulated it: "when one looks at 'the reality of socialist life' in socialist realism, one is looking not just at a metaphor for reality, but reality as metaphorical."[28] The frantic process, in which art boils over from the incessant attempts to capture the flames of reality, even seems to affect language itself, ever creating new words to represent the present. When we move from the demand "that all artistic creativity have a high ideological level [*nivel të lartë ideologjik*],"[29] to the phrase "[i]n the majority of our literary-artistic creativity, which is characterized by its high artistic level and level of ideas [*nga niveli i lartë ideor e artistik*], our new man finds himself,"[30] and finally to the qualification "a very high ideo-artistic level [*me nivel shumë të lartë ideoartistik*],"[31] we are witness to an adjectivic merger, a grammaticalization, where art and ideology are compressed together in the neologism "ideo-artistic"[32] that captures the essence, if there were such a thing, of Albanian socialist realism. Borges speaks of a language on the northern hemisphere of Tlön that only consists of adjectives. This could have been one.

—

In an anachronistic postscript to his story, postdated to 1947, Borges describes the "Tlönification" of the world after the discovery – perhaps we are already here dealing with a *hrön* – of the complete set of forty volumes of *The First Encyclopaedia of Tlön*:

> Almost immediately, reality "caved in" at more than one point. The truth is, it wanted to cave in. Ten years ago, any symmetry, any system with an appearance of order – dialectical materialism, anti-Semitism, Nazism – could spellbind and hypnotize mankind. How could the world not fall under the sway of Tlön, how could it not yield to the vast and minutely detailed evidence of an ordered planet? [...] Numismatics, pharmacology, and archaeology have been reformed. I understand that biology and mathematics are also awaiting their next avatar... [...] If my projections are correct, a hundred years from now someone will discover the hundred volumes of *The Second Encyclopaedia of Tlön*."[33]

The parallel drawn here between Tlön and totalitarian world views should not surprise us, and we could argue that its influence on cer-

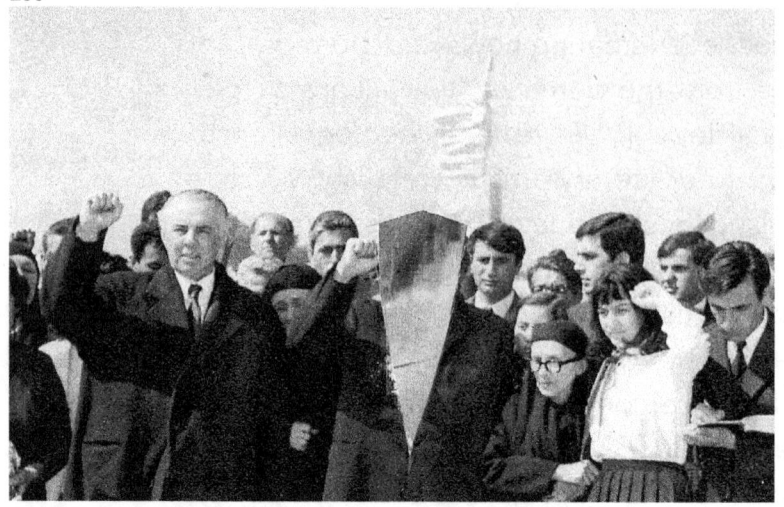

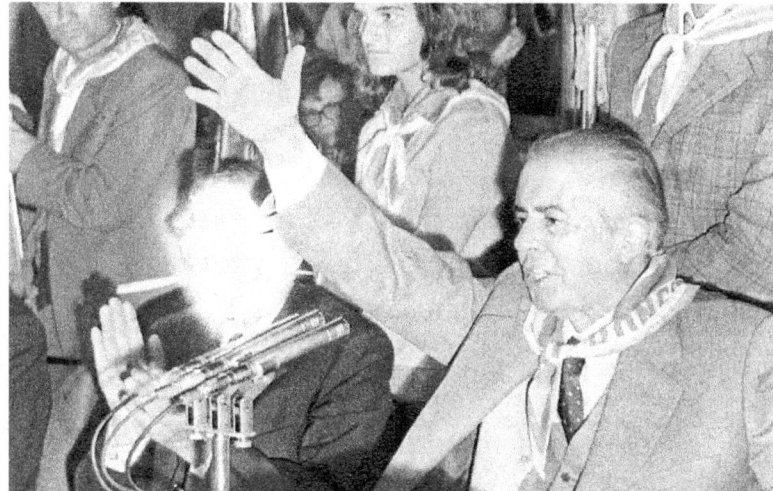

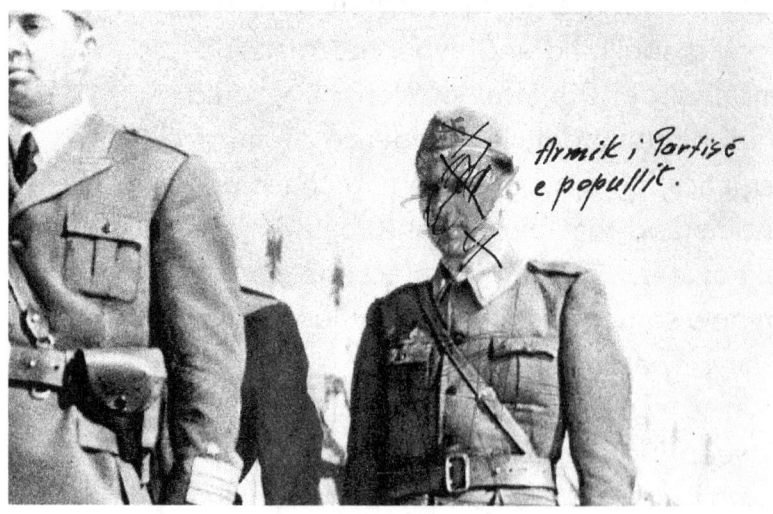

Removed faces of Mehmet Shehu
from *Gju me gju me popullin* (Tirana:
8 Nëntori, 1978).

Fytyrat e fshira e Mehmet Shehut nga
Gju me gju me popullin (Tiranë: 8
Nëntori, 1978).

tain types of artistic and cultural production has in fact been quite extensive, and not only as regards the hypotheses of Albanian socialist realist art that we have attempted to excavate from the dirt of history. For what, we should ask, are the grave mounds of the Illyrian tribes that were the "first" to inhabit the Balkan peninsula other than *hrönir* "found" by the eager Albanian archeologists of the socialist period?[34] And what about national hero Skënderbeg, who seems be uncovered in each of the Western Balkan countries with a fresh ideologically inflected heritage. For as Borges suggests, "[t]he systematic production of *hrönir* [...] has been of invaluable aid to archaeologists, making it possible not only to interrogate but even to modify the past, which is now no less plastic, no less malleable than the future."[35] The language of Albanian socialist realism, as I have suggested above, is fully consistent with the Tlönian world view, and therefore the *hrön*-like aspects of its visual and monumental art production should not surprise us. Nor should we be held back by a supposedly clearly demarcated distinction between fact and fiction. If anything, this is an opposition that is irrelevant to Albanian socialist realism as much as it is inexpressible on Tlön.[36]

Although the suggestion that the entirety of the country succumbed to this extreme form of idealism may be exaggerated, it must be admitted that the ideology that infused and nourished Albanian socialist realism in the years leading up to Hoxha's death not only resulted in these types of retroactive depictions of a genealogy of nationalist heroes and their artifacts up to Illyrian times, it also entailed the retroactive and collective *erasure* of the depiction of anyone fallen out of political grace – and there were many. As historian Elidor Mëhilli suggests, "History unfolded not only in the spaces of tomorrow but also in the blank spaces of the past – waiting to be partially erased, rearranged, rewritten."[37] In 1981, the entire nation grabbed their pens and erased Mehmet Shehu from every single publication in perhaps one of the most definitive gestures of socialist realism. Once again, *esse est percipi.*

—

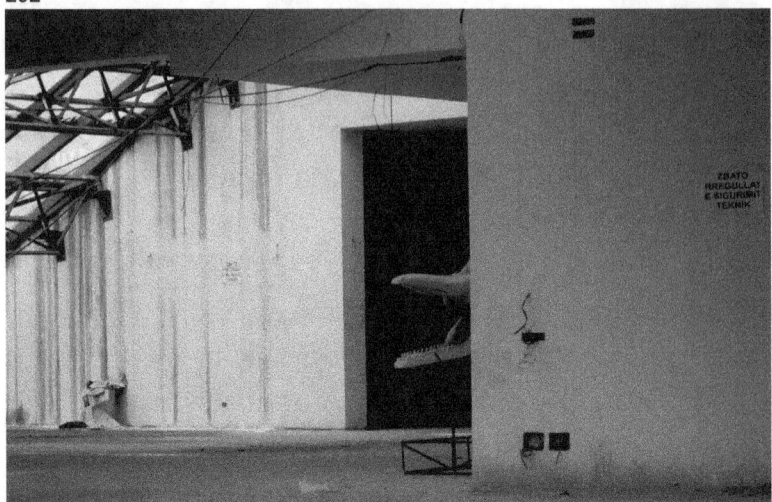

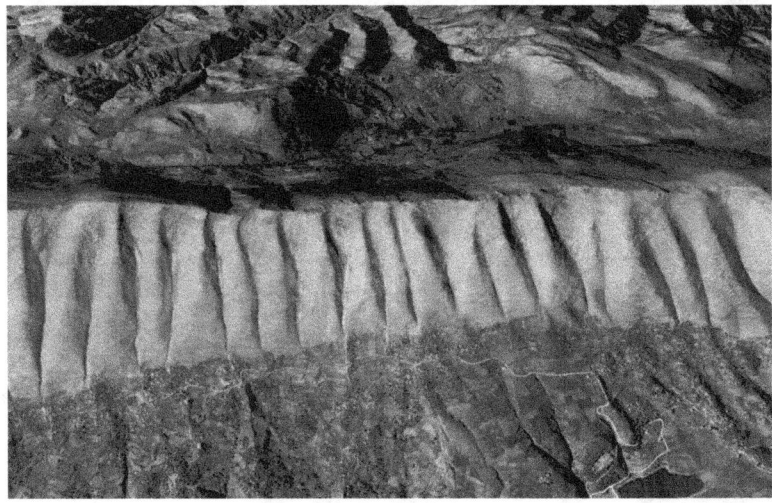

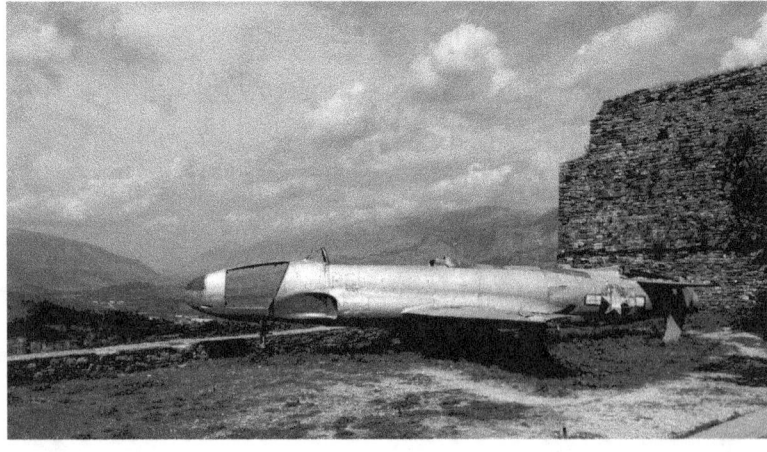

The model of the cachalot skeleton in the former Enver Hoxha Museum, 2011.

Modeli i skeletit të kashalotit brenda ish-Muzeut të Enver Hoxhës, 2011.

Image of Mt. Shpirag before the intervention of *NEVER*, 2011.

Pamja e Malit Shpirag para ndërhyrjes së *NEVER*, 2011.

Armando Lulaj, *US Spy Plane*, c-print, 80 x 120 cm, 2014.

Armando Lulaj, *Avion amerikan spiunazhi*, stampim me ngjyrë, 80 x 120 cm, 2014.

It is in response to these continuous attempts of the Albanian socialist state to produce *hrönir* and elevate the symbol to the highest level of reality that we should interpret the artistic work of Armando Lulaj, which, now that the socialist project has been prematurely aborted, has perfected the laborious process of unearthing or fabricating them – the difference is impossible to make. All the artifacts that populate his work have a vague and sketchy quality, overgrown with weeds, forgotten in museums, lost in time and space with hardly a single photograph or archival document to prove their existence. In fact, Lulaj himself often has to "produce" the documentation necessary for these artifacts to exist in the eye of political and artistic bureaucracies alike, and sometimes even has to resort to *copying* a *hrön* so that it may exist: The skeleton of the cachalot in *It Wears as It Grows*, of which copy was carried around the streets in Tirana, but whose existence inside the Natural History Museum is only supported by the single archival indication "whale skeleton"; in *NEVER*, the inscription "ENVER," overgrown by weeds and with no remaining photograph in the national archives, only lingering in the memory of a handful of villagers; an American military plane in *Recapitulation*, rusting outside the castle walls of Gjirokastër, which has been seemingly erased from US archives and documentation of which is practically inaccessible due to opaque references to "diplomatic sensitivity." Even one of the few depictions of planes in Albanian art and important contextual element in *Recapitulation* Spiro Kristo's painting *Flying Day (The Pilots of Division 7594, Rinas)*, was without archival file, belonging to a long-forgotten owner, orphaned on the walls of the National Gallery of Arts. Objects, copies, photographs, documentation, all of them hang together through a handful of eye-witnesses.

In precisely this sense, the oeuvre of Armando Lulaj is a coherent and rigorous contemporary response to Albanian socialist realist cultural production, both in terms of artistic and archeological artifacts, not mired by shame or false modesty about its supposedly art historical irrelevance. In fact, it seems to be the result of what is nothing but a thoroughly emancipatory gesture, in which Albanian socialist realism is recast as the consummation of conceptual art. If we abandon the outdated model of the artist as author, and no longer view the socialist artistic production in Albania from the perspective of single, individual artists, but rather as an ideologically driven machinery that encompasses an entire conceptual chain ranging from the Central Committee down to the artist in his studio, the actual production process of art works from socialist realist runs entirely parallel to that of conceptual art.

As Sol LeWitt famously stated in 1967, "When an artist uses a conceptual form of art, it means that all the planning and decisions are made beforehand and the execution is a perfunctory affair. The idea becomes a machine that makes the art."[38] This indeed comes very close to Hoxha's conception of socialist realist art, working from scientific predictions and like a Turing machine representing reality "flame by flame." In fact, it is precisely his ideas on socialist realist art that "produce" it in the exact same way that socialist realist art produces reality. Conceptual, as adjective, is here a synonym for "ideo-artistic." The institutional and bureaucratic aspects of socialist realist art production – the plenums, debates, organizations, material allocations, work plans, etc. – follow naturally, in the same way that many conceptual artists imposed strict regulations on their own modes of productivity. And whereas the latter ventured to strip themselves of any authorship, the former's authorship was diffused through the many collaborative efforts and removed through the bureaucratic apparatus. In this sense, the "death of the author" promulgated through various theoretical circuits in the West was still very modest compared to his death in Albanian art, in the sense the Western-style authorial death was self-imposed and moreover allowed for an enormous authorial output about this death itself; those who claimed his death definitely did not renounce their own authorship. This imposed death – may we say murder – of the author under socialist realism at the same time accounts for the fact that by far the majority of artists active under socialist realism have been unable to "regain" their authorial voice and style after 1990, mostly lapsing into a seemingly desire-driven, sensuous form of semi-abstraction.

The work of Armando Lulaj traces the few remaining pieces of evidence of this murder. Dealing with objects whose authorship and ownership is contested or unknown, he makes them his own, although he never adopts the language of authorship himself. The texts that accompany his films are always slightly condensed historical narratives without any specific authorial quality, sketching out the minimal framework for the viewer the gain access to the work. The filmic images, interspersed with archival footage, suggest a performative catalogue of archeological gestures and actions – reconstruction, measuring, displacement – without clearly establishing objects and objectives. His work thus appropriates and affirms the vagueness of the *hrönir* that are its quasi-objects as the only truthful way to deal with them and their ideologically charged past, articulating itself in an artistic language of mere adjectives.

1.   Cited from Petre Petrov, "The Industry of Truing: Socialist Realism, Reality, Realization," *Slavic Review* 70.4 (2011): 873–92, at 889.
2.   Jorge Luis Borges, "Tlön, Uqbar, Orbis Tertius," in *Collected Fictions*, trans. Andrew Hurley (New York: Penguin, 1998), 68–81, at 73.
3.   Ibid., 72.
4.   Ibid., 72–3.
5.   Ibid., 78.
6.   Ibid., 77–78.
7.   Eda Čufer, "Enjoy Me, Abuse Me, I am Your Artist: Cultural Politics, Their Monuments, Their Ruins," in *East Art Map: Contemporary Art and Eastern Europe*, ed. Irwin (London: Afterall, 2006), 362–83, at 374–5: "In principle, communism did not have an international cultural policy within the framework of its political bloc, and if cultural exchanges did take place at the state level, we can be sure that those who were at odds with the logic of the regime took no part in them whatsoever." See also Eva Forgacs, "How the New Left Invented East-European Art," *Centropa* 3.2 (2003).
8.   To name three major publications: Boris Groys, *The Total Art of Stalinism: Avant-Garde, Aesthetic Dictatorship, and Beyond*, trans. Charles Rougle (New York: Verso, 2011); Evegeny Dobrenko, *Political Economy of Socialist Realism*, trans. Jesse M. Savage (New Haven: Yale University Press, 2007); Igor Golomstock, *Totalitarian Art in the Soviet Union, the Third Reich, Fascist Italy and the People's Republic of China*, trans. Robert Chandler (New York: Overlook, 2011).
9.   Set off, in part, by the publication of Camilla Gray, *The Great Experiment: Russian Art 1863–1922* (London: Thames and Hudson, 1962). For an overview of this rapprochement, see Jürgen Harten, "From the Black Square to the White Flag," in *East Art Map: Contemporary Art and Eastern Europe*, ed. Irwin (London: Afterall, 2006), 384–9.
10.   See for an excellent overview Irwin (ed.), East Art Map: Contemporary Art and Eastern Europe (London: Afterall, 2006).
11.   Cf. Čufer, "Enjoy Me," 375.
12.   Gëzim Qëndro's *Le surréalisme socialiste: L'autopsie de l'utopie* (Paris: L'Harmattan, 2014) remains the only monograph devoted solely to an analysis of Albanian socialist realism to date.
13.   Raino Isto, "In It We Should See Our Own Revolution Moving Forward, Rising Up": Socialist Realism, National Subjecthood, and the Chronotope of Albanian History in the Vlora Independence Monument," MA Thesis (University of Maryland, 2014), 29 n. 62: "The

emphasis on continuity between the artists of the National Awakening and socialist realism also allowed the influence of Russian socialist realism to be almost completely elided." Isto's blog *afterart* is an invaluable resource for those wishing to explore Albanian socialist realism: http://afterart.wordpress.com/

14.   Clement Greenberg, "Avant-Garde and Kitsch," in *Collected Essays and Criticism* (Chicago: University of Chicago Press, 1986). See for an analysis of the impact of Greenberg's and other Western narratives on East European art history, Ana Peraica, "A Corruption of the 'Grand Narrative' of Art," in *East Art Map*, 472–6.

15.   Cf. Isto, "'In It We Should See Our Own Revolution Moving Forward, Rising Up,'" 27.

16.   Bernd Fischer, "Enver Hoxha and the Stalinist Dictatorship in Albania," in *Balkan Strongmen: Dictators and Authoritarian Rulers of Southeast Europe*, ed. Bernd J. Fischer (London: Hurst, 2007), 239–68, at 264.

17.   In fact, everyday life was to be avoided as representational theme. See the chapter "La quotidiennité comme résistance" in Qëndro, *Le surréalisme socialiste*.

18.   Enver Hoxha, *Mbi letërsinë dhe artin (nëntor 1942–nëntor 1976)* (Tiranë: 8 Nëntori, 1977).

19.   Ibid., 241: "Revolucionizimi i mëtejshëm i jetës së vendit nuk mund të kuptohet pa zhvillimin e pa thellimin e revolucionit

ideologjik e kulturor." For the entire speech see Instituti i Studimeve Marksiste–Leniniste pranë KQ të PPSH, *Dokumente kryesore të Partisë së Punës të Shqipërisë*, v. 5, 1966–1970 (Tirana, 1974), 61–200. Available online at http://enver-hoxha.net/content/content_shqip/librat/ppsh_dokumenta_kryesore/dokumenta_kryesore_5.htm. Unless noted otherwise, all translation from Albanian are by the author.

20.   See for an excellent treatment of Albanian ideological lingo, Ardian Verhbiu, *Shqipja totalitare: Tipare të ligjërimit publik në Shqipërinë e viteve 1945–1990* (Tirana: Çabej, 2007).

21.   Hoxha, *Mbi letërsinë e artin*, 253–4: "Partia shtron detyrën që letërsia dhe artet të bëhen një armë e fuqishme në duart e Partisë për edukimin e punonjësve në radhët e para të luftës për të edukuar një rini të pastër ideologjikisht e moralisht, që gjithë krijimtaria artistike të ketë një nivel të lartë ideologjik, të përshkohet nga fryma revolucionare luftarake e Partisë si dhe nga një frymë e shëndoshë kombëtare. Partia kërkon që letërsia dhe artet të pasqyrojnë më gjerë luftën, punën dhe jetën e popullit punonjës, idealet dhe aspiratat e tij, ndjenjat e tij fisnike, karakterin e tij heroik, thjeshtësinë dhe madhështinë e tij, hovin e tij revolucionar, të pasqyrojnë me vërtetësi dhe në zhvillimin e vet revolucionar realitetin dhe aktualitetin tonë, që në qendër të krijimtarisë të vihen heronjtë e

kohës sonë: punëtorët, fshatarët, ushtarët, intelektualët popullorë dhe kuadrot revolucionarë, njerëzit e rinj, të edukuar nga Partia, ata që me vetëmohim e heroizëm punojnë e luftojnë për ndërtimin e socializmit, për mbrojtjen e për lulëzimin e atdheut socialist, që institucionet artistike dhe kulturore të udhëhiqen kurdoherë nga kërkesat ideopolitike të Partisë, të luftojnë e të demaskojnë ideologjinë borgjeze, me qëllim që të ushtrojnë në masat një ndikim edukativ revolucionar, të jenë të popullit dhe për popullin."

22.   Edi Muka, "Albanian Socialist Realism or the Theology of Power," in *East Art Map*, 131–140, at 131. This resonates with the argument made by Groys in "Educating the Masses: Socialist Realist Art," in *Art Power* (Cambridge, MA: MIT Press, 2008), 141–8, at 146: "Whereas the market dominated, even defined, Western mass culture, Stalinist culture was noncommercial, even anti-commercial. Its aim was not to please the greater public but to educate, to inspire, to guide it. (Art should be realist in form and socialist in content, in other words.)"

23.   Isto, "'In It We Should See Our Own Revolution Moving Forward, Rising Up,'" 31, n. 66.

24.   Hoxha, *Mbi letërsinë e artin*, 292–3: "Realizmi socialist është pasqyrimi me besnikëri i jetës socialiste që po ndërtojmë në të gjitha aspektet e saj, i transformimeve kolosale materiale dhe me temp revolucionar që pëson

vendi ynë, shoqëria jonë, njerëzit tanë në bazë të teorisë marksiste-leniniste dhe në bazë të masave e vendimeve të përpunuara nga Partia jonë. Por ky realizëm socialist nuk paraqitet aspak në forma statike, të ngurta; ai zien, është në zhvillim të përhershëm e të vazhdueshëm, nëpërmjet një lufte të të kundërtave, nëpërmjet një lufte klase, nëpërmjet luftës të së resë kundër së vjetrës: Ky realizëm socialist, i paraqitur dhe i kuptuar kështu, është i lidhur me të tanishmen dhe me perspektivën. E tanishmja pregatit të ardhshmen dhe këtë të ardhshme nuk e pregatit nëpërmjet ëndërrimeve dhe imagjinateve ireale, por nëpërmjet parashikimeve shkencore materialiste, të drejtuara nga ligje të zbuluara, të cilat shkencërisht ndihmojnë për të zbuluar të reja."
25. Ibid., 290–1: "Në qoftë se krijimtaria jonë letraro-artistike e realizmit socialist nuk i përgjigjet sa duhet aktualitet, nuk është vënë plotësisht në vijën e parë të luftës së Partisë dhe të masave punonjëse për thellimin e pandërprerë të revolucionit, kjo nuk do të thotë se ajo ka dalë jashtë radhëve të kësaj lufte dhe duhet menjanuar, se çdo vepër e re që do të pasqyrojë flakë për flakë realitetin, do të krijohet nga hiçi."
26. Petrov, "The Industry of Truing," 884.
27. Andon Kuqali, "Kritika të orientojë e të hapë horizonte për të ardhmen," *Nëndori* 19.4 (1972), 77–82, 82: "Krijimi i figurës

artistike si një figurë kuptimplote e përgjithësuese [...] është një detyrë me përgjegjësi të madhe ideologjike, e cila lidhet me kalimin në metaforë, me krahasime figurative, me simbole. Këto përbëjnë shkallën më të lartë të realizmit artistik." I thank Raino Isto for this reference.
28. Raino Isto, "'Kritika të Orientojë e të Hapë Horizonte': Some Comments and Resources Related to Aesthetic Criticism in Communist Albania," *afterart*, August 23, 2014: https://afterart.wordpress.com/2014/08/23/kritika-te-orientoje-e-te-hape-horizonte-some-comments-and-resources-related-to-aesthetic-criticism-in-communist-albania/ (accessed March 10, 2015).
29. Hoxha, *Mbi letërsinë e artin*, 253: "gjithë krijimtaria artistike të ketë një nivel të lartë ideologjik."
30. Ibid., 314: "Në pjesën më të madhe të krijimtarisë sonë letraro-artistike, që karakterizohet nga niveli i lartë ideor e artistik, njeriu ynë i ri gjen vetëveten."
31. Ibid., 315: "një art me nivel shumë të lartë ideoartistik."
32. Elsewhere we also find the more common adjective "ideo-political" [*ideopolitik*] and "ideo-esthetical" [*ideoestetik*] (Hoxha, *Mbi letërsinë e artin*, 411), and even "ideo-emotional" [*ideoemotional*] (Kuqali, "Kritika të orientojë e të hapë horizonte për të ardhmen," 81).
33. Kuqali, "Kritika të orientojë e të hapë horizonte për të ardhmen," 81.
34. The recreation or "discovery" of historical presence under the

pressure of ideology – the production of hrönir – is of course not exclusive to Albania. We may point to a contemporary example described elsewhere in this catalogue, where Jonas Staal describes the retroactive production of cultural artifacts of the Kurdish independent cantons in Rojava (see this volume, 76).
35. Kuqali, "Kritika të orientojë e të hapë horizonte për të ardhmen," 77–78.
36. It is typical that another scholar, Ani Kokobobo, has also adopted a literary model to discuss socialist realist ideology, in which she speaks of "philosophical madness" resulting in a "mad and arbitrary reality" and draws parallels with the disintegration of reality in socialist Albania into a Baudrillardian "hyperreality." See "Bureaucracy of Dreams: Surrealist Socialism and Surrealist Awakening in Ismail Kadare's *The Palace of Dreams*," *Slavic Review* 70.3 (2011): 524–44.
37. See Elidor Mëhilli, "Written. (Erased.) Rewritten." in Armando Lulaj, *Albanian Trilogy: A Series of Devious Stratagems*, ed. Marco Scotini (Berlin: Sternberg, 2015): 43–61.
38. Sol LeWitt, "Paragraphs on Conceptual Art," in *Conceptual Art: A Critical Anthology*, ed. Alexander Alberro and Blake Stimson (Cambridge, MA: MIT Press, 1999), 12–16, at 12.

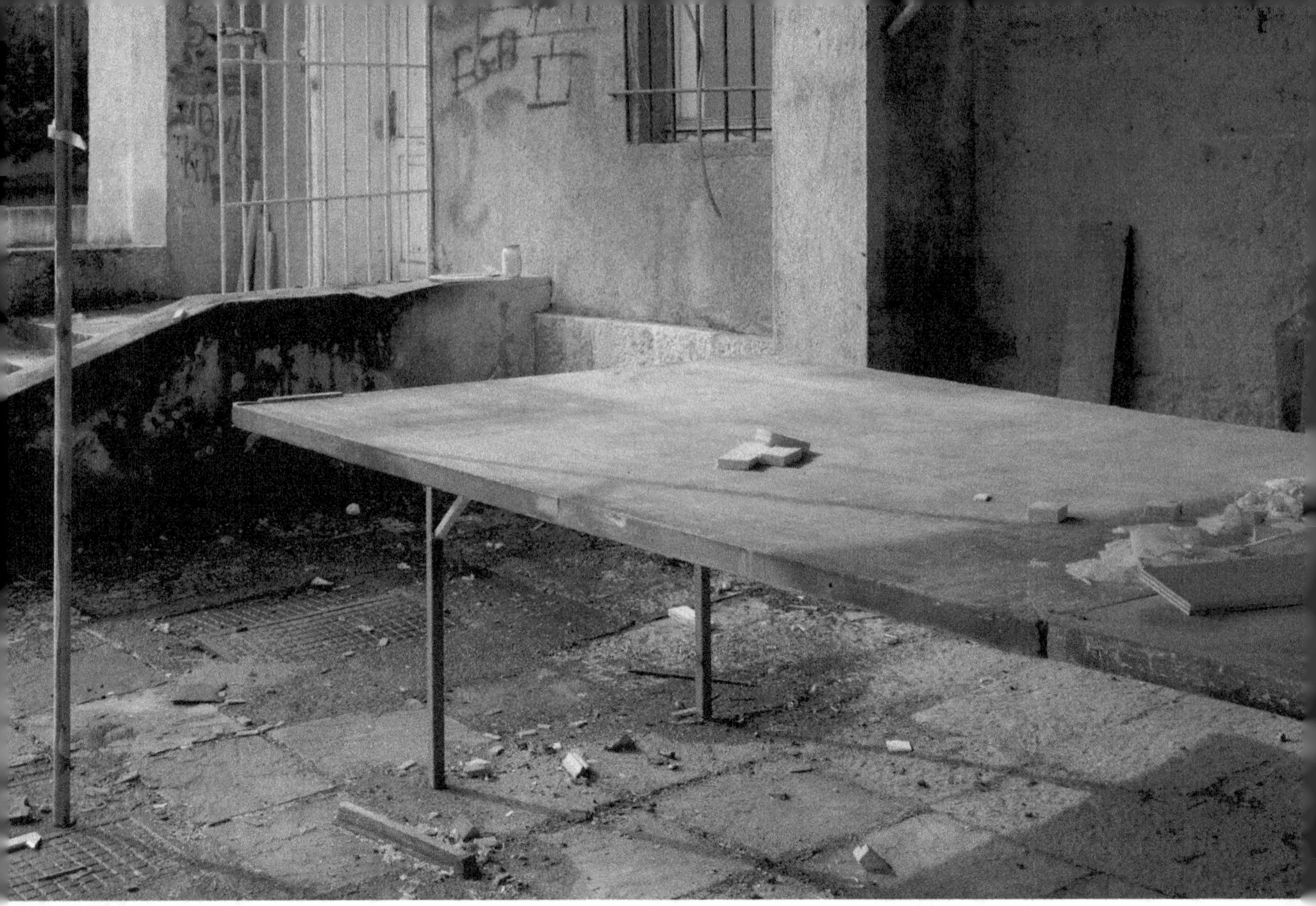

Workers Leaving the Studio. Looking Away from Socialist Realism. is a project of Mihnea Mircan and Vincent W.J. van Gerven Oei, realized by The Department of Eagles and the National Gallery of Arts, Tirana.

Punëtrorët dalin nga studioja. Duke mos parë më realizëm socialist. është një projekt i Mihnea Mircan dhe Vincent W.J. van Gerven Oei që u realizua nga Departamenti i Shqiponjave dhe Galeria Kombëtare e Artit, Tiranë.

This project was funded by the Prince Claus Fund, Amsterdam, the Netherlands.

Ky projekt u financua nga Fondacioni "Prince Claus", Amsterdam, Hollandë.

C Fonds

Prince Claus Fund *for* Culture and Development

Editor
Redaktor
Vincent W.J. van Gerven Oei

Translations
Përkthime
Jonida Gashi, Genti Gjikola,
Vincent W.J. van Gerven Oei

Design
Dizajn
Vincent W.J. van Gerven Oei

Images
Pamje
Marco Mazzi

18, 20, 22: Courtesy of Santiago Sierra;
26, 162 (top): Courtesy of the National
Gallery of Arts, Tirana, Albania; 46–57
(top): Courtesy of Jonas Staal; 86, 90,
94, 98: Photography by Adrian Sabau,
courtesy of Ciprian Mureşan; 113, 118:
Courtesy of IRWIN; 140, 141 Courtesy
of Sarah Vanagt; 166, 174–5, 186–9,
192 (center, bottom), 202 (bottom):
Courtesy of Armando Lulaj; 190:
Courtesy of Debatikcenter Film; 191:
Courtesy of Debatikcenter Film and
Paolo Maria Deanesi Gallery; 192 (top):
Courtesy of ATSh; 202 (top): Courtesy
of Pim van der Heiden; 202 (center):
Google Earth.

Thanks
Falenderime
Morena Dushku Palloj, Mumtas
Dhrami, Embassy of the Netherlands
in Tirana, Ermir Grezda, Genti Gjikoli,
Iliada Korçari, Sotir Kosta, Anastas
Kostandini, Eugen Kristo, Nelo
Llukaçi, Kujtim Qama, Edi Rama,
Skerdi Sulovari, Shpëtim Reçi, Artan
Shabani, Sali Shijaku, Zef Shoshi,
Thoma Thomai, Suzana Varvarica & the
technical and restauration team of the
National Gallery of Arts.

www.ingramcontent.com/pod-product-compliance
Lightning Source LLC
Chambersburg PA
CBHW080957170526
45158CB00010B/2829